How exciting it would be to spend five minutes with John Bunyan every day for one year—perhaps in his home or before his hearth, in his prison cell or before his pulpit—to hear his testimony of salvation, to sit under his preaching, and to listen to him muse upon such glorious doctrines as justification, imputation, the fear of God, and the free offer of the gospel. That opportunity is now possible in this Christ-centered, gospel-saturated, and experiential collection of John Bunyan's personal and theological reflections. May the Lord richly bless your year with the persecuted tinker, brilliant allegorist, and fiery preacher of Bedford!

JOEL R. BEEKE
Chancellor and Professor of Homiletics & Systematic Theology
Puritan Reformed Theological Seminary
Grand Rapids, Michigan

John Bunyan knew by experience the richness and freeness of God's love and grace. And, as a result, his corpus is powerfully drenched with heartfelt, biblical Christianity. It is a privilege to be able to recommend this new selection of daily readings from Bunyan's grace-filled works. May the Puritan preacher speak afresh in our days through these expertly-chosen excerpts and encourage the readers of this devotional to live lives that honour Christ as Bunyan so powerfully did in his day.

MICHAEL A. G. AZAD HAYKIN
Professor of Church History
The Southern Baptist Theological Seminary
Louisville, Kentucky

"No sin against God can be little because it is against the great God of heaven and earth; but if the sinner can find out a little god, it may be easy to find out little sins." Thousands of such pertinent quotables penetrate this book. Soul-health and mind-delight combine as advantages that consistently accrue to the reader of John Bunyan. Bunyan was a tinker, Roger Duke is a "pipe-fitter." They are brothers not only in their useful trades but in their desire for knowledge of the holy. This 365-day journey through the works of Bunyan will nourish the spirit and give a good grasp of the sanctified literary treasury that constitute the Bunyan corpus of literary production. Dr. Duke has brought forth from Bunyan an excellent treat to look forward to every day.

TOM NETTLES
Senior Professor of Historical Theology
The Southern Baptist Theological Seminary
Louisville, Kentucky

When it comes to doctrinal clarity, theological vigor, and applicational warmth, there may be no greater Puritan writer than John Bunyan. His was a heart full of love for the Lord, His Word, and His people, and to read his writings is to encounter the Balm of Gilead that cleanses, renews, and strengthens the weary heart. Dr. Duke has done a great service by compiling these daily readings from Bunyan, and I warmly commend it to all.

JACOB TANNER
Pastor, Christ Keystone Church, Middleburg, Pennsylvania
Author, *The Tinker's Progress: The Life and Times of John Bunyan*

John Bunyan Daily Readings

Edited by

Roger D. Duke

CHRISTIAN HERITAGE

Softback ISBN: 978-1-5271-1172-1
Ebook ISBN: 978-1-5271-1212-4

Published in 2024
in the
Christian Heritage Imprint
by
Christian Focus Publications,
Geanies House, Fearn, Tain, Ross-shire,
IV20 1TW, Scotland, UK
www.christianfocus.com

Cover design by Daniel van Straaten

Printed in India by Imprint Press

Dedicated to

Katie Melinda Young Duke

In Our 50th Year of Marriage
(50th Anniversary October 5th, 2024)

Her Family of Origin Called Her "Linda"
Her Grandchildren Call Her "Kay Kay"
I Call Her "Kate"

The Scripture declares:
"Her children have arisen up and call her blessed:
her husband also, and I praise her."
Proverbs 31:28 (KJV, personalized).

"She has done me good and not evil all the days of her life."
Proverbs 31:12 (KJV, personalized).

Since Then,
She Has Been:
My Wife
My Lover
The Mother of My Children
My Best Friend
My Confidant
My Encourager
My Business Partner
My Fellow Laborer in the Lord's Vineyard.
The Doctor and Nurse of My Family
The Primary Caretaker of Our Special Needs Adult Son Dale
The Glue That Binds Our Little Tribe Together

I cannot fathom what my life would have been without her!

INTRODUCTION

Since 1678 when it was first published *The Pilgrim's Progress* has been read by and influenced millions of Christians as well as others. For many years, if a family had any books in the household, they probably included a well-worn copy of the *Authorized Version* of the *Bible* and a copy of *The Pilgrim's Progress.* Some may have even read Bunyan's personal testimony of salvation found in: *Grace Abounding to the Chief of Sinners: A Brief Relation of the Exceeding Mercy of God in Christ to His Poor Servant.*

This editor had three special emphases in mind when he accepted, with a great deal of joy and excitement, the offer to bring forth such a volume from Bunyan's writings:

1. That Bunyan's writings would be a spiritual blessing to all who had not read anything beyond the above two named volumes.
2. That this devotional could expose the readers to a broader knowledge of Bunyan's sixty some other works that are largely unknown to evangelical audiences.
3. That it would be a worthy addition to the *Daily Readings* series put forth by the good folk at Christian Focus Press.

Here we furnish a monthly index of each volume consulted from where the daily excerpts were drawn:

January: *Grace Abounding to the Chief of Sinners: A Brief Relation of the Exceeding Mercy of God in Christ to His Poor Servant.*

February: *My Confession of Faith (or A Confession of My Faith and a Reason of My Practice, or, With Who, and Who Not, I can Hold Church-fellowship, or the Communion of Saints).*

March: *Paul's Departure and Crown (or An Exposition Upon 2 Timothy 4:6-8).*

April: *Saved by Grace (or a Discourse of the Grace of God).*

May: *The Strait Gate (or Great Difficulty of Going to Heaven).*

June: *Justification by an Imputed Righteousness (or No Way to Heaven but by Jesus Christ),* Part 1.

July: *Justification by an Imputed Righteousness (or No Way to Heaven but by Jesus Christ),* Part 2.

August: *The Desire of the Righteous Granted: (or A Discourse of the Righteous Man's Desires),* Part 1.

September: *The Desire of the Righteous Granted: (or A Discourse of the Righteous Man's Desires),* Part 2.

October: *Christ a Complete Saviour (or The Intercession of Christ and Who Are Privileged In).*

November: *A Treatise of the Fear of God (or Showing What It Is and How Distinguished from that Which Is Not So).*

December: Was excerpted from three Bunyan sources:

1. *Bunyan's Dying Sayings.*
2. *Bunyan's Last Sermon*, Preached July 1688, taken from the Gospel of John 1:13, "Which were born, not of blood, nor the will of the flesh, nor of the will of man, but of God" (KJV).
3. *Come and Welcome to Jesus Christ.*

It is the editor and publisher's hope that your Christian life will be edified as you read this humble offering.

Roger D. Duke
June, 2024

JANUARY 1

A Child of Disobedience

... [And] they may come to their senses and escape from the snare of the devil, after being captured by him to do his will.
2 TIMOTHY 2:26

As for my own natural life, for the time that I was without God in the world, it was indeed according to the course of this world, and "the spirit that now worketh in the children of disobedience" (Eph. 2:2). It was my delight to be "taken captive by the devil at his will" (2 Tim. 2:26).

So settled and rooted was I in these things, that they became as a second nature to me; the which, as I also have with soberness considered since, did so offend the Lord, that even in my childhood he did scare and frighten me with fearful dreams, and did terrify me with dreadful visions; for often, after I had spent this and the other day in sin.

I was greatly afflicted and troubled with the thoughts of the day of judgment, and that both night and day, and should tremble at the thoughts of the fearful torments of hell-fire; still fearing that it would be my lot to be found at last amongst those devils and hellish fiends, who are there bound down with the chains and bonds of eternal darkness, "unto the judgment of the great day."

In these days, the thoughts of religion were very grievous to me; I could neither endure it myself, nor that any other one should; so that, when I have seen some read in those books that concerned Christian piety, it would be as it were a prison to me. Then I said unto God, "Depart from me, for I desire not the knowledge of thy ways" (Job 21:14). I was now void of all good consideration, heaven and hell were both out of sight and mind; and as for saving and damning, they were least in my thoughts.

JANUARY 2

Rain on the Just and the Unjust

The toil of the fool wearies him, for he does not know the way to the city.

ECCLESIASTES 10:15

But God did not utterly leave me, but followed me still, not now with convictions, but judgments; yet such as were mixed with mercy. For once I fell into a creek of the sea, and hardly escaped drowning. Another time I fell out of a boat into Bedford river, but mercy yet preserved me alive. Another time, being in the field with one of my companions, it chanced that a poisonous snake passed over the highway; so I, having a stick in my hand, struck her over the back; and having stunned her, I forced open her mouth with my stick, and plucked her sting out with my fingers; by which act, had not God been merciful unto me, I might, by my desperateness, have brought myself to mine end.

This also have I taken notice of with thanksgiving; when I was a soldier, I, with others, were drawn out to go to such a place to besiege it; but when I was just ready to go, one of the company desired to go in my room; to which, when I had consented, he took my place; and coming to the siege, as he stood sentinel, he was shot into the head with a musket bullet, and died.

Here, as I said, were judgments and mercy, but neither of them did awaken my soul to righteousness; wherefore I sinned still, and grew more and more rebellious against God, and careless of my own salvation.

[I thought in my lost condition.] Thus man, while blind, doth wander, but wearies himself with vanity, for he knows not the way to the city of God (Eccles. 10:15).

JANUARY 3

The Log and the Speck

You hypocrite, first take the log out of your own eye, and then you will see clearly to take the speck out of your brother's eye.
MATTHEW 7:5

Wherefore I fell to some outward reformation, both in my words and life, and did set the commandments before me for my way to heaven; which commandments I also did strive to keep, and, as I thought, did keep them pretty well sometimes, and then I should have comfort; yet now and then should break one, and so afflict my conscience; but then I should repent, and say I was sorry for it, and promise God to do better next time, and there get help again, "for then I thought I pleased God as well as any man in England."

Thus I continued about a year; all which time our neighbours did take me to be a very godly man, a new and religious man, and did marvel much to see such a great and famous alteration in my life and manners; and, indeed, so it was, though yet I knew not Christ, nor grace, nor faith, nor hope; and, truly, as I have well seen since, had then died, my state had been most fearful; well, this, I say, continued about a twelvemonth or more.

Now, therefore, they began to praise, to commend, and to speak well of me, both to my face, and behind my back. Now, I was, as they said, become godly; now, I was become a right honest man. But, oh! When I understood that these were their words and opinions of men, it pleased me mighty well. Yet, I was nothing but a poor, painted hypocrite, yet I loved to be talked of as one that was truly godly. I was proud of my godliness, and, indeed, I did all I did, either to be seen of, or to be well spoken of, by man. And thus, I continued for about a twelvemonth or more.

JANUARY 4

God Visits the Soul

Blessed be the God and Father of our Lord Jesus Christ, [who] ... hath begotten us again unto a lively hope by the resurrection of the Jesus Christ from the dead.

1 PETER 1:3 KJV

But upon a day, the good providence of God did cast me to Bedford, to work on my calling; and in one of the streets of that town, I came where there were three or four poor women sitting at a door in the sun, and talking about the things of God; and being now willing to hear them discourse, I drew near to hear what they said, for I was now a brisk talker also myself in the matters of religion, but now I may say, I heard, but I understood not; for they were far above, out of my reach; for their talk was about a new birth, the work of God on their hearts, also how they were convinced of their miserable state by nature; they talked how God had visited their souls with his love in the Lord Jesus, and with what words and promises they had been refreshed, comforted, and supported against the temptations of the devil. Moreover, they reasoned of the suggestions and temptations of Satan in particular; and told to each other by which they had been afflicted, and how they were borne up under his assaults. They also discoursed of their own wretchedness of heart, of their unbelief; and did contemn, slight, and abhor their own righteousness, as filthy and insufficient to do them any good.

And I thought they spoke as if joy did make them speak; they spoke with such pleasantness of Scripture language, and with such appearance of grace in all they said, that they were to me, as if they had found a new world, as if they were people that dwelt alone and were not to be reckoned among their neighbours.

JANUARY 5

The Folly of the Froward

A perverse heart shall be far from me, I will know nothing of evil.

PSALM 101:4

O Lord, I am a fool, and not able to know the truth from error: Lord, leave me not to my own blindness, either to approve of, or condemn this doctrine [of Christ]; if it be of God, let me not despise it; if it be of the devil, let me not embrace it. Lord, I lay my soul, in this matter, only at thy foot; let me not be deceived, I humbly beseech thee.

One thing I may not omit: There was a young man in our town, to whom my heart before was knit more than to any other, but he being a most wicked creature for cursing, and swearing, and whoring, I now shook him off, and forsook his company; but about a quarter of a year after I had left him, I met him in a certain lane, and asked him how he did? He, after his old swearing and mad way, answered, I am well. But why do you swear and curse like this Harry? What will become of you if you die in this condition? He answered me annoyed! What would the devil do for company if it were not for men like me?

But God, who had, as I hope, designed me for better things, kept me in the fear of his name, and did not suffer me to accept such cursed principles. And blessed be God, who put it into my heart to cry to him to be kept and directed, still distrusting my own wisdom; for I have since seen even the effect of that prayer, in his preserving me not only from ranting errors, but from those also that have sprung up since. The Bible was precious to me in those days.

JANUARY 6

God Shows His Mercy

So, then it depends not on human will or exertion, but on God, who has mercy.

ROMANS 9:16

So ... I tried at first to look over the business of faith, yet in a little time, I better consider the matter, was willing to put myself upon .... trial, whether I had faith or not. But, in my grief, poor wretch, so ignorant and brutish was I, that I knew to this day no more how to do it, than I know how to begin and accomplish ... [a] rare and curious piece of art, which I never yet saw nor considered.

Neither yet could I attain to any comfortable persuasion that I had faith in Christ; but instead of having satisfaction, here I began to find my soul to be assaulted with fresh doubts about my future happiness; especially with such as these, whether I was elected? But how if the day of grace should now be past and gone?

By these ... temptations I was very much afflicted and disquieted; sometimes by one, and sometimes by the other of them. And first, to speak of that about my questioning my election, I found at this time, that though I was in a flame to find the way to heaven and glory, and though nothing could beat me off from this, yet this question did so offend and discourage me! I was, especially at some times, as if the very strength of my body also had been taken away by the force and power [of these thoughts]. This Scripture did also seem to me to trample upon all my desires, "It is not of him that willeth, nor of him that runneth, but of God that showeth mercy" (Rom. 9:16).

JANUARY 7

The Beginnings of a Peaceful Mind

You keep him in perfect peace whose mind is stayed on you, because he trusts in you.

ISAIAH 26:3

By these things I was driven to my wits' end, not knowing what to say, or how to answer these temptations. Indeed, I little thought that Satan had thus assaulted me, but that rather it was my own prudence. Thus, to start the question: that the elect only attained eternal life, that I, without scruple, did heartily close with Christ. But that I was one of them—there lay all the questions.

Therefore, for several days, I was greatly assaulted and perplexed. Often, when I was walking, ready to sink [in despair] where I went, with faintness in my mind. But one day, after I had been so many weeks oppressed and cast down, I was now quite ready to give up the ghost of all my hopes of ever attaining life, that sentence fell with weight upon my spirit, "Look at the generations of old and see; did ever any trust in the Lord, and was so unnerved?"

Thus I continued for over a year, and could not find the place; but at last, casting my eye into the Apocrypha books I found it in Ecclesiasticus 2:10. This, at first, did somewhat daunt me. Because, by this time, I had got more experience of the love and kindness of God, it troubled me the less; especially when I considered, that though it was not in those texts that we call holy and canonical, yet forasmuch as this sentence was the sum and substance of many of the promises, it was my duty to take the comfort of it; and I bless God for that Word, for it was of God to me: that Word doth still, at times, shine before my face.

JANUARY 8

Has Christ Called Me?

Wherefore the rather, brethren, give diligence to make your calling and election sure. ...

2 PETER 1:10, KJV

How lovely now was everyone in my eyes that I thought to be converted [both] men and women! They looked like and walked like a people that carried the broad seal of heaven about them. Oh! I saw the lot had fallen to them in pleasant places, and they had a goodly heritage (Ps. 16:6). But that which made me sick was that of Christ, in Mark, He went up into a mountain and called to him whom he would, and they came unto him (Mark 3:13).

This Scripture made me faint and fear, yet it kindled fire in my soul. That which made me fear was this—that Christ should have no liking to me, for he called "whom he would." But oh! the glory that I saw in that condition did still so engage my heart that I could seldom read of any that Christ did call. But I presently wished: Would I had been in their clothes; would I had been born Peter; would I had been born John; or would I had been by and had heard him when he called them, how would I have cried, O Lord, call me also. But oh! I feared he would not call me!

And truly the Lord let me go thus many months together and showed me nothing. Neither that I was already nor should be called hereafter. But at last, after much time spent, and many groans to God, that I might be made partaker of the holy and heavenly calling, that Word came in upon me—"I will cleanse their blood that I have not cleansed, for the Lord dwelleth in Zion" (Joel 3:21).

JANUARY 9

An Uneasy Conscience

A man's spirit will endure sickness but a crushed spirit who can bear?

PROVERBS 18:14

Further, in these days I should find my heart to shut itself up against the Lord. Against his Holy Word. I have found my unbelief to set, as it were, the shoulder to the door to keep him out. And when I have with many a bitter sigh cried, good Lord! Break it open; Lord, break these gates of brass, and cut these bars of iron in two pieces (Ps. 107:16). Yet that Word would sometimes create in my heart a peaceable pause, "I girded [prepared] thee, though thou hast not known me" (Isa. 45:5).

But all this while as to the act of sinning, I never was more tender than now; I dare not take a pin or a stick, though but so big as a straw, for my conscience now was sore, and would hurt at every touch; I could not now tell how to speak my words, for fear I should misplace them. Oh, how gingerly did I then go in all I did or said! I found myself as in a muddy bog that shook if I did but stir; and was there left both of God and Christ, and the Spirit, and all good things.

But, I observe, though I was such a great sinner before conversion, yet God never much charged the guilt of the sins of my ignorance upon me. Only he showed me I was lost if I had not Christ, because I had been a sinner; I saw that I wanted a perfect righteousness to present me without fault before God, and this righteousness was nowhere to be found, but in the person of Jesus Christ. ... I was thus afflicted with the fears of my own damnation.

JANUARY 10

Tempted and Tried

For this reason, when I could bear it no longer ... for fear that somehow the tempter had tempted you and our labour would be in vain.

1 THESSALONIANS 3:5

For about the space of a month after, a very great storm came down upon me, which handled me twenty times worse than all I had met with before. It came stealing [in] upon me, now by one piece, then by another. First, all my comfort was taken from me. Then darkness seized upon me, after which, whole floods of blasphemies, both against God, Christ, and the Scriptures, were poured upon my spirit, to my great confusion and astonishment. These blasphemous thoughts also stirred up questions in me. [These] against the very being of God, and of his only beloved Son; as, whether there were, in truth, a God, or Christ, or not? And [even] whether the holy Scriptures were not rather a fable, and cunning story, than the holy and pure Word of God?

The tempter would also much assault me with this: How can you tell but that the Turks had as good Scriptures to prove their Mahomet [Mohammed] the Saviour, as we must prove our Jesus is? And, could I think, that so many ten thousand, in so many countries and kingdoms, should be without the knowledge of the right way to heaven. If there were indeed a heaven, and that we only, who live in a corner of the earth, should alone be blessed therewith? Everyone doth think his own religion right, both Jews and Moors, and Pagans! And how if all our faith, and Christ, and Scriptures, should be but a think-so too?

While I was in this temptation, I should often find my mind suddenly put upon it, to curse and swear, or to speak some grievous thing against God, or Christ his Son, and of the Scriptures.

JANUARY 11

No Peace for Mind

"There is no peace," says my God, "for the wicked."

ISAIAH 57:21

In these days, when I have heard others talk of what was the sin against the Holy Ghost, then would the tempter so provoke me to desire to sin that sin. But it was as if I could not, must not, neither should be quiet until I had committed it. If it were to be committed by speaking of such a word, then I would have been as if my mouth would have spoken that word. And in so strong a measure was this temptation upon me, that often I have been ready to clap my hand under my chin—to hold my mouth from opening. And to that end also I have had thoughts at other times—to leap with my head downward—into some muck hill hole or other, to keep my mouth from speaking! This Scripture did also tear and rend my soul, during these distractions, "The wicked are like the troubled sea when it cannot rest, whose waters cast up mire and dirt."

And now my heart was, at times, exceedingly hard. I was very dejected to think that this should be my lot. I saw some could mourn and lament their sin. And others, again, could rejoice, and bless God for Christ. And others could quietly talk of, and with gladness remember, the Word of God. While I was only in the storm or tempest. This much sunk me: I thought my condition was alone. I should, therefore, much bewail my bad ... [luck]. But get out of, or get rid of, these things, I could not.

While this temptation lasted, which was about a year, I could attend upon none of the ordinances of God but with sore and great affliction. Yea, then I was most distressed with blasphemies.

JANUARY 12

Peace through Christ's Blood

... and through him [Christ] to reconcile to himself all things, whether on earth or in heaven making peace by the blood of his cross.

COLOSSIANS 1:20

I remember that one day, as I was traveling into the country and musing on the wickedness and blasphemy of my heart, and considering of the enmity that was in me against God that Scripture came in my mind, He hath "made peace through the blood of his cross" (Col. 1:20). By which I was made to see, both again, and again, and again, that day—that God and my soul were friends by this blood. Yes, I saw that the justice of God and my sinful soul could embrace and kiss each other through this blood. This was a good day for me; I hope I shall not forget it!

At another time, as I sat by the fire in my house, and musing on my wretchedness, the Lord made that also a precious Word unto me, "Since therefore the children share flesh and blood, he himself likewise partook of the same things, that through death he might destroy the one who has the power of death, that is, the devil, and deliver all those who through fear of death were subject to lifelong slavery" (Heb. 2:14-15). I thought that the glory of these words was then so weighty on me that I was, both once and twice, ready to faint from extreme emotion! Yet not with grief and trouble, but with solid joy and peace.

At this time, I sat under the ministry of holy Mr. Gifford, whose preaching, by God's grace, was much for my stability. He pressed us to take special heed to cry mightily to God that he would convince us of the reality [of the gospel], and set us down therein, by his own Spirit, in the holy Word. For, said he, if you do otherwise then temptations will come.

JANUARY 13

Another Comforter

And I will ask the Father, and he will give you another Helper, to be with you forever.

JOHN 14:16

And now, methought, I began to investigate the Bible with new eyes and read as I never did before. And . . . the epistles of the apostle Paul were sweet and pleasant to me. Indeed, I was then never out of the Bible, either by reading or meditation. [I was] still crying out to God that I might know the truth, and way to heaven and glory.

And as I went on and read, I lighted on that passage, "To one is given by the Spirit the word of wisdom; to another the word of knowledge by the same Spirit; and to another faith" (1 Cor. 12:8-9). And though, as I have since seen that by this Scripture the Holy Ghost intends, in special things extraordinary, yet on me it did then fasten with conviction. I did want things ordinary, even that understanding and wisdom that other Christians had. On this word I mused and could not tell what to do.

No, said I with myself, though I am convinced that I am an ignorant sort and that I want those blessed gifts of knowledge and understanding that other good people have. Yet, at a venture, I will conclude I am not altogether faithless, though I know not what faith is. For it had been showed me and that too as I have since seen, and that by Satan, that those who conclude themselves in a faithless state, have neither rest nor quiet in their souls; and I was loath to fall quite into despair.

Wherefore, by this suggestion, I was for a while made afraid to see my want of faith. But God would not suffer me thus to undo and destroy my soul, but did continually, against this my blind and sad conclusion, create still within me such suppositions.

JANUARY 14

To Leave Christ or Not?

They went out from us, but they were not of us; for if they had been of us, they would have continued with us. But they went out, that it might become plain that they all are not of us.

1 JOHN 2:19

And now I found that I loved Christ dearly. But I thought my soul clung unto him and my affections clung unto him. I felt love for him as hot as fire. But I did quickly find that my great love was but little. I who had, as I thought, such burning love to Jesus Christ, could let him go again for a very small thing! God can tell how to abase us and can hide pride from man. Quickly after this my love for him was tried.

For after the Lord had thus graciously delivered me from this great and sore temptation and had set me down so sweetly in the faith of his holy gospel and had given me such strong consolation and blessed evidence from heaven touching my interest in his love through Christ; the tempter came upon me again, and that with a more grievous and dreadful temptation than before.

And the temptation was this: To sell and part with this most blessed Christ and to exchange him for the things of this life. The temptation lay upon me for the space of a year and did follow me so continually that I was not rid of it one day in a month. No, not even one hour in many days together, the only time being when I was asleep.

And though, in my judgment, I was persuaded that those who were once effectually in Christ, as I hoped, through his grace, I had seen myself, that I could never lose him forever.

JANUARY 15

Holy or Profane Like Esau?

And the blood of Jesus his Son cleanses us from all sin.

1 JOHN 1:7B

In addition, that Scripture did seize upon my soul, "Lest there be any fornicator, or profane person, as Esau, who for one morsel of meat sold his birthright. For ye know how that afterward, when he would have inherited the blessing, he was rejected: for he found no place of repentance, though he sought it carefully with tears" (Heb. 12:16-17).

Now, I was one bound, I felt myself shut out unto the judgment to come. Nothing now for two years together would abide with me, but damnation, and an expectation of damnation.

These words were to my soul like fetters of brass to my legs, in the continual sound of which I went together for several months. But about ten or eleven o'clock one day, as I was walking under a hedge, full of sorrow and guilt, God knows that I was bemoaning myself for this hard hap [fortune], that such a thought should arise within me. Suddenly this sentence bolted in upon me, the blood of Christ remits all guilt! At this I made a stand in my spirit; when this word took hold upon me!

Now I began to conceive peace in my soul. At the same time also I had my sin, and the blood of Christ thus represented to me. That my sin, when compared to the blood of Christ, was no more to me, than a little clot or stone before me in this vast and wide field that I saw. This gave me good encouragement for the space of two or three hours. Now I thought I saw, by faith, the Son of God, as suffering for my sins. But because it did not last; I therefore sunk in my spirit under exceeding guilt again.

JANUARY 16

Presumptuous Sinner?

Keep back your servant also from presumptuous sins; let them not have dominion over me!

Psalm 19:13

Then again, being unwilling to perish, I began to compare my sin with others; to see if I could find that any of those that were saved had done as I did. So, I considered David's adultery and murder, and found them the most heinous crimes. They were committed after he received light and grace. I saw his transgressions were only such as were against the law of Moses. The Lord Christ could deliver him. But mine was against His gospel. Yes, I sinned against the mediator. "I had sold my Saviour"!

Should I not be publicly executed, when I considered that; besides the guilt that possessed me, I should be so void of grace? What must this great sin be? It must be the great transgression (Ps. 19:13)? Must that wicked one [the devil] touch my soul (1 John 5:18)? Oh, what stings did I find in all these sentences!

What, is there only one sin that is unpardonable? But one sin that would put away the soul without the reach of God's mercy; and I must be guilty of it? It must be?! Is there but one sin among so many millions of sins, for which there is no forgiveness? And must I commit this one sin? Oh, unhappy sin! Oh, unhappy man! These things would break and confound my spirit so much that I did not know what to do? I thought, at times, they would have brought me to my wits' end. And still, to aggravate my misery, the thought would run through my mind, "Ye know how that afterward, when [Esau] would have inherited the blessing, he was rejected." Oh! No one knows the terrors of those days like I do!

JANUARY 17

Am I a Rebel?

But if you refuse and rebel, you shall be eaten by the sword; for the mouth of the Lord has spoken.

ISAIAH 1:20

Then I was struck into a very great trembling. So much that at times I could, for whole days together, feel my very body, as well as my mind, to shake and totter under the sense of the dreadful judgment of God. This should fall on those that have sinned that most fearful and unpardonable sin. I also felt such a clogging and heat in my stomach, by reason of this terror; that I was especially at some times, as if my breastbone would have split in sunder. Then I thought of that concerning Judas, who, by his falling headlong, burst asunder and all his bowels gushed out (Acts 1:18).

I feared also that this was the mark that the Lord set on Cain. I even continued to fear and tremble, under the heavy load of guilt that he had charged on him for the blood of his brother Abel. Thus, did I ... shrink under the burden that was upon me. The burden which also did so oppress me, that I could neither stand, nor go, nor lie, either at rest or quiet.

Yet that saying would sometimes come to my mind, He hath received gifts for the rebellious (Ps. 68:18). "The rebellious," I thought; surely, they are such as once were under subjection to their prince. Even those who, after they have sworn subjection to his government ... have taken up arms against him, I thought [it] is my very condition! Once I loved ... [Christ], feared him, served him; but now I am a rebel. I have sold him, I said, "Let him go if he will; but yet he has gifts for rebels, and then why not for me?"

JANUARY 18

Post Tenebras Lux
(After Darkness Light)

See that you do not refuse him who is speaking. For if they did not escape when they refused him who warned them on earth, much less will we escape if we reject him who warns from heaven.

HEBREWS 12:25

Once as I was walking back and forth in a good man's shop, I bemoaned in my sad and doleful state. I afflicted myself with self-abhorrence for this wicked and ungodly thought. I lamented this hard hap [fortune] of mine. That I should commit so great a sin, greatly fearing I should not be pardoned. Praying in my heart, that if this sin of mine did differ from that against the Holy Ghost, the Lord would show it me. And now ready to sink with fear; suddenly there was, as if there had rushed in at the window, the noise of wind upon me. But very pleasant as if I heard a voice speaking, "Didst [thou] ever refuse to be justified by the blood of Christ?" And, then my whole life and profession past was in a moment opened to me. Wherein I was made to see that deliberately I had not. So, my heart answered groaningly, then fell, with power, that Word of God upon me, "See that ye refuse not him that speaketh" (Heb. 12:25). This made a strange seizure upon my spirit; it brought light with it. And it commanded a silence in my heart of all those tumultuous thoughts that before did use—like hellhounds—to roar and bellow and make a hideous noise within me. It showed me that Jesus Christ had yet a word of grace and mercy for me. That he had not, as I had feared, quite forsaken and cast off my soul. Rather, this was a kind of a chide for my proneness to desperation. It was a kind of a threatening me—if I did not—despite my sins and the heinousness of them, [that I should] venture my salvation upon the Son of God.

JANUARY 19

The Saviour Turned Lion and Destroyer

For the great day of ... wrath has come, who can stand?
REVELATION 6:17

Now, the most free and full and gracious words of the gospel were the greatest torment to me. Nothing so afflicted me as the thoughts of Jesus Christ, the remembrance of a Saviour. Because I had cast him off! It brought forth the villainy of my sin and my loss of salvation to [my] mind. For nothing did twinge my conscience like this. Every time I thought of the Lord Jesus: of his grace, love, goodness, kindness, gentleness, meekness, death, blood, promises and blessed exhortations, comforts, and consolations; they all went to my soul like a sword. All these considerations of the Lord Jesus, these thoughts would make place for themselves in my heart. Yes, this is the Jesus, the loving Saviour, the Son of God, whom thou hast parted with, whom you slighted, despised, and abused! This is the only Saviour, the only Redeemer, the only one that could so love sinners as to wash them from their sins in his own most precious blood. But you have no part nor lot in this Jesus, you have put him from you, you have said [such] in your heart. Let him go if he will.

Now, therefore, you are severed from him; *you have* severed yourself from him. Behold, his goodness; but you are no partaker of it. Oh, I thought, what have I lost! What have I parted with! What have I disinherited my poor soul of! Oh! It is sad to be destroyed by the grace and mercy of God; to have the Lamb, the Saviour, turn lion and destroyer (Rev. 6).

JANUARY 20

Only Temporary Relief

If you, O Lord, should mark iniquities, O Lord, who could stand? But with you there is forgiveness, that you may be feared.

Psalm 130:3-4

And as I was thus in musing and in my studies, I considered how to love the Lord and to express my love to him. It came to me, "If thou, Lord, shouldest mark iniquities, O Lord, who shall stand? But there is forgiveness with thee, that thou mayest be feared" (Ps. 130:3-4). These were good words to me, especially the latter part. Especially, that there is forgiveness with the Lord that he might be feared. This I understood that he might be loved and had in reverence. For it was thus made known to me. The great God did set so high esteem [on] the love of his poor creatures; that rather than go without their love he would pardon their transgressions.

And now was that word fulfilled in me, and I was also refreshed by it. Then they shall be ashamed and confounded, "and never open their mouth anymore because of their shame, when I am pacified toward them for all that they have done, saith the Lord God" (Ezek. 16:63). Thus, I thought in my soul at this time, [I was] forever set at liberty from being again afflicted with my former guilt and amazement.

But now [again] was the word of the gospel forced from my soul, so that no promise or encouragement was to be found in the Bible for me. And now would that saying work upon my spirit to afflict me, "Rejoice not, O Israel, for joy as other people" (Hosea 9:1). For I saw indeed there was cause of rejoicing for those that held to Jesus. But as for me, I had cut myself off by my transgressions, and left myself neither foothold, nor handhold, amongst all the stays and props in the precious Word of Life.

JANUARY 21

Sustained by Prayer

But he said to me, "My grace is sufficient for you, my power is made perfect in weakness."

2 CORINTHIANS 12:9

At another time, I remember I was again much under the question, Whether the blood of Christ was sufficient to save my soul? In which doubt I continued from morning till about seven or eight at night; until I was quite worn out with fear. These words did sound suddenly within my heart, He is able! But I thought this word "ABLE" was spoke so loud to me; it showed such a great word, it seemed to be writ in great letters. And it ended [my] my fears just like that. I mean for a time it stayed with me—about a day. I never had such an experience in all my life, either before or after that.

But one morning, when I was again at prayer, and trembling under the fear that no word of God could help me, that piece of a sentence darted in upon me, "My grace is sufficient." I thought I felt secure, as if there might be hope. But, oh how good a thing it is for God to send his Word! For about a fortnight [15 days] before I was looking at this very place [in the Scriptures], and then I thought it could not come near my soul with comfort. Then I thought God's grace was not large enough for me; no, not [nearly] large enough! But now, it was as if it had arms so wide that it could not only enclose me, but many more besides.

By these words I was sustained, yet not without exceeding conflicts. For the space of seven or eight weeks, my peace would be in and out, sometimes twenty times a day. Therefore, I still did pray to God that he would help me to apply the whole sentence, "My grace is sufficient."

JANUARY 22

Striving

All the Father gives me will come to me, and whoever comes to me I will never cast out.

JOHN 6:37

Thus, I was confounded, not knowing what to do, nor how to be satisfied with this question: Whether the Scriptures could agree in the salvation of my soul? I quaked at the apostles! I knew their words were true and that they must stand for ever.

This Scripture did most sweetly visit my soul: "And him that cometh to me I will in no wise cast out" (John 6:37). Oh, the comfort that I have had from this Word, "in no wise"! But Satan would greatly labour to pull this promise from me, telling of me that Christ did not mean me. [But] I was a sinner of lower rank, who had done as I had done?

But I answered Satan—there is in this Word no such exception—but "him that comes"! HIM, any *him*; "him that cometh to me I will in no wise cast out." And this I well remember still; that of all the cunning Satan used to take this Scripture from me, yet he never did so much as put this question to me. But do you come rightly? Because [then] I saw that to come aright was to come as I was, a vile and ungodly sinner. I had to cast myself at the feet of [His] mercy, condemning myself for sin. If ever Satan and I did strive for any Word of God in all my life, it was for this good word of Christ; he at one end and I at the other. Oh, what struggle Satan and I had! It was for verse in John's Gospel I say—we did so tug and strive—he pulled, and I pulled. But God be praised, I got the better of him. I got some sweetness from the experience.

JANUARY 23

Personal Apostacy Considered

For it is impossible, in the case of those who have once been enlightened, who have tasted the heavenly gift, and have shared in the Holy Spirit, and have tasted the goodness of the word of God and the powers of the age to come and then have fallen away, to restore them again to repentance. ...

HEBREWS 6:4-6

When I had, with much deliberation, considered the matter [of apostacy], I could not conclude that the Lord had comforted me. I thought I should not come close to those most fearful and terrible Scriptures.

When I came to these Scriptures, I found their expression changed. Then they looked not so grimly to me as before I thought they did. *First,* I came to the sixth chapter of the Hebrews, yet trembling for fear it should strike me! When I had considered it, I found the falling intended was a falling away completely. That is, as I conceived, a falling from, and an absolute denial of the gospel of remission of sins by Christ, for from them the apostle begins his argument (vv 1-3). *Secondly,* I found that this falling away must be openly; even in the view of the world, even so as "to put Christ to an open shame." *Thirdly*, I found that those he intended were forever shut up of God—in blindness, hardness, and impenitency. It is impossible they should be renewed again unto repentance. By all these particulars, I found, to God's everlasting praise, my sin was not the sin in this place intended.

First, I confessed I was fallen, but not fallen away from the profession of faith in Jesus unto eternal life. *Secondly*, I confessed that I had put Jesus Christ to shame by my sin—but not to open shame. I did not deny him before men, nor condemn him as a fruitless one before the world. *Thirdly*, nor did I find that God had shut me up or denied me to come. Though I found it hard work indeed to come to him by sorrow and repentance. Blessed be God for unsearchable grace.

JANUARY 24

Christ Exalted

The LORD says to my Lord: "Sit at my right hand, until I make your enemies your footstool."

PSALM 110:1

Here I lived for some time, very sweetly at peace with God through Christ. Oh, I thought, Christ! Christ! There was nothing but Christ that was before my eyes. I was not only looking upon this and the other benefits of Christ—his blood, burial, or resurrection—[as parts]. But [finally] considered him as a whole Christ! In him, all these and all other of his virtues, relations, offices, and operations met together. Because he sat on the right hand of God in heaven.

It was glorious for me to see his exaltation and the worth and prevalence of all his benefits. And it was because of this: Now I could look from myself to him and should reckon all these graces of God that now were ... [great] to me. In Christ, my Lord and Saviour! Now Christ was all! All my wisdom, all my righteousness, all my sanctification, and all my redemption.

Further, the Lord did also lead me into the mystery of union with the Son of God. That I was joined to him, that I was flesh of his flesh, and bone of his bone, and now was that a sweet word to me in Ephesians 5:30 ["For we are members of his body"]. By this also was my faith in him, as my righteousness, the more confirmed to me. For if he and I were one, then his righteousness was mine, his merits mine, his victory also mine. Now could I see myself in heaven and earth at once. In heaven by my Christ, by my head, by my righteousness and life, though on earth by my body or person.

JANUARY 25

Where Is There a Refuge?

To them were given Shechem, the city of refuge for the manslayer, with its pastureland in the hill country of Ephraim, Gezer its pasturelands ...

JOSHUA 21:21

Another cause of temptation was that I had tempted God. On this manner did I do it. Upon a time, my wife was great with child. Her pangs were fierce and strong upon her as if she would have immediately fallen into labour and been delivered of an untimely birth. Now, at this very time it was, that I had been so strongly tempted to question the being of God. When my wife lay crying by me; I said with all secrecy imaginable, even thinking [and praying] in my heart: "Lord, if you will now remove this sad affliction from my wife and cause that she be troubled no more this night, then I shall know that thou can discern the most secret thoughts of the heart."

I had no sooner said it in my heart; than her pangs were taken from her, and she was cast into a deep sleep, and so she continued till morning! At this I greatly marveled, not knowing what to think[?] I was shown in my heart how the Lord revealed he knew my secret thoughts—which was a great astonishment unto me for several weeks after.

The Scriptures now also were wonderful things unto me. I saw that the truth of them were the keys of the kingdom of heaven. Those that the Scriptures favor must inherit bliss, but those that they oppose and condemn must perish forever. Oh! this Word, "Whose soever sins ye remit, they are remitted unto them; and whose soever sins ye retain, they are retained." Now I saw the apostles to be the elders of the city of refuge, those that they were to receive in, were received to life. But those that they shut out were to be slain by the avenger of blood.

JANUARY 26

Temptations Galore

But let a man examine himself, and so let him eat of the bread, and drink of the cup.

1 CORINTHIANS 11:28

Now I shall go forward to give you a relation of the Lord's dealings with me; of his dealings with me at different seasons, and of the temptations I did meet. I shall begin with what I met when I first did join in fellowship with the people [church] of God in Bedford. After I had propounded to the church that my desire was to walk in the order and ordinances of Christ with them and [I] was also admitted by them [to membership]. While I thought of that blessed ordinance of Christ, which was his last supper with his disciples before his death; that Scripture "This do in remembrance of me" (Luke 22:19) was made a very precious Word unto me. For by it the Lord did come down upon my conscience with the discovery of his death for my sins. I then felt as if he plunged me in the virtue of the same. Behold, I had not been a partaker at that ordinance for long, but such fierce and sad temptations did always attend me. Both to blaspheme the ordinance; and to wish some deadly thing on those who also ate it. Unless I should at any time be guilty of consenting to these wicked and fearful thoughts I was forced to bend myself all the while to pray to God to keep me from such blasphemies. And, to cry to God to bless the bread and cup to them as it went from mouth to mouth. The reason for this temptation I have thought since was this: Because I did not take it with that reverence when at first I approached to partake of it.

JANUARY 27

A Joyful Breakthrough

And he cried out, "Jesus, Son of David, have mercy on me!"
LUKE 18:38

At another time, though just before I was well and savoury [peaceful] in my spirit, yet suddenly there fell upon me a great cloud of darkness, which did so hide from me the things of God and Christ, that it was as if I had never seen or known them in my life.

Then with joy I told my wife, O now I know, I know! [For] ... that night was a good night to me, I never had a few better. I longed for the company of some of God's people that I might have imparted unto them what God had showed me. Christ was a precious Christ to my soul that night. I could scarce lie in my bed for joy, and peace, and triumph through Christ. This great glory did not continue upon me until morning, yet that twelfth [chapter] of the author to the Hebrews (Heb. 12:22-23) was a blessed Scripture to me for many days together after this.

The words are these,

> Ye are come unto mount Sion, and unto the city of the living God, the heavenly Jerusalem, and to an innumerable company of angels, to the general assembly and church of the firstborn, which are written in heaven, and to God the judge of all, and to the spirits of just men made perfect, and to Jesus the mediator of the new covenant, and to the blood of sprinkling, that speaketh better things than that of Abel.

Through this blessed sentence the Lord led me over and over, first to this word, and then to that, and showed me wonderful glory in every one of them. These words also have oft[en] since this time been great refreshment to my spirit. Blessed be God for having mercy on me.

JANUARY 28

Call to the Ministry, Part 1

Then I said, "Here I am! Send me."

Isaiah 6:8

And now I am speaking my experience, I will in this place thrust in a word or two concerning my preaching the Word and God's dealing with me. For after I had been about five or six years awakened [converted], I helped myself to see both the want and worth of Jesus Christ our Lord. I also ventured my soul upon him. Some of the most able among the saints, did perceive that God had counted me worthy to understand something of his will in his holy and blessed Word. And [He] had given me utterance, in some measure to express what I saw to others for edification. Therefore, they desired for me, with much earnestness, that I would be willing to take in hand, in one of the meetings, to speak [preach] a word of exhortation unto them.

Wherefore, the church desired, after prayer to the Lord—with fasting—I was more particularly called forth and appointed to a more ordinary and public preaching of the word. Not only to, and amongst them that believed, but also to offer the gospel to those who had not yet received the faith. And about that time, I did evidently find in my mind a secret pricking for the task. And I bless God, not for desire of vain glory. But at that time, I was most sorely afflicted with the fiery darts of the devil concerning my eternal state.

Yet I could not be content, unless I was found in the exercise of my gift, unto which also I was greatly animated, not only by the continual desires of the godly, but also by that saying of Paul to the Corinthians, "... [T]he household of Stephanas ... devoted themselves to the service of the saints" (1 Cor. 16:15).

JANUARY 29

Call to the Ministry, Part 2

Each one should be fully convinced in his own mind.

ROMANS 14:5B

When I went first to preach the Word abroad, the doctors and priests [ministers] of the country did open wide against me. But I was persuaded of this, not to render railing for railing. But to see how many of the carnal professors I could convince of their miserable state by the law, and of their want and worth of Christ. For I thought, this shall answer for me in time to come, when ... [my work will be vindicated] before their faces.

I never cared to meddle with things that were controversial and in dispute among the saints, especially things of the lower nature. Yet it pleased me much to contend with great earnestness for the word of faith and the remission of sins by the death and sufferings of Jesus. But I say as to other things, I should leave them alone. Because I saw they engendered strife; because they neither, in doing nor in leaving undone commended us to God. Besides, I saw the work before me, did run in another channel, even to carry an [evangelical] awakening word. To that, therefore, did I stick and adhere.

I never endeavored to, nor dare make use of other men's lines [sermons]. Though I condemn not all that do. For I verily thought and found by experience; that what had been taught to me by the Word and Spirit of Christ, could be spoken, maintained, and stood to be the soundest and best-established conscience. And though I will not now speak all that I know in this matter, yet my experience hath more interest in that text of Scripture than many amongst men are aware.

JANUARY 30

Call to the Ministry, Part 3

The fruit of the righteous is a tree of life, and whoever captures souls is wise.

PROVERBS 11:30

If any of those who were awakened by my ministry did after that fall back, as sometimes too many did, I can truly say their loss has been more to me than if one of my own children, begotten of my body, had been going to their grave. I may speak without an offense to the Lord, nothing hath gone so near me as that—unless it was the fear of the loss of the salvation of my own soul. My heart had been so wrapped up in the glory of this excellent work; I counted myself more blessed and honored of God by this than if he had made me the emperor of the Christian world, or the lord of all the glory of the earth without it! O these words, "He which converteth the sinner from the error of his way shall save a soul from death" (James 5:20). "The fruit of the righteous is a tree of life; and he that winneth souls is wise" (Prov. 11:30). "They that be wise shall shine as the brightness of the firmament; and they that turn many to righteousness as the stars for ever and ever" (Dan. 12:3). "For what is our hope, or joy, or crown of rejoicing? Are not even ye in the presence of our Lord Jesus Christ at his coming? For ye are our glory and joy" (1 Thess. 2:19-20). These, I say, with many others of a like nature have been great refreshments to me.

I have observed, that where I have had a work to do for God, I have had first, God moving upon my spirit to desire I might preach there. I have also observed that such and such souls have been strongly set upon my heart, and I was stirred up to wish for their salvation.

JANUARY 31

Call to the Ministry, Part 4

My little children, for whom I am again in the anguish of childbirth, until Christ is formed in you.

GALATIANS 4:19

In my preaching I have really been in pain, and have, as it were, travailed to bring forth children to God. Neither could I be satisfied unless some fruits appeared in my work. If I were fruitless, it mattered not who commended me. But if I were fruitful, I cared not who did condemn. I have thought of that, "Lo, children are an heritage of the Lord. ... Happy is the man that hath filled his quiver full of them" (Ps. 127:3-5).

Sometimes, again, when I had been preaching, I was violently assaulted with thoughts of blasphemy. And I was strongly tempted to speak the words with my mouth before the congregation. I have also been tempted to do so even when I have begun to speak the Word with much clearness, evidence, and liberty of speech. Before the ending of that opportunity, I was so blind and so separated from me the things I was speaking. And I was also so focused on my speech; to utterance before the people that I had not known or remembered what I was about to say. It was as if my head had been in a bag all the time when I was trying to preach.

Again, when at other times I have been about to preach upon some smart and scorching portion of the Word; I found the tempter suggest: What, will you preach this? This condemns yourself! Of this your own soul is guilty! You cannot preach this at all, or if you do, you will be cut into pieces so to make a way for your own escape. Instead of awakening others, you will lay that guilt upon your own soul, and you will never get out from under it.

FEBRUARY 1

I Believe in the Holy Trinity

Hear, O Israel: "The LORD our God, the LORD is one."

DEUTERONOMY 6:4

I believe that there is but one, only true God, and there is none other but he. *To us there is but one God the Father of whom are all things. And this is life eternal that they might know thee, the only true God* (Mark 12:32; 1 Cor. 8:8; John 17:3; Acts 17:24).

I believe that this God is Almighty, Eternal, Invisible, Incomprehensible. *I am the Almighty God, walk before me and be thou perfect. The eternal God is thy refuge. Now unto the king eternal, Immortal, Invisible, the only wise God, be honor and glory for ever and ever.* (Gen. 17:1; Deut. 33:26-27; 1 Tim. 1:17; Job 11:7; Rom. 11:33).

I believe that this God is unspeakably perfect in all his attributes of power, wisdom, justice, truth, holiness, mercy, love, his power is said to be *eternal,* his understanding and wisdom, *infinite*; he is called the *just Lord* in opposition to all things; he is said to be truth itself and the God thereof: There is no one as holy as the Lord. *God is love. Canst thou by searching find out God; canst thou find out the Almighty unto perfection?* (Rom. 1:20; Ps. 147:5, Zeph. 3:5; 2 Thess. 2:10; Deut. 32:4; Job 11:7).

I believe that in the Godhead, there are *three persons* or subsistence. *There are three that bare record in heaven. The Father, the Word, and the Holy Ghost.* (1 John 5:7; see also: Gen. 1:26; 3:22; 11:7; Isa. 6:8).

I believe that these three are in Nature, Essence, and Eternity, *equally one. These three are one.*(1 John 5:7).

FEBRUARY 2

I Believe in the World to Come

To him who sits on the throne and to the Lamb be blessing and honor and glory and might forever and ever!

REVELATION 5:13B

I believe *there is a world to come* (Heb. 2:5, 6:5).

I believe that there shall be a resurrection of the dead, both just, and unjust.

> Many that sleep in the dust of the earth shall awake, some to everlasting life, and some to everlasting shame and contempt. Marvel not at this. For the hour is coming, in the which all that are in their graves shall hear his voice, and shall come forth, they that have done good, to the resurrection of life, and they that have done evil, to the resurrection of damnation (Acts 24:15; Dan. 12:2; John 5:28).

I believe that they that shall be counted worthy of that world, and of the resurrection from the dead, neither marry nor are given in marriage, neither can they die any more, *for they are equal to the Angels, and are the children of God, being the children of the resurrection* (Luke 20:34-36).

I believe that those that dye impenitent, shall be tormented with the devil and his angels, and shall be cast with them into the Lake that burns with fire and brimstone, *where their worm dies not, and the fire is not quenched* (Rev. 21:8; Mark 9:43, 48; Matt. 25:41, 46; John 5:29).

I believe, that because God is naturally holy and just, even as he is good and merciful; therefore (all having sinned) none can be saved, *without the means of a redeemer.*

> Then he is gracious unto him, and saith, deliver him from going down to the pit, I have found a ransom. We have redemption through his blood, even the forgiveness of our sins. For which out shedding of blood, is no remission (Job 33:24; Col. 1:14. Heb. 9:22).

FEBRUARY 3

I Believe in Christ as Redeemer

... You were ... ransomed ... with the precious blood of Christ, like that of a lamb without blemish or spot.

1 PETER 1:18-19

I believe that Jesus Christ our Lord himself is the redeemer.

> They remembered that God was their rock, and the high God their redeemer. Forasmuch as ye know, that ye were not redeemed, with corruptible things, as silver and gold, from your empty conversation received by tradition from your Fathers; But with the precious blood of Christ, as of a Lamb without blemish; and without spot.

I believe that the great reason why the Lord, the second person in the Godhead, did clothe himself with our flesh and blood, was that he might be capable of obtaining the redemption, that before the world, was intended for us.

> Forasmuch then as the children were made partakers of flesh and blood, he also himself likewise took part of the same; (mark) that through death he might destroy him that had the power of death, that is the devil, and deliver them who through fear of death, were all their lifetime subject to bondage. When the fulness of the time was come, God sent forth his Son made of a woman, made under the Law to redeem them that were under the Law. Wherefore it behooved him in all things to be made like unto his brethren; that he might be a merciful, and faithful high priest in things pertaining to God; To make reconciliation for the sins of the people. For in that himself hath suffered being tempted, he is able also to support them that are tempted. Christ hath redeemed us from the curse of the Law, being made a curse for us. As it is written cursed is every one that is hung on a tree. That the blessing of Abraham might come upon the Gentiles, through faith in Jesus Christ (Heb. 2:14-15; Gal. 4:4; Heb. 2:17-18; Gal. 3:13-14).

FEBRUARY 4

I Believe in the Virgin Birth

Therefore, the LORD himself will give you a sign. Behold, the virgin shall conceive and bear a son, and shall call his name Immanuel.

ISAIAH 7:14

I believe that the time when ... [Jesus] clothed himself with our flesh, was in the days of the reign of *Caesar Augustus*. Then I say, and not till then, was the word made flesh, or clothed with our nature.

> And it came to pass in those days, that there went out a decree from *Caesar Augustus*, that all the world should be taxed; And Joseph went up from Galilee, out of the City of Nazareth unto Judah, unto the city of David, which is called Bethlehem; because he was of the house and lineage of David, to be taxed with Mary his espoused wife being great with child. And so, it was ... the days were accomplished, that she should be delivered. (Luke 2:1-6)

And this child was he of whom godly Simeon was told by the Holy Ghost, when he said, that he should not see death until he had seen the Lord Christ (John 1:14; 1 Tim. 3:16; Luke 2:1-3, 6:25-27).

I believe, therefore that this very child, as before testified is both God and man, the Christ of the living God.

> And this shall be a sign unto you; you shall find the babe wrapped in swaddling clothes lying in a manger. But while he thought on these things, behold the Angel of the Lord appeared unto him; saying, Joseph, thou son of David, fear not to take unto you Mary your wife, for that which is conceived in her is of the Holy Ghost. And she shall bring forth a son, and thou shalt call his name Jesus; for he shall save his people from their sins. (Luke 2:7, 12; Matt. 1:21-22).

FEBRUARY 5

I Believe Christ Is Our Righteousness

The Lord *is our righteousness.*

Jeremiah 33:16b

I believe that the righteousness and redemption by which we believe makes us stand just before God. And we are saved from the curse of the Law; is that righteousness and redemption that consists in the personal acts and performances of this child Jesus—this God-man the Lord's Christ. I [also believe], that it is his personal fulfilling of the law for us ... [he satisfies] the utmost requirement of the justice of God. "Do not think (Jesus said) that I am come to destroy the Law, or the Prophets; I am not come to destroy, but to fulfill" (Matt. 5:17). By which means he became the end of the Law for righteousness to everyone that believeth (Rom. 10:4). "For what the Law could not do in that it was weak through the flesh; God sending his own son in the likeness of sinful flesh, and for sin, condemned sin in the flesh." (Rom. 8:3). So, finishing transgressions and making an end of sins and making reconciliation for iniquity, he brought in everlasting righteousness.

I believe, that for the completion of this work, he was always sinless. He did always the things that pleased God's Justice. [I believe] that every one of his acts; both of doing and suffering and rising again from the dead were really and infinitely perfect—being done by him as [THE] God-man: Wherefore, his acts before he died are called, the righteousness of God. His blood the blood of God; and herein we perceive the love of God in that he laid down his life for us. The Godhead which gave virtue to all the acts of human nature, was then in perfect union with it, when he hung upon the cross for our sins.

FEBRUARY 6

I Believe Christ Is Exalted

The LORD says to my Lord: "Sit at my right hand until I make your enemies your footstool."

PSALM 110:1

I believe that the righteousness that saves the sinner from the wrath to come, is properly and personally Christ's and ours as we have union with him. God, by his grace imputes it to us.

> Yea doubtless, I count all things loss for the excellency of the knowledge of Christ Jesus my Lord, for whom I have suffered the loss of all things, and do count them but dung that I may win Christ and be found in him, not having my own righteousness, which is of the Law, but that which is through the faith of Christ, the righteousness which is of God by faith (Phil. 3:8-9)

> For of him are ye in Christ Jesus, who of God is made unto us wisdom and righteousness, and sanctification, and redemption. (1 Cor. 1:30)

I believe God, as the reward of Christ's undertakings for us, hath exalted him to his own right hand, as our mediator, and given him a name above every name. And God hath made him Lord of all, and judge of the quick [living] and the dead. And in all this that we who believe might take courage to believe and hope in God. And being found in fashion as a man, he humbled himself unto death, even the death of the cross, (where he died for our sins). Wherefore God hath highly exalted him; and given him a name above every name. That at the name of Jesus every knee should bow, both of things in heaven, and things in earth, and things that are under the earth. And that every tongue should confess that Jesus Christ is Lord to the glory of God the Father (read Philippians 2).

FEBRUARY 7

I Believe in the Shed Blood

He entered once for all into the holy places, not by means of the blood of goats and calves, but by means of his own blood, thus securing eternal redemption.

HEBREWS 9:12

I believe, that being on the right hand of God in heaven, Christ doth effectually exercise the office of his excellent priesthood, and mediatorship. He presents himself continually before God, in the righteousness, which is accomplished for us when he was in the world. By the efficacy of his blood, he not only went into the holy place, but being there he obtained eternal redemption for us. Now, as receiving the worth and merit of His blood from the Father; he does bestow upon us grace, repentance, faith, and the remission of sins. Yes, he also received for us the Holy Ghost to be sent unto us, to confirm our adoption and glory. For if he were on earth, he should not be a Priest; seeing then we have a great high priest, that is entered into the heavens—Jesus the son of God. Let us hold fast our profession. For there is one God, and one mediator between God and men—the man Christ Jesus. For by his own blood, he entered the holy place, having obtained eternal redemption for us. For Christ is not entered into the holy places made with hands, which are the figure of the true; but into heaven itself, now to appear in the presence of God for us. Therefore, being by the right hand of God exalted; and having received of the Father, the promise of the Holy Ghost; he hath shed forth this which we now see and hear (Heb. 8:4; 1 Tim. 2:5; Heb. 9:12, 24; Act 5:31).

FEBRUARY 8

I Believe in Imputed Righteousness

Blessed is the man against whom the LORD counts no iniquity, and in whose spirit there is no deceit.

PSALM 32:2

I [also] believe, that [while he is] there, he shall continue till the restitution of all things, and then he shall come again in Glory, and shall sit in judgment upon all flesh.

And I believe that according to his sentence, so shall their judgment be.

I believe we are sinful creatures in ourselves, that no good thing done by us, can procure from God the imputation of the righteousness of Jesus Christ. But that the imputation is an act of grace—a free gift without our deserving it. Being justified freely by his grace through the redemption that is in Jesus Christ. He called us, and saved us, with a holy calling, not according to our works, but according to his own purpose and grace, which was given us in Christ Jesus. (Rom. 3:24, 5:17; 2 Tim. 1:9).

FEBRUARY 9

I Believe His Righteousness Is Received by Faith

And he [Abraham] believed the LORD, and He counted it to him as righteousness.

GENESIS 15:6

I believe that the offer of his righteousness, as tendered in the gospel, is to be received by faith. We are still in the very act of receiving it, judging ourselves sinners in our selves. Oh, wretched man that I am! Who shall deliver me from the body of this death? I thank God through Jesus Christ. Believe on the Lord Jesus Christ, and thou shalt be saved. The gospel is preached in all nations for the obedience of faith. Being justified freely by his grace, through the redemption that is in Jesus Christ. Whom God hath set forth to be a propitiation (a sacrifice to appease the displeasure of God) through faith in his blood. [This] declares his righteousness for the remission of sins that are passed [over by] the forbearance of God. To declare ... at this time his righteousness; that he might be just, and the justifier of him that believeth on Jesus. Therefore, men and brethren, ... this man is preached unto you the forgiveness of sins. And by him all that believe are justified from all things, from which they could not be justified by the law of Moses (Rom. 7:24; Acts 16:31; Rom. 3:24-25; Acts 13:38-39).

I believe that this faith, in respect to the imputation of this righteousness avails for justification before God. It is put forth itself in such ways as purely respect the offer of a gift. It is received, accepted, embraced, and trusted. As many as received him to them he gave power to become the sons of God, even to them that believe on his name. This is a faithful saying, and worthy of all acceptation that Jesus Christ came into the world to save sinners; of whom I am chief. (John 12:1; Tim. 1:15; Heb. 11:13; Eph. 1:13).

FEBRUARY 10

I Believe God Chooses

And when the Gentiles heard this, they began rejoicing and glorifying the Word of the Lord, and as many as were appointed to eternal life believed.

ACTS 13:48

I believe that the faith that [saves] is not to be found with any but those in whom the Spirit of God by mighty power does work it. All others, being fearful and incredulous, dare not venture their souls and eternity upon it. And consequently, it is called the faith that is wrought by the exceeding great and mighty power of God: The faith that is of the operation of God. And therefore, it is that others are said to be fearful and so unbelieving. These, with other ungodly sinners, must have their part in the lake of fire (Eph. 1:18-19; Col. 2:12; Eph. 2:8; Phil. 1:19; Rev. 21:8).

I believe that this faith is effectually wrought in none, but those which before the world, were appointed unto glory. And as many as were ordained unto eternal life believed. That he might make known the riches of his glory—upon the vessels of mercy—which he had before prepared to receive glory. We give thanks unto God always for you all, making mention always of you in our prayers. Remembering without ceasing your work of faith, and labour of love, and patience of hope in our Lord Jesus Christ in the sight of God. We know brethren, beloved, your election of God, but of the rest ... [Jesus] says, you believed not because ye are not of my sheep. Therefore, they could not believe, because [Isaiah] said: He hath blinded their eyes, and hardened their hearts that they should not see with their eyes; nor understand with their heart, and I should heal them. (Isa. 6:10).

FEBRUARY 11

I Believe We Are His Workmanship

For we are his workmanship, created in Christ Jesus for good works, which God prepared beforehand, that we should walk in them.

EPHESIANS 2:10

I believe that election is free and permanent, being founded in [God's] grace and unchangeable will of God. Even so then at this present time there is a remnant according to the election of grace. And if by grace, then it is no more of works; otherwise, grace is no more grace. But if it be of works, then it is no more of grace, otherwise work is no more work. Nevertheless, the foundation of God stands sure, having this seal: The Lord knows who are his. In whom also we have obtained an inheritance, being predestinated, according to the purpose of him who worketh all things after the counsel of his own will (Rom. 11:5-6; 2 Tim. 2:19; Eph. 1:11).

I believe that the decree of election is so far off from making any foreseen works in us as the ground or cause of the choice. And consequently, it is said: We are predestined to be conformed to the image of his Son. Not because we are; but we should be holy and without blame before him in love. For we are his workmanship, created in Christ Jesus, unto good works, which God hath before ordained that we should walk in them. He blessed us according as he chose us in Christ. And hence it is again that the salvation and calling of which we are now made partakers, is no other than what was given us in Christ Jesus before the world began—according to his eternal purpose which he purposed in Christ Jesus our Lord (Eph. 1:3-4, 2:10; 3:8-11; 2 Tim. 1:9; Rom. 8:26).

FEBRUARY 12

I Believe We Are Elect In Christ

Blessed be the God and Father of our Lord Jesus Christ, who has blessed us in Christ with every spiritual blessing in the heavenly places, even as he chose us in him before the foundation of the world, that we should be holy and blameless before him.

EPHESIANS 1:3-4

I believe that Christ Jesus is he in whom the elect are always considered; and that without him there is neither election, grace, nor salvation. Having predestinated us to the adoption of children by Jesus Christ to himself; according to the good pleasure of his will—to the praise of the glory of his grace. Where he has made us accepted in the beloved, in whom we have redemption through his blood, the forgiveness of sins according to the riches of his grace. That in the dispensation of the fullness of times; he might gather together in one all things in Christ which are in heaven. And gather all things that are in earth even in him. Neither is their salvation in any other: For there is none other name under heaven given among men, whereby we must be saved (Eph. 1:5-7, 10; Acts 4:12).

I believe that there is no impediment attending the election [elect] of God that can hinder their conversion and eternal salvation. Moreover, whom he did predestinate them he also called. And whom he called them he also justified. And whom he justified them he also glorified. What shall we say to these things; if God be for us, who can be against us? Who shall lay anything to the charge of God's elect? It is not God that justifies? Who is he that condemns? What then? Israel hath not obtained that which he seeks. But the election [elect] hath obtained it and the rest were blinded. For Israel hath not been forsaken nor Judah of his God the Lord of hosts. Though their land was filled with sin even against the holy one of Israel (Rom. 8:30-34, 11:7; Jer. 51:5; Acts 9:12-15).

FEBRUARY 13

God Only Justifies Sinners

[For all] ... are justified by his grace as a gift, through the redemption that is in Christ Jesus.

ROMANS 3:23-24

I believe also, That the power of imputing righteousness resideth only in God by Christ:

1. Sin being the transgression of the law.

2. The soul that hath sinned being his creature, and the righteousness also his, and his only. "Even as David also describeth the blessedness of the man, unto whom God imputeth righteousness without works, saying, Blessed are they whose iniquities are forgiven, and whose sins are covered. Blessed is the man to whom the Lord will not impute sin" (Rom. 4:6-8). Hence therefore it is said again, that men "shall abundantly utter the memory of thy great goodness, and shall sing of thy righteousness" (Ps. 145:7). "For he saith to Moses, I will have mercy on whom I will have mercy, and I will have compassion on whom I will have compassion. So, then it is not of him that willeth, nor of him that runneth, but of God that showeth mercy" (Rom. 9:15-16).

3. I believe the offer of this righteousness, as tendered in the gospel, is to be received by faith; we still in the very act of receiving it, judging ourselves sinners in ourselves. "Oh wretched man that I am! who shall deliver me from the body of this death? I thank God through Jesus Christ" (Rom. 7:24-25). "Believe on the Lord Jesus Christ, and thou shalt be saved" (Acts 16:31). The gospel is preached in all nations for the obedience of faith. "Being justified freely by his grace through the redemption that is in Christ Jesus; whom God hath set forth to be a propitiation, [a sacrifice to appease the displeasure of God] through faith in his blood. To declare his righteousness for the remission of sins that are past through the forbearance of God."

FEBRUARY 14

I Believe God's Word Quickens the Dead

When he had said these things, he cried out with a loud voice, "Lazarus, come forth."

JOHN 11:43

I believe, that to have an effectual calling the Holy Ghost must accompany the word of the gospel and with mighty power: I mean; that calling which is of God is made to be the fruit of electing love. I know, says Paul to the Thessalonians: "brethren, beloved your election of God. For our gospel came not unto you in word only; but also in power, and in the Holy Ghost, and in much assurance" (1 Thess. 1:4-5). Otherwise, men will not, cannot, hear and turn [or repent]. Samuel was called four times, before he knew the voice of him that spoke from heaven. It is said of them [the Israelites] in Hosea, as the prophets called them, so they went from them. And instead of turning to them, [they] sacrificed to Balaam, and burnt incense to graven images (1 Sam. 4:6, 10; Hos. 11:2).

The reason being: Because men by nature, are not only dead in sins but enemies in their minds by reason of wicked works. The call then is this: Awake you who sleep and arise from the dead, and Christ shall give you light (Eph. 5:14). Understand; therefore, that effectual calling is like that word of Christ that raised Lazarus from the dead: A word attended with an arm, that was omnipotent. Lazarus come forth—was a word to the dead—but not only so: It was a word for the dead; a word that raised him from the dead; a word that outwent all opposition; and that brought him forth of the grave though bound hand and foot (John 11:43; Eph. 2:1-2; Heb. 10:32; Gal. 1:15; Acts 9)!

FEBRUARY 15

I Believe God Effectually Awakens the Sinner

For this very reason, make every effort to supplement your faith with virtue, and virtue with knowledge.

2 PETER 1:5

An effectual awakening about the evil of sin, and especially of unbelief (John 16:9). And therefore, when the Lord God called Adam, he also made [known] unto him, an effectual discovery of sin; insomuch that he did strip him of all his righteousness (Gen. 3). Thus, he also served as the healer. It was such an awakening, he saw he was without Christ, without hope, and a stranger to the commonwealth of Israel, and without God in the world (Acts 16:29-30; Eph. 2:12). Oh, the dread and amazement that the guilt of sin brings with it when it is revealed by the God of heaven: [Nothing] like to it is the sight of mercy, when it pleased God, who called us by his grace, to reveal his Son in us.

In effectual calling, there is a great awakening about the world to come, and the glory of unseen things, the resurrection of the dead and eternal judgment; the salvation that God hath prepared for them that love him. And the blessedness that will attend us and be upon us at the coming of our Lord Jesus Christ; are all great things in the soul that is under the awakening calls of God. And hence we are said to be called to glory, to the obtaining of the Glory of our Lord Jesus Christ (1 Thess. 2:12; 2 Thess. 2:13-14).

In effectual calling, there is also a sanctifying virtue; And hence we are said to be called with a holy calling, with a heavenly calling: Called to glory and virtue. But ye are a chosen generation, a royal priesthood, a holy nation, a peculiar people, that you should shew forth the praises of him who hath called you out of darkness into his marvelous light (Heb. 3:1; 1 Thess. 4:7; 1 Pet. 1:8-9).

FEBRUARY 16

I Believe God Awakes the Dead

So, the captain came and said to him [Jonah], "What do you mean, you sleeper?"

JONAH 1:6

And hence it is that calling; it is sometimes expressed by quickening, awakening, illuminating, or bringing them forth of darkness to light that amazed and astonished those who witnessed it. For it is a strange thing for a man that lay long dead, or never saw the light with his eyes to be raised out of the grave; Or for him to be made to see that which he could not so much as once think of before—so it is with effectual calling (1 Pet. 2:9). Hence ... Peter said, he hath called us out of darkness into his marvelous light (Eph. 4:21; Acts 7:2). In effectual calling the voice of God is heard, and the gates of heaven are opened—when God called Abraham, he appeared to him in glory.

FEBRUARY 17

Turn to God in Repentance

Say to them, "As I live, declares the LORD God, I have no pleasure in the death of the wicked, but that the wicked turn from his way and live; turn back, turn back from your evil way, for why will you die, O House of Israel?"

EZEKIEL 33:11

[I believe] repentance is a turning of the heart to God in Christ: A turning from sin and the devil and darkness to the goodness and grace, and holiness that is in him. Wherefore they of olden day are said to repent because they came to loathe and abhor themselves for all their abominations. I abhor myself; said Job, and repent in dust, and ashes (Ezek. 6:9, 2:43, 36:31; Job 42:5-6).

Godly repentance: Doth not only affect the soul with the loathsome nature of sin that is past; but fills the heart with godly hatred of sins that yet may come. When Moses feared that through his being overburdened, with the care of the children of Israel, some unruly, or sinful passions might shew themselves in him—what did he say? I beseech thee kill me out of hand, if I have found grace in thy sight, and let me not see my wretchedness. (Num. 14:13-15).

Consider how Paul called godly repentance wrought in the upright Corinthians. Behold he said this same thing that you sorrowed after a godly sort: What carefulness it wrought in you? What clearing of yourselves? Yes, what fear? Yes, what vehement desire and what zeal, what revenge? In all things you have approved yourselves to be clear in this matter (2 Cor. 7:9-11).

FEBRUARY 18

Repentance unto Life

When they heard these things they fell silent. And they glorified God, saying, "Then to the Gentiles also God has granted repentance that leads to life."

ACTS 11:18

[I believe repentance] ... produces love. Wherefore Paul when he had put the church in remembrance that they were called of God; added concerning brotherly love they had no need that he should write unto them. If God be so kind to us, to forgive us our sins, to save our souls, and to give us the kingdom of heaven; let these be motives beyond all others to provoke us to love again. Further, if we who are beloved of God are made members of one man's body all partakers of his grace; clothed all with his glorious righteousness; and are together appointed to be the children of the next world; why should we not love one another?

Beloved, if God so loved us we ought also to love one another (1 John 4:11). And truly so we shall if the true grace of God be upon us. Because we also see them to be the called of Jesus. Travelers that are of the same country, love and take pleasure in one another when they meet in a strange land. We sojourn here in a strange country; with them that are heirs together with us of the promised kingdom and glory (Heb. 11:9). Now as I say, this holy love produces works by its love. Love in God, and Christ, when discovered, compels us to love.

The name, and word, and truth of God in Christ together with the sincerity of this grace; of faith, and holiness that is in us, are the delightful objects of this love.

FEBRUARY 19

I Trust God's Word

The grass withers, the flower fades, but the Word of God will stand forever.

ISAIAH 40:8

Touching ... [that] Word of God, I thus believe and confess. That all the holy Scriptures are the Words of God. All Scriptures are given by inspiration of God. For the prophecy of the Scripture came not in old time by the will of man; but holy men of God, speak as they were moved by the Holy Ghost [2 Pet. 1:20-21].

I believe that the holy Scriptures, of themselves, without the addition of human inventions, can make the man of God perfect in all things; and thoroughly furnished unto all good works. They are able to make one wise unto salvation through faith in Jesus Christ. And to you in all other things, that either respect the worship of God or walking before all men [2 Tim. 3:16-17].

I believe the great end why God committed the Scriptures to writing was: That we might be instructed in Christ, taught how to believe, encouraged to patience and hope. So, the grace that is to be brought unto us at the revelation of Jesus Christ; we might understand what is sin, and how to avoid the commission of them (John 20:31; 1 John 5:13; Rom. 15:4). Concerning the works of men (David said) by the word of thy lips, I have kept myself from the paths of the destroyer. Through your precepts I get understanding; therefore, I hate every false way. I have hidden thy word in my heart that I might not sin against thee [Ps. 17].

I believe that ... [the Scriptures] cannot be broken, but will certainly be fulfilled in all the prophecies, threatenings, and promises, either to the salvation, or damnation of men.

FEBRUARY 20

I Believe God Is Sovereign Over All

And He made from one man every nation of mankind to live on all the face of the earth, having determined allotted periods and the boundaries of their dwelling place.

ACTS 17:26

I believe Jesus Christ, by the word of the Scriptures, will judge all men at the day of doom. For that [judgment] is the book of the Law of the Lord according to Paul's Gospel.

I believe that this God made the world, and all things that are therein. For in six days the Lord made heaven and earth, the sea, and all that is in them. Also, that after the time of the making thereof, ... [He gave] it to the children of men and preserved it for the children of God—for all that would be born in all the ages to come. When the most high divided to the nations their inheritance, when he separated the sons of Adam; he set the bounds of the people according to the number of the children of Israel. For as he made of one blood all nations of men for to dwell upon the face of the earth; so, he hath determined the times before appointed, and the bounds of their habitation.

FEBRUARY 21

I Believe In God Ordained Government

Then he said to them, "Therefore render to Caesar the things that are Caesar's, and to God the things that are God's."

MATTHEW 22:21

I believe that magistracy [the office of magistrate] is God's ordinance, which he hath appointed for the government of the whole world. And that it is a judgment of God, to be without those ministers of God, which he hath ordained to put wickedness to shame.

Whosoever therefore resisted the power, resisted the ordinance of God; they that resist shall receive to themselves damnation [judgment]. For rulers are not a terror to good works but to evil works. Will you not then be afraid of the power, do that which is good and you shalt have praise of the same. For ... [the magistrate] is the minister of God to you for good. But if you do that which is evil, be afraid, for he beareth not the sword in vain.

For he is the minister of God, a revenger to execute wrath upon him that doth evil. Wherefore, you must need to be subject, not only for wrath, but also for conscience's sake. For because of this you need to pay tribute also; for they are God's ministers attending continually unto this very thing. Many are the mercies we receive from a well-qualified magistrate. And if any shall at any time be otherwise inclined, let us shew our Christianity by patient suffering for well-doing—that it shall please God.

FEBRUARY 22

With Whom Shall I Worship?

I appeal to you, brothers, to watch out for those who cause divisions and create obstacles contrary to the doctrine that you have been taught: avoid them.

ROMANS 16:17

Now then, I dare not have communion with them that profess not faith and holiness or that are not visible saints by calling. But note that by this assertion, I meddle not with the [God's] elect. But as he is a visible saint by calling neither do I exclude the secret hypocrite, if he is hidden from me by visible saintship [one who is a confessed and practicing Christian]. Wherefore I dare not have communion with men from this single supposition, that they may be elect. Neither dare I exclude the other from a single supposing that he may be a secret hypocrite. I meddle not here with these things. I only exclude him that is not a visible saint. Now he that is visibly or openly prophane, cannot be then a visible saint. For the one that is a visible saint must profess faith, and repentance, and consequently holiness of life: And with none other dare I communicate [fellowship in worship].

FEBRUARY 23

Reasons For My Worship Practice: Reason One

So Moses cut two tablets of stone like the first. And he rose early in the morning and went up on Mount Sinai, as the Lord had commanded him, and took in his hand two tablets of stone.

EXODUS 34:4

First, because God himself hath so strictly put the difference both by word and deed. For from the beginning, he did not only put a difference between the seed of the woman and the children of the wicked, only the instinct of grace and change of the mind as his own. But did cast out from his presence the father of all the ungodly. Even cursed Cain when he showed himself to be openly prophane. God banished him to go into the land of the [renegade] or vagabond. Away from God's face, so the privileges of the communion of saints was ever after hidden from him (Gen. 3:15; 4).

Besides, when after this through the policy of Satan, the children of Cain and the seed of Seth did commix themselves in worship. By that means they corrupted the way of God: What followed first, God judged it wickedness. He raised up Noah to preach against it, and after that, because they would not be reclaimed, he brought the flood, upon the whole world of these ungodly; and saved only Noah alive because he had kept himself righteous (Gen. 6:1-3; 11:1, 13). Here I could enlarge abundantly, and add many more instances of alike nature, but I am here only for a truth upon things.

FEBRUARY 24

Reasons For My Worship Practice: Reason Two

... [I]n admitting foreigners, uncircumcised in heart and flesh, to be in my sanctuary, profaning my temple, when you offer to me my food, the fat and the blood. You have broken my covenant, in addition to all your abominations.

EZEKIEL 44:7

Secondly, because it is so often commanded in the Scriptures that all the congregation should be holy. I am the Lord your God, ye shall therefore sanctify yourselves; For ye shall be holy for I am holy. Ye shall be holy, for I the Lord your God am holy. Sanctify yourselves therefore and be ye holy, for I am the Lord your God. Besides, the gates of the temple were to be shut against all others. Open the gates, that the righteous nation that keeps the truth may enter in: This gate of the Lord into which the righteous shall enter. Thus, says the Lord, no stranger uncircumcised in heart or uncircumcised in flesh shall enter into my sanctuary or any stranger which is amongst the children of Israel. For the things of worship are holy. Be ye holy that bear the vessels of the Lord. Because all the limits and bounds of communion are holy. This is the law of the house: Upon the top of the mountain the whole limit thereof shall be most holy. Behold this is the law of the house.

FEBRUARY 25

Reasons For My Worship Practice: Reason Three

To the church of God that is in Corinth, to those sanctified in Christ Jesus, called to be saints together with all those who in every place call upon the name of the Lord Jesus Christ, both their Lord and ours.

1 CORINTHIANS 1:2

Thirdly, I dare not have communion with them [who are not practicing saints]. Because the example of New Testament churches before us have been a community of visible saints. Paul writes to the Roman church thus: To all that are at Rome, beloved of God, called to be saints, and to the rest of the churches ... Thus, you see under what denomination [or name] those persons went of old who were counted worthy to be members of a visible church of Christ. Besides this, the members of such churches go under such character[istics] as these:

1. The called of Christ Jesus (Rom. 1:6).
2. Men that have drank into the spirit of Jesus Christ (1 Cor. 12:13).
3. Persons in whom was God the Father (Eph. 4:6).
4. They were all made partakers of the joy of the gospel (Phil. 1:7).
5. Persons that were circumcised inwardly (Col. 2:11).
6. Persons that turned to God from idols to serve the living and true God (1 Thess. 1:4).
7. Those that were the body of Christ and members in particulars [and] ... these attributes could be visibly seen; ... [then] they made profession of faith, of holiness, of repentance, of love to Christ, and of self-denial at their receiving into [church] fellowship.

FEBRUARY 26

Reasons For My Worship Practice: Reason Four

Therefore go out from their midst, and be separate from them, says the LORD, and touch no unclean thing; then I will welcome you.

2 CORINTHIANS 6:17

Fourth, I dare not hold communion with the open prophane:

1. Because it is promised to the church, that she shall dwell by herself. That is, she is a church, and spiritual. Lo(ok)! The people shall dwell alone and shall not be reckoned among the nations (Num. 23:9).
2. Because this is their privilege. But you are a chosen generation, a royal priesthood, a holy nation, a peculiar people [of his own]. [So] that you should show forth the praises of him, who has called you out of darkness into his marvelous light (1 Pet. 2:9-10).
3. Because this is the fruit of the death of Christ, who gave himself for us, that he might redeem as from all iniquity and purify unto himself a peculiar people [of his own] zealous of good works (Titus 2:14).
4. Because this is the commandment: Save yourselves from the untoward [perverse] generation (Acts 2:40).
5. Because with such it is not possible [that] we should have true and spiritual communion. Be not unequally yoked together with unbelievers: For what fellowship hath righteousness with unrighteousness? And what communion hath light with darkness? And what concord hath Christ with Belial [the Evil One]? Or what part does the one who believes have with an infidel? Or what agreement hath the temple of God with idols? For you are the temple of the living God; as God said, I will dwell in them and walk in them, and I will be their God [2 Cor. 6:14-18].

FEBRUARY 27

Reasons For My Worship Practice: Reasons Five and Six

You shall not plow with an ox and a donkey together.
DEUTERONOMY 22:10

Fifthly, I dare not hold communion with the open prophane.

1. Because this would be plowing with on ox and an ass together: Heavenly things suit best for communion in heavenly matters (Deut. 22:10).
2. It subjected not the nature of our discipline, which is not forced, but free in a professed subjection to the will and commandment of Christ: Others being excluded by God's own prohibition (Lev. 1:3; Rom. 6:17; 2 Cor. 8:12). Paul also exhorted Timothy to follow righteousness, faith, charity, peace, etc. ([These] are the bowels (the seat of pity, tenderness, and courage) of church communion); he said do it with those who call on the name of the Lord, out of a pure heart (2 Tim. 2:22).

Sixthly, in a word, to hold communion with the open prophane is most pernicious and destructive.

1. It was the wicked multitude that fell into lusting and that tempted Christ in the desert (Num. 11:4).
2. It was the prophane heathen, from whom Israel learned to worship idols. They were mingled among the heathen, learned their works, and served their idols, which became a snare to them (Ps. 106:25-27).
3. It was this [inter]mingled people that God hath threatened to bring a plague with those deadly punishments of his. With which he threatened to punish Babylon herself: Saying; A sword is upon her mighty [men], her chariots and treasures; a sword also shall be upon the mingled people that are in the midst of her [Jer. 50:35-38].

FEBRUARY 28

Do Not Marvel At My Worship Practice(s)

A mixed multitude also went up with them, and very much livestock, both flocks and herds.

Exodus 12:38

And no marvel!

1. [A] mixed communion polluted the ordinances of God: Say to the rebels saith the Lord God. Let it suffice you for all your abominations: That you have brought into my sanctuary strangers, uncircumcised in heart, and uncircumcised in flesh. These in my sanctuary to pollute it; even my house when you offered my bread and the fat, and the blood. And they have broken my covenant because of all their abominations (Ezek. 44:6-8).
2. It violated the Law: her priests have violated my law and profaned my holy things. They have put no difference, between the holy and prophane; neither have they shewed difference between the unclean, and the clean (Ezek. 22:6).
3, It profaned the holiness of God: Judah hath dealt treacherously and an abomination is committed in Israel and Jerusalem: For Judah hath profaned the holiness of the Lord which he loved, and hath married the daughter of a strange God (Mal. 2:11).
4. It defiled the truly gracious[!]: Do you not know that a little leaven leavens the whole lump: Look diligently therefore lest any root of bitterness springing up trouble you, and thereby many be defiled (1 Cor. 5:6; Heb. 12:15-16).

Lastly, to conclude, as I have said, it provoked God to punish with severe judgments: And [we should] therefore heed well[!]

As I said before, the drowning of the whole world was occasioned, by the sons of God commixing themselves with the daughters of men; and the corruption of worship that followed (Gen. 6–7).

FEBRUARY 29

I Will Not Fellowship With The Profane

And the earth opened its mouth and swallowed them up, with their households and all the people who belonged to Korah and all their goods.

NUMBERS 16:32

Hear how Paul handles the point [of the profane]. This he said: 'That the things which the Gentiles do when they openly prophane sacrifice. They sacrifice to devils, and not to God. And I would not have you to have fellowship with devils. You cannot drink the cup of the Lord and the cup of devils. You cannot be partakers of the table of the Lord of the table of devils, [Dare] we provoke the Lord to jealousy? Are we stronger than he is?' (1 Cor. 10:21-23). I conclude that therefore it is an evil and dangerous thing to hold church communion with the openly prophane and ungodly. It pollutes his ordinances. It violates his law. It profanes his holiness. It defiles his people and provokes the Lord to severe and terrible judgments.

I might here greatly enlarge but I only intend brevity. Yet let me tell you: That when Nehemiah understood, by the book of the law of the Lord, that the Ammonite and the Moabite should not come into the congregation of God; they separated [them] from Israel all the mixed multitude. Many have pleaded for the profane that they should abide in the Church of God. But such have not considered that God's wrath always has with great indignation been shown against such offenders and their conceits. Indeed, they like not to plead for them under that notion but rather as Korah and his company. All the entire congregation is holy. But it makes no matter by what name they are called, if by their deeds they show themselves openly wicked.

MARCH 1

Ready To Be Offered

For I am already being poured out as a drink offering, and the time of my departure has come. I have fought the good fight, I have finished the race, I have kept the faith.

2 TIMOTHY 4:6-7

These words were, by the apostle Paul, written to Timothy. Whom, he had begotten in the faith by the preaching of the gospel of Christ. In ... [this gospel] are many things of great concern both for instruction and consolation. Some things of which I shall open unto you for your profit and edification. But before I come to the words themselves, as they are a relation of Paul's case, I shall point out something from them as they depend upon the words going before them. That being, a vehement exhortation to Timothy to be constant and faithful in his work. Which, in brief can be summed up in these particulars: Foremost: A solemn binding charge before God and Jesus Christ our Lord that Timothy should constantly preach the Word! Preach whether in or out of season; reproving, rebuking, and exhorting with all long-suffering and doctrine. And so, because of that ungodly spirit that would possess professors after ... [Paul] was dead. For the time would come, he saith; that they will not endure sound doctrine neither sound reproof nor sound trial of their state and condition by the Word. But after their own lusts shall they heap to themselves teachers, having itching ears—the plague that once God threatened to rebellious Israel (Deut. 28:27). And they will be turned unto fables. Much like this is that in the Acts of the Apostles: For I know this [Paul declared], that after my departing shall grievous wolves enter in among you, not sparing the flock. Also, from your own selves shall men arise speaking perverse things to draw away disciples after them. Therefore watch, and remember, that by the space of three years, I ceased not to warn every night and day with tears (Acts 20:29-31).

MARCH 2

Ready to Endure Hardship

Share in suffering as a good soldier of Jesus Christ.

2 TIMOTHY 2:3

[Learn first] that the murders and outrage our brethren suffer at the hands of wicked men should not discourage those that live a full and faithful performance of their duty to God and man. Whatever may be the consequences of such [holy living]. Or when we see our brethren before us fall to the earth by death, through the violence of the enemies of God for their holy and Christian profession; we should desire to make good their ground against them [even] though our turn should be next. We should valiantly do in this matter as is the custom of soldiers in war. Take great care that the ground [gained] be maintained, and the front [line be] kept full and complete. Therefore, Paul said to Timothy, endure hardness as a good soldier of Jesus Christ. Paul said in one place, we should not be moved by these afflictions, but endure by resisting even unto blood. Paul said in another place, don't be ashamed of the testimony of our Lord nor of me his prisoner. Stand up! Like valiant worthies as the ministers of my God. And don't fly every man to his own while the cause, and ways, and brethren of our Lord are buffeted and condemned by the world. And remember those that keep the charge of the Lord when most go a-whoring[1] from their God.

1 "a-whoring" is a reference to going after other gods as idols or turning to the world and its ways. "Whoring' is often used in the Old Testament by the prophets as a metaphor for Israel's idol worship.

MARCH 3

To Be Offered

For I am now ready to be offered, and the time of my departure is at hand.

2 TIMOTHY 4:6 KJV

Paul, by saying he was "to be offered" alluded to some of the sacrifices that of old[1] were under the law. Thereby signified to Timothy that his death and martyrdom for the gospel should be both sweet in the nostrils of God and of great profit to his church in this world—for so were the sacrifices of old. Paul ... lifted his eyes up higher than simply to look upon death as it is the common fate of [all] men. He had good reason to do it for his death was [to be] violent [as] it was also for Christ and ... his church and truth. And as it is usual with Paul ... to set out the suffering of the saints which they undergo for the name and testimony of Jesus. Yes, he will have our prayers as a sacrifice, our praises as a thanksgiving, and [our self] mortification as sacrifices.

Paul further insinuates ... in his epistles ... to the Colossians, "I now rejoice in my sufferings for you, and fill up that which is behind of the afflictions of Christ in my flesh, for his body's sake, which is the church" (Col. 1:24). But this he meant: That as Christ was offered in sacrifice for his church as a Saviour, so Paul would offer himself as a sacrifice for Christ's church; as a saint, as a minister, and as one that was counted faithful. "Yea," he said, "and if I be offered upon the sacrifice and service of your faith, I joy, and rejoice with you all" (Phil. 2:17). This, then, teaches us several things worthy of our consideration.

---

1 Bunyan no doubt believes that Paul here refers to the Old Testament sacrifices of bulls and goats to God.

MARCH 4

Things Worthy Of Our Consideration

And most of the brothers, having become confident in the Lord by my imprisonment, are much more bold to speak the word without fear.

PHILIPPIANS 1:14

First: That the blood of the saints, that they lose for his name, is a sweet savour to God. And so says the Holy Ghost, "Precious in the sight of the Lord is the death of his saints" (Ps. 116:15). And again, "He shall redeem their soul from deceit and violence, and precious shall their blood be in his sight" (Ps. 72:14).

Second: Those that suffer for Christ are of great benefit to his church, as the sacrifices of old were confirming and strengthening to Israel. Wherefore, Paul said his bonds encouraged his brethren and made them much more bold in the way of God to speak his word without fear.

Third: The sufferings or offering of the saints in sacrifice is of great use and advantage to the gospel: Of use I say [in] many ways. (1.) The blood of the saints defends it; (2.) confirms it; and (3.) redeems [what] ... has been lost in antichristian darkness.

They do thereby defend and preserve it from those that would take it from us or from those that would impose another upon us. "I am set," saith Paul, "for the defense of the gospel," and my sufferings have fallen out for the furtherance of it (Phil. 1:12, 17). That is, ... [the gospel] hath not only continued to hold its ground but hath also got more by my contentions, sufferings, and hazards for it.

That the truth of the gospel might be continued with you, he declares. So again he confesses, I suffer, so that the gospel may be preserved entire that the souls that are yet unborn may have the benefit of it—with eternal glory.

MARCH 5

Christian Suffering Produces Virtue

But we rejoice in our sufferings, knowing that suffering produces endurance, and endurance produces character, and character produces hope.

ROMANS 5:3-4

The sufferings of the saints are of a redeeming virtue; by their patient enduring and losing their blood for the Word they recover the truths of God. [These truths] ... have been buried in antichristian rubbish from that soil and slur that hath for a long time cleaved unto them. Wherefore it is said: They overcame him, the beast, "by the blood of the Lamb, and by the word of their testimony, and they loved not their lives unto the death" (Rev. 12:11). They overcame him; they recovered the truth from under his aspersions and delivered it from all its enemies. David said, "The words of the Lord are—as silver tried in a furnace of earth, purified seven times" (Ps. 12:6). What is this furnace of earth but the body of the saints of God in which the Word is tried as by [the] fire in persecution. Yea, [it is] "purified seven times;" [it] is brought forth at last by the death of the Christians in its purity before the world. How hath the headship and lordship of Christ with many other doctrines of God been taken away from the Pope by the sufferings of our brethren before us? While their flesh did fry in the flames, the Word of God was cleansed. By such means purified in these their earthen furnaces [bodies] and so delivered to us. The lamps of Gideon were then discovered when his soldiers' pitchers were broken. If our pitchers were broken for the Lord and his gospel's sake; those lamps will then be discovered that before lying hid and unseen (Judg. 7:15-22). Much use might be made of this good doctrine.

MARCH 6

The Blood Of Persecution Cries Out

And the LORD said, "What have you done? The voice of your brother's blood is crying to me from the ground."

GENESIS 4:10

The judgment that is made of our sufferings by carnal men is nothing at all to be heeded. They see not the glory that is wrapped up in our cause: nor the innocence and goodness of our conscience in our enduring of these afflictions; they judge according to the flesh [and] according to outward appearance. For so ... we seem to lie under contempt and to be in a disgraceful condition. But all things here are converted to another use and end. That which is contemptible when persons are guilty, is honorable when persons are clear. And that which brings shame when persons are buffeted for their faults, is thankworthy in those that endure grief, suffering wrongfully (1 Pet. 2:19-22).

We learn also from this, the reason why some in days before us have made light of the rage of the world; but they have laughed at destruction when it cometh (Job 5:21-22). Therefore, [says Paul] I take pleasure in infirmities, in reproaches, in necessities, in persecutions, in distresses—for Christ's sake. Let those that suffer for theft and murder hang down their heads like a bulrush and carry it like those that are going to [be] hung. But let those whose trials are for the Word of God know by these very things they are dignified [distinguished, exalted].

Learn also in this to be confident, that thy sufferings have their sound and a voice before God and men. First, before God, to provoke him to vengeance "when he maketh inquisition for blood" (Ps. 9:12; Gen. 4:9-11). The blood of Abel cried until it brought down wrath upon Cain; and so did the blood of Christ and his apostles, till it had laid Jerusalem upon heaps. Secondly, thy blood will also have a voice before men and that possibly for their good.

MARCH 7

Counted To Be Slaughtered

Yet for your sake we are killed all the day long; we are regarded as sheep to be slaughtered.

PSALM 44:22

The enemies of God and his truth ... [are] never want [or lack of] will and malice to oppose the Word of God. They are also always in readiness to murder and slaughter the saints as the prophet cries to Jerusalem did; "Behold the princes of Israel, everyone was in thee to their power to shed blood" (Ezek. 22:6). That is, they had [the] will and malice always at hand to oppose the upright in heart. Our Lord Jesus also said, "they are they that kill the body." For though it is a truth that God's hand is always safe upon the hilt of their sword. Yet by them we are killed all day long and accounted as sheep for the slaughter (Ps. 44:22; Rom. 8:36). That is: in their desires always as well as by their deeds when they are ... [set free]....

Paul's kinsman said to the captain: "There lie in wait for him of them more than forty men, which have bound themselves with a curse, that they will neither eat nor drink till they have killed him and now are they ready" (Acts 23:12-13, 21). And consequently it is by the Word they are called dragons, lions, bears, wolves, leopards, dogs, and the like. All which are beasts of prey, and delight to live by the death of others. Paul, therefore, seeing and knowing that this readiness was in his enemies to pour out his bowels [entrails] to the earth he cried out to Timothy, saying; "make thou full proof of thy ministry, for I am now ready to be slain; I am now ready to be offered" (2 Tim. 4:5-6). These words thus understood may be useful in many ways.

MARCH 8

Whom To Fear?

I tell you, my friends, do not fear those who kill the body, and after that have nothing more that they can do.

LUKE 12:4

To show us we live, not because of any good nature or inclination that is in our enemies towards us; for they, as to their wills are ready to destroy us. But they are in the hand of God, in whose hand is also our times (Ps. 31:15). Wherefore, though by the will of our enemies, we are always delivered to death, yet "behold we live" (2 Cor. 6:9). Therefore, in this sense it may be said, "Where is the fury of the oppressor?" It is not in his power of disposal; therefore, here it may be said again he is not "ready to destroy" (Isa. 51:13). The cup that God's people in all ages have drunk—even the cup of affliction and persecution—it is not in the hand of the enemy but in the hand of God; and he, not they, [did] pour out of the same (Ps. 75:8). So that they with all their raging waves have banks and bounds set to them; by which they are limited within their range even as the chained bear. "Surely the wrath of men shall praise thee, the remainder of wrath you shall restrain" (Ps. 76:10; Job 38:10-11).

This should encourage us not to forsake the way of our Lord Jesus when threatened by our adversaries. Because they are in his chain: Indeed, they are ready in their wills to destroy us. But as to power and liberty to do it that is not at all with them. Who would fear to go even by the very nose of a lion, if his chain would not cause him to hurt us. It is too much below the spirit of a Christian to fear a man that shall die. For the Lord our Maker preserves even the hairs of our head.

MARCH 9

Am I Ready To Be Sacrificed?

For I am already being poured out as a drink offering, and the time of my departure has come.

2 TIMOTHY 4:6

[Paul declared,] "I am ready ... not to be bound only, but also to die at Jerusalem for the name of the Lord Jesus" (Acts 21:13). That also implies as much where he said, "Neither count I my life dear unto myself, so that I might finish my course with joy, and the ministry which I have received of the Lord Jesus, to testify the gospel of the grace of God" (Acts 20:24). As ... [Paul's] enemies, then, were ready and willing in their hearts so he was ready and willing in his. This man was like to those mighty men of Solomon, that were ready prepared for the war and waited on the king. [They were] fit to be sent at any time upon the most sharp and pinching service (2 Chron. 17:12-19). A thing fitly becoming all the saints, but chiefly those that minister in the word and doctrine. Understand these words ... and they also teach us many things; both for conviction and for edification.

Here we see that a Christian's heart should be unclenched from this world. For he that is ready to be made a sacrifice for Christ and his blessed Word, he must be one that is not entangled with the affairs of this life: How else can he please him who hath chosen him to be a soldier? Thus, was it with this blessed man [Paul]. He was brought to God's foot with Abraham and crucified to this world with Christ. He had passed a sentence of death upon all earthly pleasures and profits beforehand, that they might not deaden his spirit when he came to suffer for his profession.

MARCH 10

Accepting Christ's Reproach Willingly

By faith Moses, when he was come to years, refused to be called the son of Pharaoh's daughter. ... Esteeming the reproach of Christ greater riches that the treasures in Egypt: for he had respect unto the recompense of reward.

HEBREWS 11:24, 26 (KJV)

[Paul's willingness to be sacrificed] shows us the true effects of a right sight and sense of the sufferings that attend the gospel. They shall become truly profitable to those that shall bear them aright. What made ... [Paul] ready? It was for sufferings ... [that] made him ready for them because he saw they wrought out for him a "far more exceeding and eternal weight of glory?" (2 Cor. 4:17). This made Moses also spurn a crown and a kingdom; to look with a disdainful eye upon all the glory of Egypt. He saw the reward that was laid up in heaven for those that suffered for Christ. Therefore, "he refused to be called the son of Pharaoh's daughter; choosing rather to suffer affliction with the people of God than to enjoy the pleasures of sin for a season; esteeming the reproach of Christ greater riches than the treasures in Egypt: for he had respect unto the recompense of reward. By faith he forsook Egypt, not fearing the wrath of the king, for he endured, as seeing him who is invisible." Everyone cannot thus look upon the afflictions and temptations that attend the gospel. No! Not everyone that professes it. This can be seen by their shrinking and shirking at the noise of the trumpet and alarm to war. They can be content as cowards in a garrison to lie still under some smaller pieces of service. When upon hearing the Word and entering in; to follow with loving in word and in tongue and the like [suits them]. But to "go forth unto him without the camp, bearing his reproach" and to be in jeopardy every hour for the truth of the glorious gospel—that they dare not do.

MARCH 11

A Weight Of Eternal Glory

For this light momentary affliction is preparing for us an eternal weight of glory beyond all comparison.

2 CORINTHIANS 4:17

What made ... [Paul] ready for [sufferings]? He saw they wrought for him a "far more exceeding and eternal weight of glory." This made Moses also spurn at a crown and a kingdom; to look with a disdainful eye upon all the glory of Egypt. He saw the reward that was laid up in heaven for those that suffered for Christ.

By this readiness we may discern who are unfeignedly [heartfelt] willing to find out that they may do the whole will of God. Even those that are already made willing to suffer for his sake, they are still inquiring: "Lord, what wouldst thou have me to do?" not mattering nor regarding the cross and distress that attends it. "The Holy Ghost witnessed to me," Paul saith, that "in every city, saying that bonds and afflictions abide me. But none of these things move me, neither count I my life dear unto myself, so that I may finish my course with joy" (Acts 20:23-24). He believed heavenly things would countervail all the trouble and sorrow that attends them. This, therefore, sharply rebukes those that can be glad to be ignorant of the knowledge of some truths; especially of them that are persecuted. Still answering those that charge them with walking irregularly that they do but according to their light. Whereas the hearts that be full of love to the name and glory of Christ will in quiet return and come. Yea and be glad, if they find the words of God and will eat them with savour and sweet delight, how bitter soever they are to the belly: Because of that testimony they bind us up to maintain before peoples, and nations, and kings (Rev. 10:10-11). "I am now ready to be offered."

MARCH 12

Redeeming The Time

Look carefully then how you walk, not as unwise but as wise, making the best use of the time, because the days are evil.

EPHESIANS 5:15-16

Another thing to be considered in the words of the apostle when he said, "I am now ready," doth signify that now he had done that work that God had appointed him to do in the world. "I am now ready" because I have done my work. This is further manifest by the following words of the text: "I am now ready to be offered, and the time of my departure is at hand." Namely my time to depart this world. The words also that follow are much to the purpose, "I have fought a good fight, I have finished my course." This is much like that of our Lord Jesus. "I have finished the work which thou gave me to do" (John 17:4). Now then, put all these things together. Namely that I am to be offered as a sacrifice and for this my enemies are ready; my heart is also ready. And because I have done my work, I am therefore every way ready. This is a frame and condition that deserved not only to stand in the Word of God for Paul's everlasting praise, but to be a provoking argument to all that read or hear of it to follow the same steps. I shall therefore, to help it forward, according to grace received, draw one conclusion from the words and speak a few words to it. The conclusion is this: That it is the duty and wisdom of those that fear God so to manage their time and work that he hath allotted unto them. That they may not have part of their work to do when they should be departing the world.

MARCH 13

Do It With All Your Might

For we must all appear before the judgment seat of Christ, so that each one may receive what is due for what he has done in the body, whether good or evil.

2 CORINTHIANS 5:10

This truth I might further urge from the very words of the text, they were written on purpose by Paul to stir up Timothy and all the godly to press hard after this very thing. But to [re]mind you of some other Scriptures that press it hard [on us] as a duty.

That this is the duty and wisdom of those that fear God, you may see by Christ's exhortation to watchfulness, and to prepare for his second coming: "Therefore be ye also ready; for in an hour you think not, the Son of man cometh" (Matt. 24:44). These words, as they are spoken to stir up the godly to be ready to meet their Lord at his coming. So, because the godly must meet him as well in his judgments and providences here as at his personal appearance at the last day. Therefore, they should be diligent to be fitting themselves to meet him in all such dispensations. "And because," saith God, "I will do this unto thee; prepare to meet thy God, O Israel" (Amos 4:12).

Now death is one of the most certain of those dispensations. Yes, such that it leaves to those no help or means to perform forever that which you should want it what is lacking to your work. Wherefore Solomon also doth press us to this very work and from this consideration: "whatsoever thy hand finds to do—do it with thy might. For there is no work, nor device, nor knowledge, nor wisdom, in the grave, where you are going" (Eccles. 9:10). Balk nothing of your duty, neither defer to do it. For you are on your way to thy grave and there you cannot finish anything that by neglect you have left undone. Therefore, be diligent while life lasts.

MARCH 14

As You See The Day Approach

But encouraging one another, and all the more as you see the Day drawing near.

HEBREWS 10:25B

[One] Scripture is in Peter's epistle to those that were scattered abroad: "Seeing," he said, "that ye look for such things, be diligent, that ye may be found of him in peace" (2 Pet. 3:14). He is there discoursing of the coming of Christ to judge. And from the certainty and dread of that day he does press them on to continual diligence and is to be understood as that of Paul to Timothy. [One should be] ... diligently watching in all things; that as ... [Paul] said again that they may stand complete in all the will of God; not lacking this or that of the work which was given them to do of God and this world (2 Tim. 4:5). Much might be said for further proof of this duty. But to give you some examples of the godly men of old, whereby it will appear, that as it is our duty to do it so it is also our wisdom.

And consequently, it is said of Enoch, that he "walked with God" (Gen. 5:22), and of Noah, that he was faithful in his generation and "walked with God" (Gen. 6:9). That is, they kept in touch with him, keeping up with the work and duty that every day required. Not doing their duty by fits and by starts but in a fervent spirit they served the Lord. So again, it is said of Abraham, that his work was to walk before God in a way of faith and self-denial which he with diligence performed. And therefore, the Holy Ghost saith he "died in a good old age" (Gen. 25:8).

MARCH 15

Faithful Unto Death

Be faithful unto death, and I will give you the crown of life.
REVELATION 2:10B

Jacob, when he blessed his sons, as he lay upon his deathbed before them, does sweetly comfort himself with this after all his toil and travel saying: "I have waited for thy salvation, O Lord." As if he had said, Lord, I have faithfully walked before thee in the days of my pilgrimage, through the help and power of thy grace. And now having nothing to do but to die, I lie waiting for thy coming to gather me up to thyself and my father: So, when he "had made an end of commanding his sons ... he gathered up his feet into the bed, and yielded up the ghost, and was gathered unto his people" (Gen. 49:18-33). Caleb and Joshua are said to be men of excellent spirit, because they were faithful in this their work (Num. 14:24). David was eminent this way and had done his work before his death-day came: "After he had served his own generation by the will of God," he then "fell on sleep" (Acts 13:36). Which in the Old Testament is signified by three passages,

1. By his losing his heat before his death, thereby showing his work for God was done he now only waited to die.
2. By that passage, "these are the last words of David," even the wind up of all the doctrines of that sweet Psalmist of Israel (2 Sam. 23:1-2).
3. That in the Psalms is very significant, "The prayers of David the son of Jesse are ended" (Ps. 72:20). In the whole they all do doubtless speak forth this in the main. David made great conscience of walking with God, by labouring to drive his work before him, that his work and life might meet together: For that indeed is a good man's wisdom.

MARCH 16

This One Thing I Do!

Brothers, I do not consider that I have made it my own. But one thing I do: forgetting what lies behind and straining forward to what lies ahead.

PHILIPPIANS 3:13

Job had great consciousness also as to this very thing as he witnesses both God's testimony and his own conscience for him (Job 1:8, 31). Elijah had brought his work to that issue that he had: To anoint Hazael to be king of Assyria, Jehu to be king of Israel, and Elisha prophet in his room [place]; and then [he was] to be caught up into heaven (1 Kings 19:15-16). What shall I say? I might come to Hezekiah, Jehoshaphat, Josias. With old Simeon also, whose days were lengthened chiefly not because he was behind with God and his conscience as to his work for God in the world. But to see with his eyes now at last the Lord's Christ, a sweet forfeiting for death! Zacharias with Elizabeth his wife, that good old couple also, how tender, and doubtful were they in this matter, to walk "in all the commandments and ordinances of the Lord," in a blessed blameless way! (Luke 1:6; 2:25). Their son [John the Baptist] also is not to be left out. Who, rather than being put out of his way and hindered from fulfilling his course, would venture the loss of the love of a king and the loss of his head for a word (Mark 6:17-18). All these, with many more, are as so many mighty arguments for the praise of that I assert: To wit, that it is the duty and wisdom of those that fear God, so to manage their time and work that he hath here allotted unto them. So, they may not have part of their work [left] to do when they should be departing this world. I might urge also many reasons to enforce this truth upon you.

MARCH 17

God's Chief Design

So, whether you eat or drink, or whatever you do, do all to the glory of God.

1 CORINTHIANS 10:31

The great and chief design of God—in sending us into the world especially in converting us and possessing our souls with gifts and graces and many other benefits that we might here be to the glory of his grace—is as much as lies within us frustrated and disappointed. "This people have I formed for myself," he saith, "they shall show forth my praise" (Isa. 43:21): And again, "ye have not chosen me, but I have chosen you, and ordained you that ye should go and bring forth fruit, and that your fruit should remain" (John 15:16). God never intended, when he covered your nakedness with the righteousness of his dear Son and delivered you from the condemning power of sin and the law that you should still live as do those who know not God. "This I say therefore," said Paul, "and testify in the Lord; that ye henceforth walk not as other Gentiles, in the vanity of their mind" (Eph. 4:17). What, a Christian, and live as does the world? [!] (John 17:16). A Christian and spend your time, your strength, and parts, for things that perish in the using?

Remember, man, if the grace of God hath taken hold of thy soul, thou art a man of another world. And indeed, a subject of another and more noble kingdom—the kingdom of God, which is the kingdom of the gospel, of grace, of faith and righteousness, and the kingdom of heaven hereafter (Rom. 14:16-18). This, I say, is God's design; this is the tendency, the natural tendency of every grace of God bestowed upon thee: and herein is our Father glorified, that we bring forth much fruit (Col. 3:1-4; John 15:8).

MARCH 18

Awake O Sleeper!

Awake, O sleeper, and arise from the dead and Christ will shine on you.

EPHESIANS 5:14B

Christians should so manage their time and the work that God hath appointed them to do for his name in this world, that they may not have part thereof to do when they should be departing this world. Because, if they do not, dying will be a hard work with them especially if God awakens them about their neglect of their duty (1 Cor. 11:30-32). The way of God with his people is to visit their sins in this life; and the worst time for thee to be visited for them is when thy life is smitten down. [When] ... the dust of death, even when all natural infirmities break in like a flood upon you, sickness, fainting, pains, wearisomeness, and the like. Now I say, to be charged also with the neglect of duty when [there is] no capacity to do it. Perhaps [you will be] so feeble as scarce able to abide to hear thy dearest friend in this life speak to thee; will not this make dying hard? Yes, when you shalt seem both in thine own eyes as also in the eyes of others to fall short of the kingdom of heaven for this and the other transgression, will not this make dying hard? (Heb. 4:1-2). David found it hard, when he cried, "O spare me" a little, "that I may recover strength before I go hence and be no more" (Ps. 39:13). So again, "The sorrows of death compassed me, and the pains of hell gat hold upon me. I found trouble and sorrow: then called I upon the name of the Lord." [Yes], this will make you cry though thou be as good as David! Wherefore learn by his sorrow, as he himself also learned, at last; to serve his own generation by the will of God before he fell asleep.

MARCH 19

The Time Is At Hand!

... the day of Christ is at hand.

2 THESSALONIANS 2:2 KJV

Another reason why those that fear God should so manage their time and work for God in this world: That they may not have [some] part to do when they should be departing this life. It is, because loitering in your work does as much as in it lies, defer, and holds back the second coming of our Lord and Saviour Jesus Christ. They are not all yet come to the knowledge of the Son of God, "to the measure of the stature of the fullness of Christ" (Eph. 4:8-13). That is: To the complete making up of his body, for as Peter said: "The Lord is not slack concerning his promise, as some men count slackness, but is long-suffering to us-ward, not willing that any should perish, but that all should come to repentance" (2 Pet. 3:9). And so ... to the complete performance of all their duty and work they have [done] for God in this world. And I say, the faster the work of conversion, repentance, faith, self-denial, and the rest of the Christian duties are performed by the saints in their day; the more they make way for the coming of the Lord from heaven. Wherefore Peter again said, "Seeing then that" we look for such things, "what manner of persons ought we to be in all holy conversation and godliness, looking for, and hasting unto," [And] ... "hasting the coming of the day of God, wherein the heavens being on fire shall be dissolved, and the elements shall melt with fervent heat" (2 Pet. 3:11-12). When the bride [the Church] hath made herself ready, "the marriage of the Lamb is come" (Rev. 19:7).

MARCH 20

A Faithful Worker

Whatever you do, work heartily, as for the Lord and not for men.

COLOSSIANS 3:23

The Lord will then wait upon the world no longer when his saints are fit to receive him. As he said to Lot when he came to burn down Sodom, "Haste thee" to Zoar "for I cannot do anything till thou be come thither [out]" (Gen. 19:22). So, concerning the great day of judgment of the world which shall be also the day of blessedness and rest to the people of God. It cannot come until the Lamb's wife hath made herself ready; until all the saints that belong to glory are ready. And before I go further, what might I say to fasten this reason upon the truly gracious soul? What! Will you yet loiter in the work of your day? Will you still be unwilling to hurry along righteousness? Do you not know that you by so doing defer the coming of thy dearest Lord? Besides, that is the day of his glory, the day when he shall come in the glory of his Father and of the holy angels. And will not you by your diligence help it forwards? Must also the general assembly and church of the first-born wait upon you for their full portions of glory? Will you by doing this endeavor to keep them wrapped up still in the dust of the earth—there to dwell with the worm and corruption? The Lord awaken thee that you may see that your loitering does do this and it does also hinder your own soul of the inheritance prepared for you.

MARCH 21

We'll Work Till Jesus Comes[1]

He who goes out weeping, bearing the seed for sowing, shall come home with shouts of joy, bringing his sheaves with him.
PSALM 126:6

Another reason why saints should press hard after a complete performing their work that God hath allotted unto them is this: Because ... as they fall short in that they impair their own glory. For as the Lord hath commanded his people to work for him in this world; so, also, he of grace hath promised to reward whatever they do as Christians. For whatsoever good thing any man does the same shall he receive of the Lord, whether he be bound or free. Yes, he counts it unrighteousness to forget their work of faith and labour of love, but a righteous thing to recompense them for it in the day of our Lord Jesus (Heb. 6:10; 2 Thess. 1:6-7). This [when] well considered is of great force to prevail with those that are covetous[2] [desiring] of glory: such as Moses and Paul ... [and] the rest of that spirit. As the apostle said also to the saints at Corinth, "Be steadfast, unmovable, always abounding in the work of the Lord, forasmuch as ye know that your labour is not in vain in the Lord" (1 Cor. 15:58).

Having thus given you the reasons why God's people should be diligent in that work that God hath allotted for them to be doing for him in this world; I shall, in the next place, give you some directions as helps to help you in this work. And they are such as tend to take away those hindrances that come upon you, either by discouragement or by reason of hardness and benumbedness [insensitivity] of spirit; for great hindrances overtake God's people from [all directions].

1 Elizabeth Mills, "We'll Work Till Jesus Comes" song title.

2 Bunyan does not mean "covetous" here in a sinful way but a personal desire for God's glory.

MARCH 22

Serving Without Fear

That we, being delivered from the hand of our enemies, might serve him without fear in holiness and righteousness before him all our days.

LUKE 1:74-75

If thou would be faithful to do that work that God hath allotted you to do in this world for his name; [then] labour to live much in the favor and sense of thy freedom and liberty by Jesus Christ. That is this, if possible, [keep it] ever before you that you are a redeemed one taken out of this world and from under the curse of the law out of the power of the devil. [You are] placed in a kingdom of grace and forgiveness of sins for Christ's sake. This is of absolute use in this matter. Yes, so absolute, that it is impossible for any Christian to do his word in a Christian way without some enjoyment of it. For this, in the first [chapter] of Luke is made the very ground of all good works, both as to their nature and our continuance in them. And this is also reckoned there an essential part of that covenant that God made with our fathers; even "that he would grant unto us that we, being delivered out of the hands of our enemies, might serve him without fear, in holiness and righteousness, before him all the days of our life" (Luke 1:74-75). And if indeed this is taken away, what ground can there be laid for any man to persevere in good works? None at all! For take away grace and remission of sins for Christ's sake and you leave men nothing to help them but the terrors of the law and judgment of God. These at best, can beget but a servile and slavish spirit in that man in whom it dwells. Which spirit is so far off from being a help to us in our pursuit of good works that it makes us [that] we cannot endure that which is commanded.

MARCH 23

Trust And Obey

And Elisha sent a messenger to him saying, "Go and wash in the Jordan seven times, and your flesh shall be restored, and you shall be clean."

2 KINGS 5:10

If thou wouldst be faithful to do that work that God has allotted you to do in this world for his name; then labour to see a beauty and glory in holiness and in every good work. This tends much to the engaging of your heart, "O worship the Lord in the beauty of holiness; fear before him, all the earth" (Ps. 96:9). And for your help in this, think much on this, "Thus saith the Lord" is the wind-up of every command. For indeed, much of the glory and beauty of duties doth lie in the glory and excellency of the person that does command them. Consequently: It is that "Be it enacted by the King's most excellent Majesty" is at the head of every law. Because that law should therefore be reverenced by and be made glorious and beautiful to all. And we see upon this very account what power and place the precepts of kings do take in the hearts of their subjects. Every one loving and reverencing the statute, because there is the name of their king.

"Will you rebel against the king?" is a word that shakes the world! Well then, turn these things about for an argument to the matter in hand. Let the name of God; seeing he is wiser and better, and of more glory and beauty than kings; beget in thy heart a beauty in all things that are commanded thee of God. And indeed, if you do not act in this way, you will stumble at some of your duty and work thou must do. For some of the commands of God are in themselves, so mean and low, that take away the name of God from them, and thou wilt do as Naaman the Syrian—[who] despised instead of obeying.

MARCH 24

Dangers Of A Hard Heart

His heart is hard as a stone, hard as the lower millstone.

JOB 41:24

Would you be faithful to do that work that God has appointed you to do in this world for his name? Then make much of a trembling heart and conscience. For though the Word be the line and rule whereby we must order and govern all our actions, yet a trembling heart and tender conscience is of absolute necessity for our so doing. A hard heart can do nothing with the Word of Jesus Christ. "Hear the word of the Lord, ye that tremble at his word" (Isa. 66:5). "Serve the Lord with fear and rejoice with trembling" (Ps. 2:11). I spoke ... against a servile and slavish frame of spirit [in another place]. Therefore, you must not understand me here as if I mean now to cherish such a one. No! It is a heart that trembles for, or at the grace of God and a conscience made tender by the sprinkling of the blood of Christ. Such a conscience as is awakened both by wrath and grace by the terror and the mercy of God; for it stands with the spirit of a son to fear before his father. Yes, to fear chastenings though not to fear damnation. Let, therefore, destruction from God be a terror to thy heart, though not that destruction that attends them that perish by sin forever (Job 31:23). Though this I might add further. It may do you no harm but good, to cast an eye over your shoulder at those that now lie roaring under the vengeance of eternal fire! It may put you in mind of what you once were, and of what you must yet assuredly be, if grace by Christ prevented [you] not (Isa. 66:24). Keep, then, your conscience awake with wrath and grace, with heaven and hell.

MARCH 25

Gird Up The Loins Of Your Mind[1]

Therefore, preparing your minds for action, and being sober-minded, set your hope fully on the grace that will be brought to you at the revelation of Jesus Christ.

1 PETER 1:13

If you would be faithful to do that work that God has appointed you to do in this world for his name; then let religion be the only business to take up your thoughts and time. "Whatsoever thy hand finds to do, do it with thy might" (Eccles. 9:10). [Pursue God] with all your heart, with all thy mind, and with all thy strength. Religion, to most men is but a by-business with which they use to fill up spare hours; or as a stalking-horse[2] which is used to catch the game. How few are there in the world that have their conversation "only as becometh the gospel"! (Phil. 1:27). A heart sound in God's statutes, a heart united to the fear of God, a heart molded and fashioned by the Word of God—is a rare thing. Rare; because it is hard to find and rare because it is indeed the fruit of an excellent spirit and a token of one saved by the Lord (Ps. 119:80, 86:11). But this indifference to religion ... cannot be but a very great and sore obstruction to your faithful walking with God in this world. Gird up your loins like a man; let God and his Christ and his Word [be pre-eminent]. [Let] his people and cause be the chief [aim] in your soul. And heretofore you have afforded this world the most of your time, and travel, and study; so now convert all these to the use of religion. "As ye have yielded your members servants to uncleanness, and to iniquity unto iniquity; even so now yield your members servants to righteousness unto holiness" (Rom. 6:19). Holy things must be in every heart where this is faithfully put in practice.

1 "Gird up your loins" means to prepare for action.

2 "Stalking-horse" a false context for concealing true intentions. A form of hypocrisy.

MARCH 26

Today Is All You Have

But exhort one another every day, as long as it is called "today," that none of you may be hardened by the deceitfulness of sin.
HEBREWS 3:13

Daily bring your heart and the Word of God together that thy heart may be levelled by it and filled with it. The want of performing this sincerely is a great cause of that unfaithfulness that is in us to God. Bring then, your heart to the Word daily to try how you believe the Word today, to try how it agrees with the Word today. This is the way to make clean work daily, to keep your soul warm and living daily. "Wherewithal shall a young man cleanse his way?" said David. "By taking heed thereto according to thy Word" (Ps. 119:9). And again, "Concerning the works of men, by the word of thy lips, I have kept me from the paths of the destroyer" (Ps. 17:4). And again, "Thy Word have I hid in mine heart, that I might not sin against thee" (Ps. 119:11). He who delights "in the law of the Lord, and in his law does meditate day and night, he shall be like a tree planted by the rivers of water, that bringeth forth its fruit in its season; its leaf also shall not wither, and whatsoever he doeth shall prosper" (Ps. 1:2-3).

[Make it] a continual remembrance that to every day you do the work allotted you and that sufficient for that day are the evils that attend thee (Matt. 6:34). This remembrance set Paul upon his watch daily; made him die to himself and this world daily. And [it] provoked him also daily to wind up the spirit of his mind, transforming himself by the power of the Word from that proneness that was in his flesh to carnal things (1 Cor. 15:30-33). This will make you keep the knife at my throat in all places, and business, and company (Prov. 23:2).

MARCH 27

Yoked With Christ

For my yoke is easy, and my burden is light.

MATTHEW 11:30

Paul must go from place to place to preach, though he knew beforehand he was to be afflicted there (Acts 20:23). God may sometimes say to you as he said to his servant Moses, "Take the serpent by the tail" or as the Lord Jesus said to Peter, "Walk upon the sea" (Exod. 4:3-4). These are hard things but have not been rejected when God hath called to do them. O how willingly would our flesh and blood escape the cross of Christ! The comforts of the gospel, the sweetness of the promise, how pleasing is it to us! God will ... [lay] upon their fair neck and yoke them with Christ's yoke; for there they have a work to do, even a work of self-denial.

Let your heart be more affected with what concerns the honor of God and the profit and glory of the gospel than with what are your concernments as a man [is] with all earthly advantages. This will make you refuse things that are lawful if they appear to be inexpedient. Yes, this will make you, like the apostles of old, prefer another man's peace and edification before your own profit. And to take more pleasure in the increase of the power of godliness in any than in the increase of your corn and wine.

Reckon with your own heart every day before you lie down to sleep. And cast up both what you have received from God, done for him, and where you have also been wanting [lacking]. This will beget praise and humility and put you [to] redeeming the day that is past. Whereby you wilt be able, through the continual supplies of grace in some good measure to drive your work before you.

MARCH 28

Wisdom Versus Folly

So I turned to consider wisdom and madness and folly.
ECCLESIASTES 2:12

Sometimes, acts that seem to be foolish; as when men deny themselves those comforts, and pleasures, and friendships, and honours of the world that formerly they used to have; choose rather to associate themselves with the very objects of this world. I mean, such as carnal men count ... their ways and manners of life, though attended with a thousand calamities, more profitable, and pleasing, and delightful than all former glory. Elisha left his father's house to pour water upon the hands of Elijah. And ... the disciples left their fathers' ships and nets to live a beggarly life with Jesus Christ. As Paul did leave the feet of Gamaliel for the whip, and the stocks, and the deaths that attended the blessed gospel. One would have thought that it would have been a simple way of Peter to leave all for Christ before he knew what Christ would give him as that nineteenth [chapter] of Matthew ... imports. But Christ will have it so (v. 27). He that will save his life must lose it; and he that will lose his life in this world for Christ shall keep it to life eternal (John 12:25). I might add many things of this nature to show you what hard chapters sometimes God sets his best people. Some, when they come at the cross, will either make a stop or go no further. Or else, if they can, they will step over it. If not, they will go round about: Do not do this but take it up and kiss it and bear it after Jesus. "God forbid," saith Paul, "that I should glory, save in the cross of our Lord Jesus Christ, by whom the world is crucified unto me, and I unto the world" (Gal 6:14).

MARCH 29

A Frowning Providence

Though he slay me, I will hope in him.

JOB 13:15

Now, for your better performance of service for our Lord and Saviour Jesus Christ: O it is hard work to pocket up the reproaches of all the foolish people. As if we had found great spoil; and to suffer all their revilings, lies, and slanders, without cursing them, as Elisha did the children [of Israel]. To answer them with [our] prayers and blessings for their cursings. It is far more easy to give them taunt for taunt and reviling for reviling and to give them blow for blow. Yea, to [even] call for fire from heaven against them. But to "bless them that curse you, and to pray for them that despitefully use you and persecute you." Even of malice, of [an] old grudge, and on purpose to vex and afflict our mind to make us break out into a rage! This is work above us; now our patience should look up to unseen things. Now remember Christ's carriage to them that spilt his blood, or all is in danger of bursting and you of miscarrying in these things. I might here also dilate [enlarge] upon Job's case, and the lesson God set him, when, at one stroke, he did beat down ... [Job] (Job 1:15). O when every providence of God unto thee is like the messengers of Job, and the last to bring more heavy tidings than all that went before him (Job 1); when life, estate, wife, children, body, and soul, and all at once, seem to be struck at by heaven and earth. Here are hard lessons; now to behave myself even as a weaned child now to say, "The Lord gave, and the Lord has taken away, and blessed be the name of the Lord" (Job 1:21).

MARCH 30

Between A Rock And A Hard Place

In the fullness of his sufficiency he shall be in straits: every hand of the wicked shall come upon him.

JOB 20:22 KJV

If you would be faithful to do the work that God has appointed you to do in this world for his name. Then labour away to possess your heart with a right understanding. Labour both [for the] things that this world yields and of the things that shall be hereafter. I am confident that most, if not all the miscarriages of the saints and people of God [are that] they have their rise from deceivable thoughts here. The things of this world appear to us more [than] those that are to come. And consequently, it is that many are so hot and eager for things that be in this world, and so cold and heartless for those that be in heaven. Satan is here a mighty artist and can show us all earthly things in a multiplying glass. But when we look up to things above, we see them as through sackcloth of hair. But take ... heed, be not ruled by your sensual appetite that can only savour fleshly things. Neither be ... ruled by carnal reason which always darkens the things of heaven. But go to the Word, and as that says, so judge [yourself by it]. That tells you all things under the sun are vanity, and worse [even] vexation of spirit (Eccles. 1:2). Will you set your heart upon that which is not[hing]? "for riches certainly make themselves wings, they fly away as an eagle toward heaven" (Prov. 23:5). The same may be said for honors, pleasures, and the like; they are poor, low, base things to be entertained by a Christian's heart. The man that has most of them may "in the fullness of his sufficiency be in straits [a difficult place]" (Job 20:22).

MARCH 31

Deposits In The Heavenly Bank

And Jesus, looking at him, loved him, said to him, "You lack one thing: go, sell all that you have and give to the poor, and you will have treasure in heaven; and come, follow me."

Mark 10:21

If you would be faithful to do that work that God has appointed you do it in this world for his name? Believe then, that whatever good thing you do for him, if done according to the Word, it is not only accepted by him now; but recorded, to be remembered for you against the time to come. Yes, laid up for you as treasure in chests and coffers. To be brought out to be rewarded before both men and angels, to your eternal comfort by Jesus Christ our Lord. "Lay not up," saith Christ, "treasures upon earth, where moth and rust doth corrupt, and where thieves break through and steal; but lay up for yourselves treasures in heaven, where neither moth nor rust doth corrupt, and where thieves do not break through nor steal" (Matt. 6:19-20). The treasure here our Lord commands we should with diligence lay up in heaven, is found both in Luke and Paul to be meant by doing good work.

Luke renders it, "Sell that ye have and give alms; provide yourselves bags which wax not old, a treasure in the heavens that faileth not, where no thief approacheth, neither moth corrupteth," the latter part of the verse expounds the former (Luke 12:33).

Paul says, "Charge them that are rich in this world, that they be not high-minded, nor trust in uncertain riches, but in the living God, who giveth us richly all things to enjoy: that they do good, that they be rich in good works, ready to distribute, willing to communicate: laying up in store for themselves a good foundation against the time to come, that they may lay hold on eternal life" (1 Tim. 6:17, 19).

APRIL 1

What It Is To Be Saved?

For what will it profit a man if he gains the whole world and forfeits his soul? Or what shall a man give in return for his soul?

MATTHEW 16:26

This question supposes that there is such a thing as damnation due to man for [his] sin; "To save, to redeem, to deliver," are in general terms equivalent to all of them [who] suppose us to be in a state of thralldom [slavery] and misery. Therefore, this word "saved," in the sense that the apostle here does use it, is a word of great worth, forasmuch as the miseries from which we are saved is the misery of all most dreadful.

The miseries from which they that shall be saved shall, by their salvation be delivered, are . . . [terrible]: They are no less than sin, the curse of God, and flames of hell forever. What [is] more abominable than sin? What more [is] insupportable than the dreadful wrath of an angry God? And what is more fearful than the bottomless pit of hell? I say, what is more fearful than to be tormented there forever with the devil and his angels? Now, to "save," according to my text, is to deliver the sinner from these, with all things else that attend them. And although sinners may think that it is no hard matter to answer this question, yet I must tell you there is no man, that can feelingly know what it is to be saved, that knows not experimentally [experientially] something of the dread of these three things. It is evident, because all others do even by their practice count it a thing of no great concern, when yet it is of all other of the highest concern among men.

APRIL 2

What Shall We Do?

Now when they heard this they were cut to the heart, and said to Peter and the rest of the apostles, "Brothers, what shall we do?"

ACTS 2:37

How can ... [a man] tell what it is to be saved that hath not in his conscience groaned under the burden of sin? Yes, it is impossible that he should ever cry out with all his heart, "Men and brethren, what shall we do?"—that is, do to be saved. The man that hath no sores or aches cannot know the virtue of the salve. I mean, not know it from his own experience and therefore cannot prize, nor have that esteem of it, as he that hath received [the] cure. Clap a plaster to a well place, and that does not make its virtue to appear. Neither can he to whose flesh it is so applied, by that application understand its worth. Sinners ... that are not wounded with guilt and oppressed with the burden of sin cannot—I will say it again—cannot know in this senseless condition of yours what it is to be saved.

Again, this word "saved," as I said, concludes deliverance from the wrath of God. How, then, can he tell what it is to be saved that hath not felt the burden of the wrath of God? He—he that is astonished with and that trembles at the wrath of God—he knows best what it is to be saved (Acts 16:29).

But to come to the question—What is it to be saved? To be saved may either respect salvation in the whole or salvation in the parts of it or both. I think this text respects both—to wit, salvation completing, and salvation completed: For "to save" is a work of many steps. Or to be as plain as possible, "to save" is a work that hath its beginning before the world began and shall not be completed before it is ended.

APRIL 3

Preserved In Jesus Christ

To those who are called, beloved in God the Father and kept for Jesus Christ.

JUDE 1

[It] may be said "to be saved" [is] in the purpose of God before the world began. The apostle said that "he saved us, and called us with a holy calling, not according to our works, but according to his own purpose and grace, which was given us in Christ Jesus before the world began" (2 Tim. 1:9). This is the beginning of salvation, according to this beginning all things concur and fall out in conclusion— "He hath saved us according to his eternal purpose, which he purposed in Christ Jesus." God in saving may be said to save us by determining to make those means effectual for the blessed completing of our salvation. Hence, we are said "to be chosen in Christ to salvation." Again, he hath in that choice given us grace that shall complete our salvation. Yes, the text is very full, "He hath blessed us with all spiritual blessings in heavenly places in Christ, according as he hath chosen us in him before the foundation of the world" (Eph. 1:3-4).

Secondly, as we may be said to be saved in the purpose of God before the foundation of the world; so, we may be said to be saved before we are converted or called to Christ. And hence "saved" is put before "called;" "he hath saved us, and called us." He said not, he hath called us, and saved us; but he puts saving before calling (2 Tim. 1:9). So again, we are said to be "preserved in Christ and called;" he saith not called and preserved (Jude 1). Therefore, God said again, "I will pardon them whom I reserve"—Paul expounds it, those whom I have "elected and kept," and this part of salvation is accomplished through the forbearance of God.

APRIL 4

God's Grace Before Conversion

Moreover, Manasseh shed very much innocent blood, till he filled Jerusalem from one end to another, besides the sin that he made Judah to sin so that they did what was evil in the sight of the LORD.

2 KINGS 21:16.

Here lies the reason that long life is granted to the elect before conversion; and that all the sins committed and all the judgments they deserve cannot drive them out of the world before conversion. Manasseh ... was a great sinner and for the trespass which he committed he was driven from his own land and carried to Babylon. But kill him they could not though his sins had deserved death ten thousand times. But what was the reason? Why, he was not yet called! God had chosen him in Christ and laid up in him a stock of grace which must be given to Manasseh before he died. Therefore, Manasseh must be convinced, converted, and saved.

That legion of devils that was possessed with all the sins which he had committed in the time of his unregeneracy could not take away his life before his conversion (Mark 5). How many times was that poor creature, as we may easily conjecture, assaulted for his life by the devils that were in him? Yet could they not kill him even though his dwelling was near the seaside and the devils had power to drive him too. Yet they could not drive him further than the mountains that were by the seaside. Yea, they could help him often to break his chains and fetters and could also make him as mad as a bedlam. They could also prevail with him to separate from men and cut himself with stones: But kill him they could not, drown him they could not. He was saved to be called. He was, notwithstanding all this, preserved in Christ, and called. (Mark 9:22).

APRIL 5

Prevenient Mercy

Blessed be the God and Father of our Lord Jesus Christ, who has blessed us in Christ with every spiritual blessing in the heavenly places, even as he chose us in him before the foundation of the world, that we should be holy and blameless before him in love.

EPHESIANS 1:3-4

[Are you] called Christian? How many times have your sins laid you upon a sick-bed; and to you and others' thinking—at the very mouth of the grave? Yet God said concerning you, let him live for he is not yet converted. Behold, therefore, that the elect are saved before they are called. "God, who is rich in mercy, for his great love wherewith he loved us, even when we were dead in sins," hath preserved us in Christ, and called us (Eph. 2:4-5).

Now this "saving" of us arises from six causes:

1. God hath chosen us unto salvation, and therefore will not frustrate his own purposes (1 Thess. 5:9).
2. God hath given us to Christ; and his gift as well as his calling is without repentance (Rom. 11:29; John 6:37).
3. Christ hath purchased us with his blood (Rom. 5:8-9).
4. They are, by God, counted in Christ before they are converted (Eph. 1:3-4).
5. They are ordained before conversion to eternal life. Yes, to be called, to be justified, to be glorified, and therefore all this must come upon them (Rom. 8:29-30).
6. For all this he hath also appointed them their portion and measure of grace, and that before the world began.

Therefore, that they may partake of all these privileges, they are saved and called, preserved in Christ, and called.

They must be brought unto Christ, yea, drawn unto him; for "no man," saith Christ, "can come to me, except the Father which hath sent me draw him" (John 6:44). "For by grace are ye saved through faith; and that not of yourselves, it is the gift of God" (Eph. 2:8).

APRIL 6

Faith As A Gift

So, faith comes from hearing, and hearing through the word of Christ.

ROMANS 10:17

[Consider then] "Saved by faith." For although salvation begins in God's purpose and comes to us through Christ's righteousness; yet faith is not exempted from having a hand in saving us. Not that it merits ... [anything] but is given by God to those which he saves. Thereby they may embrace and put on Christ by whose righteousness they must be saved. Wherefore this faith is that which here distinguishes them that shall be saved from them that shall be damned. Consequently, it is said, "He that believeth not, shall be damned;" consequently again it is that the believers are called "the children, the heirs, and the blessed with faithful Abraham." So that the promise by faith in Jesus Christ might be given to them that believe (Gal. 3:6-9, 26; Rom. 4:13-14).

As they must be brought to [Christ], so they must be helped to lay hold on Christ by faith. For as coming to Christ, so faith, is not in our own power. Therefore, we are said to be raised up with him "through the faith of the operation of God." And again, we are said to believe, "according to the working of his mighty power, which he wrought in Christ, when he raised him from the dead" (Col. 2:12; Eph. 1:19-20). Now we are said to be saved by faith, because by faith we lay hold of, venture upon, and put on Jesus Christ for life. For life, I say, because God having made him the Saviour, hath given him life to communicate to sinners. And this life that he communicates to them is the merit of his flesh and blood. Which whoso eats and drinks by faith, hath eternal life. Because that flesh and blood has merit in its sufficiency to obtain the favor of God.

APRIL 7

Personal Perseverance Required

But the one who endures to the end will be saved.

MATTHEW 24:13

And ... let Christians cautiously distinguish betwixt the meritorious and the instrumental cause of their justification. Christ, with what he hath done and suffered, is the meritorious cause of our justification. Therefore, he is said to be made to us of God, "wisdom and righteousness." And we are said to be "justified by his blood, and saved from wrath through him," for it was his life and blood that were the price of our redemption (1 Cor. 1:30; Rom. 5:9-10). "Redeemed," says Peter, "not with corruptible things, as silver and gold," alluding to the redemption of money under the law "but with the precious blood of Christ." You are, therefore ... to make Christ Jesus the object of your faith for justification. For by his righteousness your sins must be covered from the sight of the justice of the law. "Believe on the Lord Jesus Christ, and thou shalt be saved." "For he shall save his people from their sins" (Acts 16:31; Matt. 1:21).

To be saved is to be preserved in the faith to the end. "He that shall endure unto the end, the same shall be saved" (Matt. 24:13). Not that perseverance is an accident in Christianity or a thing performed by human industry. They that are saved "are kept by the power of God, through faith unto salvation" (1 Pet. 1:3-6).

He that falls short of the state that they are saved or are possessed as saved, cannot arrive to that saved state. Wherefore, perseverance is necessary to the saving of the soul. Therefore, it is included in the complete saving of us— "Israel shall be saved in the Lord with an everlasting salvation: ye shall not be ashamed nor confounded world without end" (Isa. 45:17). Perseverance is here made necessary to the complete saving of the soul.

APRIL 8

He Is Able

Now to him who is able to keep you from stumbling and to present you blameless before the presence of his glory with great joy.

JUDE 24

... Part of salvation depends not upon human power, but upon him that has begun a good work in us (Phil. 1:6). This part of our salvation is great, and calls for no less than the power of God for our help to perform it—as will be easily granted by all those that consider—

1. That all the power and policy, malice, and rage, of the devils and hell itself are against us. Any man that understands this will conclude that to be saved is no small thing. The devil is called a god, a prince, a lion—a roaring lion. It is said that he has death and the power of it. Our perseverance, therefore, lies in the power of God—"the gates of hell shall not prevail against it."
2. All the world is against him that shall be saved. But what is one poor creature to all the world, especially if you consider that with the world is: Terror, fear, power, majesty, laws, jails, gibbets, hangings, burnings, drownings, starvings, banishments, and a thousand kinds of deaths (1 John 5:4-5; John 16:33)?
3. Add to this that all these corruptions that dwell in our flesh are against us. And not only in their nature and being, but they lust against us and war against us to "bring us into captivity to the law of sin and death" (Gal. 5:17; 1 Pet. 2:11; Rom. 7:23).
4. All the delusions in the world are against them that shall be saved, and swallowed up they would be! [If they] were ... not elect and God was not himself engaged, either by power to keep them from falling, or by grace to pardon if they fall ... to lift them up again.

APRIL 9

Fullness Of Joy

You make known to me the path of life; in your presence there is fullness of joy; at your right hand are pleasures forevermore.

PSALM 16:11

To be saved: He that is saved must, when this world can hold him no longer, have a safe-conduct to heaven. For that is the place where they that are saved must [be] to the full enjoy[ment of] their salvation. This heaven is called "the end of our faith." Because it is that which faith looks at as Peter says, "Receiving the end of your faith, even the salvation of your souls." And again, "But we are not of them who draw back unto perdition; but of them that believe to the saving of the soul" (1 Pet. 1:9; Heb. 10:39). For as I said, heaven is the place for the saved to enjoy their salvation in, with that perfect gladness that is not attainable here. Here we are saved by faith and hope of glory. But there, we that are saved shall enjoy the end of our faith and hope even the salvation of our souls. There is "Mount Zion, the heavenly Jerusalem, the general assembly and church of the firstborn." There is the "innumerable company of angels, and the spirits of just men made perfect." There is "God the judge of all and Jesus the Mediator of the new covenant." There shall our soul have as much of heaven as it can enjoy and that without intermission. Wherefore, when we come there, we shall be saved indeed! But now for a poor creature to be brought ... [there], this is the life of the point. But how shall I come ... [there]? There are heights and depths to hinder (Rom. 8:38-39).

APRIL 10

Fear At Death

And it came to pass, that the beggar died, and was carried by the angels into Abraham's bosom: and the rich man also died, and was buried.

LUKE 16:22 KJV

Suppose the poor Christian is now upon a sick-bed, beset with a thousand fears, and ten thousand at the end of that—sick-bed fears! And they are sometimes dreadful ones; fears that are begotten by the review of the sin, perhaps, of forty years' profession. Fears that are begotten by dreadful and fearful suggestions of the devil, the sight of death, and the grave. And it may be hell itself! Fears that are begotten by the withdrawing and silence of God and Christ, it may be the appearance of the devil himself. Some of these made David cry, "O spare me" a little, "that I may recover strength before I go hence, and be no more" (Ps. 39:13). "The sorrows of death," David said, "compassed me, and the pains of hell gat hold upon me; I found trouble and sorrow" (Ps. 116:3). These things; he calls the bands that the godly have in their death, and the plagues that others ... [do not know]. "They are not in trouble as other men; neither are they plagued like other men" (Ps. 73:9). But now, out of all these, the Lord will save his people: Not one sin, nor fear, nor devil shall hinder; nor the grave nor hell disappoint you. But how must this be? Why you must have a safe-conduct to heaven? What conduct? A conduct of angels: "Are they not all ministering spirits, sent forth to minister for them who shall be heirs of salvation?" (Heb. 1:14).

These angels, therefore, are not to fail them that are the saved; but must, as commissioned of God, come down from heaven to do this office for them. They must come, I say, and take the care and charge of our soul, to conduct it safely into Abraham's bosom.

APRIL 11

God's Gracious Contrivance[1]

In him we have redemption through his blood, the forgiveness of our trespasses, according to the riches of his grace.

EPHESIANS 1:7

That salvation is by grace appears in its contrivance. As their salvation was contrived by God so as was said, this salvation was undertaken by one of the three; to wit, the Son of the Father (John 1:29; Isa. 48:16).

Since there was a ... [stratagem] in heaven about the salvation of sinners on earth; yet if the result of that ... [plan] had been that we should be saved by our own good deeds, it would not have been proper for an apostle or an angel to say: "By grace ye are saved." But now, when a council is held in eternity about the salvation of sinners in time and what the result of that council shall be; that the Father, the Son, and the Holy Ghost will themselves accomplish the work of this salvation—this is grace. This is naturally grace! Grace that is rich and free! I will say it again, this is unthought-of grace. For whom could have thought that a Saviour had been in the bosom of the Father, or that the Father would have given him to be the Saviour of men; since he refused to give him to be the Saviour of angels?

Grace appears in the Son's undertaking this work. Again, could it have been thought that the Father would have sent his Son to be the Saviour? We should, for reason, have thought also that he would never have taken the work wholly upon himself; especially that fearful, dreadful, soul-astonishing, and amazing part thereof! Who could once have imagined that the Lord Jesus would have made himself so poor as to stand before God in the nauseous rags of our sins and subject himself to the curse and death that were due to our sin? By this he saved us by grace.

1 "Contrivance" is the use of skill to bring something about or create something.

APRIL 12

Mortality And Immortality

When the perishable puts on the imperishable, and the mortal puts on immortality, then shall come to pass the saying that is written: "Death is swallowed up in victory."

1 CORINTHIANS 15:54

There are three things from which this body must be saved—

1. There is that sinful filth and vileness that yet dwells in it, under which we groan earnestly all our days (2 Cor. 5:1-3).
2. There is mortality, that subjects us to age, sickness, aches, pains, diseases, and death.
3. And there is the grave and death itself for death is the last enemy that is to be destroyed. "So, when this corruptible shall have put on incorruption, and this mortal shall have put on immortality, then shall be brought to pass the saying that is written, 'Death is swallowed up in victory'" (1 Cor. 15:54).

So, when this comes to pass, then we shall be saved; then will salvation in all the parts of it meet in our glory. Then we shall be every way saved—saved in God's decree, saved in Christ's undertakings, saved by faith, saved in perseverance, saved in soul, and [saved] in body and soul together in the heavens, saved perfectly, everlastingly, gloriously.

These angels, therefore, are not to fail them that are the saved; but must, as commissioned of God, come down from heaven to do this office for them. They must come and take care and charge of our soul, to conduct it safely into Abraham's bosom. It is not our meanness [squalor] in the world, nor our weakness of faith, that shall hinder this. Nor shall the loathsomeness of our diseases make these delicate spirits shy of taking this charge upon them. Lazarus the beggar found this to be truth. A beggar so despised of the rich glutton that he was not ... [allowed] to come within his gate. A beggar full of sores and noisome putrefaction; yet behold, when he dies, the angels came from heaven to fetch him there.

APRIL 13

Changed In A Moment

[The Lord Jesus Christ] who will transform our lowly body to be like his glorious body, by the power that enables him even to subject all things to himself.

PHILIPPIANS 3:21

For our body, it shall be raised in power, in incorruption, a spiritual body and glorious (1 Cor. 15:44). The glory of which is set forth by several things—

1. It is compared to "the brightness of the firmament," and to the shining of the stars "for ever and ever" (Dan. 12:3).
2. It is compared to the shining of the sun— "Then shall the righteous shine forth as the sun in the kingdom of their Father. Who hath ears to hear, let him hear" (Matt. 13:43).
3. Their state is then to be equally glorious with angels; "But they which shall be counted worthy to obtain that world, and the resurrection from the dead, neither marry, nor are given in marriage; neither can they die any more, for they are equal unto the angels" (Luke 20:35-36).
4. It is said that then this our vile body shall be like the glorious body of Jesus Christ (Phil. 3:20-21; 1 John 3:2-3).
5. And now, when body and soul are thus united, who can imagine what glory they both possess? They will now be both in capacity, without jarring [jerking them], to serve the Lord with shouting thanksgivings, and with a crown of everlasting joy upon their heads.

In this world there cannot be that harmony and oneness of body and soul as there will be in heaven. Here the body sometimes sins against the soul, and the soul again vexes and perplexes the body with dreadful apprehensions of the wrath and judgment of God. While we be in this world, the body oft[en] hangs this way and the soul the quite contrary. But there, in heaven, they shall have that perfect union as never to jar more. But now the glory of the body shall so suit with the glory of the soul.

APRIL 14

Here We Know But In Part

But when the perfect comes, the partial will pass away.

1 CORINTHIANS 13:10.

Of the soul [in heaven]; it will then be filled in all the faculties of it with as much bliss and glory as ever it can hold.

1. The understanding shall then be perfect in knowledge—"Now we know but in part." We know God, Christ, heaven, and glory, but in part; "but when that which is perfect is come, then that which is in part shall be done away" (1 Cor. 13:10). Then shall we have perfect and everlasting visions of God, and that blessed one his Son Jesus Christ, a good thought of whom doth sometimes so fill us while in this world, that it causes "joy unspeakable and full of glory."

2. Then shall our will and affections be ever in a burning flame of love to God and his Son Jesus Christ. Our love here hath ups and downs, but there it shall be always perfect with that perfection which is not possible in this world to be enjoyed.

3. Then will our conscience have that peace and joy that neither tongue nor pen of men or angels can express.

4. Then will our memory be so enlarged to retain all things that happened to us in this world. So that with unspeakable aptness we shall call to mind all God's providences, all Satan's malice, all our own weaknesses, all the rage of men, and how God made all work together for his glory and our good to the everlasting ravishing of our hearts.

APRIL 15

The Father's Good Pleasure

Fear not, little flock, for it is your Father's good pleasure to give you the kingdom.

LUKE 12:32

How we are saved by the grace of the Father. Now this will I open unto you—

1. The Father by his grace has bound up them that shall go to heaven in an eternal decree of election. And here is the beginning of our salvation (2 Tim. 1:9). And election is reckoned not the Son's act, but the Father's— "Blessed be the God and Father of our Lord Jesus Christ, who hath blessed us with all spiritual blessings in heavenly places in Christ, according as he hath chosen us in him before the foundation of the world" (Eph. 1:3-4).

2. The Father's grace ordained and gave the Son to undertake for us our redemption. The Father sent the Son to be the Saviour of the world—"In whom we have redemption through his blood, the forgiveness of sins, according to the riches of his grace; that in the ages to come he might shew the exceeding riches of his grace, in his kindness toward us through Christ Jesus" (Eph. 1:7).

3. The Father's grace gave us to Christ to be justified by his righteousness, washed in his blood, and saved by his life.

4. The Father's grace gives the kingdom of heaven to those that he hath given to Jesus Christ—"Fear not, little flock, for it is your Father's good pleasure to give you the kingdom" (Luke 12:32).

5. The Father's grace provides and lays up in Christ, for those that he has chosen, a sufficiency of all spiritual blessings, to be communicated to them at their need, for their preservation in the faith, and faithful perseverance through this life; (2 Tim. 1:9).

APRIL 16

Graced By The Father And Son

My Father, who has given them to me, is greater than all, and no one is able to snatch them out of the Father's hand.

JOHN 10:29

The Father's grace saves us by multiplying pardons to us, for Christ's sake, day by day—"In whom we have redemption through his blood, the forgiveness of sins, according to the riches of his grace" (Eph. 1:7).

The Father's grace saves us by exercising patience and forbearance towards us all the time of our unregeneracy (Rom. 3:24).

The Father's grace saves us by holding of us fast in his hand, and by keeping of us from all the power of the enemy—"My Father," said Christ, "that gave them me, is greater than all, and no man is able to pluck them out of my Father's hand" (John 10:29).

The Father's grace saves us by accepting our persons and services, by lifting the light of his countenance upon us.

Of the grace of the Son.

I come now to speak of the grace of the Son; for as the Father puts forth his grace in the saving of the sinner, so doth the Son put forth his—"For ye know the grace of our Lord Jesus Christ, that, though he was rich, yet for your sakes he became poor, that ye through his poverty might be rich" (2 Corinthians 8:9).

Here you see also that the grace of our Lord Jesus Christ is brought in as a partner with the grace of his Father in the salvation of our souls. Now this is the grace of our Lord Jesus Christ. He was rich, but for our sakes he became poor, so that we through his poverty might be made rich.

To inquire into this grace, this condescending grace of Christ, and that by searching out how rich Jesus Christ was, and then how poor he made himself, that we through his poverty might have the riches of salvation.

APRIL 17

Jesus Became Poor For Us

For you know the grace of our Lord Jesus Christ, that though he was rich, yet for your sake he became poor, so that you by his poverty might become rich.

2 CORINTHIANS 8:9

How rich was Jesus Christ? To which I answer—Generally and Particularly:

Generally:
He was rich as the Father— "All things that the Father hath," saith he, "are mine." Jesus Christ is the Lord of all, God over all, blessed forever. "He thought it not robbery to be equal with God," being naturally and eternally God, as the Father, but of his Godhead he could not strip himself (John 10:30; 16:15; Acts 10:36; Phil. 2:6; Rom. 9:4-5).

Particularly:

1. He had the glory of dominion; he was Lord of all the creatures; they were under him upon a double account—(a) as he was their creator (Col. 1:16); (b) as he was made the heir of God (Heb. 1:2).
2. Therefore the glory of worship, reverence, and fear from all creatures, was due unto him. The worship, obedience, subjection, and service of angels were due unto him. The fear, honor, and glory of kings, and princes, and judges of the earth were due unto him (Ps. 148).
3. But above all, the glory of communion with his Father was his. I say, the glory of that unspeakable communion that he had with the Father before his incarnation, which alone was worth ten thousand worlds, that was ever his.

APRIL 18

Not Even A Bed

And Jesus said to him, "Foxes have holes, and birds of the air have nests, but the Son of Man has nowhere to lay his head."
MATTHEW 8:20

Now ... heaven he forsook for our sakes—"He came into the world to save sinners" (1 Tim. 1:15).

[1.] He was made lower than the angels for the suffering of death (Heb. 2:9). When he was born, he made himself as he said, a worm, or one of no reputation. He became the reproach and byword of the people. He was born in a stable, laid in a manger, earned his bread with his labour, being by trade a carpenter (Ps. 22:6; Phil. 2:7; Luke 2:7; Mark 6:3). When he [proceeded] himself to his ministry, he lived upon the charity of the people. When other men went to their own houses, Jesus went to the Mount of Olives. Hark, what he said ... [concerning] this—"Foxes have holes, and birds of the air have nests, but the Son of man hath not where to lay his head." He denied himself this world's good (Luke 8:2-3; 9:58; John 7:35; 8:1).

[2.] Again, as he was Prince of life, he for our sakes laid down that also. For so ... [strong was] the matter that he or we must die. But the grace that was in his heart wrought with him to lay down his life: "He gave his life a ransom for many." He laid down his life that we might have life. He gave his flesh and blood for the life of the world. He laid down his life for his sheep.

[3.] Again, he was Prince of peace but he forsook his peace also. He laid aside peace with the world and chose upon that account to be a man of sorrows and acquainted with grief. Therefore, was persecuted from his cradle to his cross, by kings, [by] rulers.

APRIL 19

The Great Need Of Repentance

The time is fulfilled, and the kingdom of God is at hand: repent and believe in the Gospel.

MARK 1:15

Take a catalogue of ... [what salvation means]: "Believe on the Lord Jesus Christ, and thou shalt be saved" (Mark 16:16; Acts 16:31). "If thou shalt confess with thy mouth the Lord Jesus, and shalt believe in thine heart that God hath raised him from the dead thou shalt be saved."

[A caution.] But, sinner, if you would indeed be saved, beware of these four things—

1. Beware of delaying repentance; delays are dangerous and damnable. They are dangerous because they harden the heart. They are damnable because their tendency is to make you outstand [resist] the time of grace (Ps. 95:7; Heb. 3-12).
2. Beware of resting in the word of the kingdom without the spirit and power of the kingdom of the gospel. For the gospel coming in word only saves nobody, for the kingdom of God or the gospel where it comes to salvation is not in word but in power (1 Thess. 1:4-6; 1 Cor. 4:19).
3. Take heed of living in a profession, a life that is provoking to God. For that is the way to make him cast thee away in his anger.
4. Take heed that your inside and outside are alike. And both [are] conformable to the Word of his grace. Labour to be like the living creatures which you may read of in the book of the prophet Ezekiel, whose appearance and themselves were one (Ezek. 10:22).

In all this, I have advertised you not to be content without the power and Spirit of God in your hearts. For without him you partake of none of the grace of the Father or Son but will certainly miss the salvation of the soul.

April 20

Sola Gratia

Through him we have also obtained access by faith into this grace in which we stand, and we rejoice in hope of the glory of God.

Romans 5:2

That salvation is by grace appears in its contrivance [stratagem]. Again, as their salvation was contrived by God; so was said, this salvation was undertaken by one of the three: To wit, the Son of the Father (John 1:29; Isa. 48:16).

Had there been a contrivance in heaven about the salvation of sinners on earth? Yet if the result of that contrivance had been that we should be saved by our own good deeds, it would not have been proper for an apostle or an angel to say: "By grace ye are saved." But now when a council is held in eternity about the salvation of sinners in time and when the result of that council shall be; that the Father, the Son, and the Holy Ghost will themselves accomplish the work of this salvation. This is grace, this is naturally grace, grace that is rich and free. Yea, this is unthought-of grace. I will say it again, this is unthought-of grace. For whom could have thought that a Saviour had been in the bosom of the Father, or that the Father would have given him to be the Saviour of men, since he refused to give him to be the Saviour of angels (Heb. 2:16-17)?

Again, could it have been thought that the Father would have sent his Son to be the Saviour? We should, in reason, have thought also that he would never have taken the work wholly upon himself. Especially that fearful, dreadful, soul-astonishing, and amazing part thereof! Who could once have imagined that the Lord Jesus would have made himself so poor as to stand before God in the nauseous rags of our sins and subject himself to the curse and death that were due to our sin? But thus, he did to save us by grace.

APRIL 21

Chosen In Christ

For many are called, but few are chosen.

MATTHEW 22:14

Blessed be the God and Father of our Lord Jesus Christ, who hath blessed us with all spiritual blessings in heavenly places in Christ: according as he hath chosen us in him before the foundation of the world.

EPHESIANS 1:3-4

Grace appears in the terms and conditions of which salvation is made. Again, if we consider the terms and conditions upon which this salvation is made ... to them that are saved, it will further appear we are saved by grace.

1. The things that immediately concern our justification and salvation, they are offered, yea, given to us freely, and we are commanded to receive them by faith. Sinner, hold up thy lap. God so loved the world, that he gave his Son, that he gives his righteousness, that he gives his Spirit, and the kingdom of heaven (John 3:16; Rom. 5:17; 2 Cor. 1:21-22; Luke 12:32).
2. He also gives repentance, he gives faith, and gives everlasting consolation, and good hope through grace (Acts 5:30-31; Phil. 1:29; 2 Thess. 2:16).
3. He gives pardon and gives more grace to keep us from sinking into hell than we have sin to sink us in thither [there] (Acts 5:31; Prov. 3:34; John 4:6; 1 Pet. 5:5).
4. He has made all these things over to us in a covenant of grace. We call it a covenant of grace because it is set in opposition to the covenant of works. And because it is established to us in the doings of Christ, founded in his blood, established upon the best promises made to him, and to us by him.

APRIL 22

What Is Man?

What is man, that you make so much of him, and that you set your heart on him?

Job 7:17

An enemy to God: By nature, he is an enemy to God, an enemy in his mind. "The carnal mind is enmity against God, for it is not subject to the law of God, neither indeed can be" (Rom. 8:7; Col. 1:21).

A slave to sin: So that the state of man was this—he was not only overly persuaded ... to sin against God. But he drank this sin, like water, into his very nature, mingled it with every faculty of his soul and member of his body. By the means of which he became alienated from God, and an enemy to him in his very heart. And will you, O Lord, as the Scripture has it, "And you do open your eyes upon such a one?" (Job 14:3). Yea, open your heart and take this man, not into judgment, but into mercy with thee?

In covenant with death and hell: Further, man by his sin had not only given himself to be a captive slave to the devil; but continues in his sin. He made head[way] against his God, struck up a covenant with death, and made an agreement with hell. But for God to open his eyes upon such a one, and to take hold of him by riches of grace, this is amazing (Isa. 28:16-18).

"Now when I passed by you, and looked upon you, behold, your time was the time of love. I spread my skirt over you and covered your nakedness. Yea, I swore unto you and entered into a covenant with you, said the Lord God and you became mine." Sinner, see further into the chapter, Ezekiel 16. All this is the grace of God, every word in this text smells of grace.

APRIL 23

Grace Is The Carriage

Therefore, we are ambassadors for Christ, God making his appeal through us. We implore you on behalf of Christ, be reconciled to God.

2 CORINTHIANS 5:20

The carriage of God to man and of man to God in his conversion.

Of God's Carriage to Man.

[God] ... comes to him while he is in his sins, in [by] his [atoning] blood. He comes to him now, not in the heat and fire of his jealousy, but "in the cool of the day," in [God's] unspeakable gentleness, mercy, pity, and bowels of love. Not in clothing himself with vengeance, but in a way of entreaty and meekly beseeches the sinner to be reconciled unto him (2 Cor. 5:19-20).

It is expected among men that he which gives the offense should be the first in seeking peace. But sinner, betwixt God and man it is not so; not that we loved God, not that we chose God. But "God was in Christ, reconciling the world unto himself, not imputing their trespasses unto them." God is the first that seeks peace; and ... in a way of entreaty he bids his ministers pray you in Christ's stead: "as though God did beseech you by us, we pray you, in Christ's stead, be ye reconciled to God." O sinner, will you not open [your heart]? Behold, God the Father and his Son Jesus Christ stand both at the door of your heart, beseeching [begging] there for favor from you that you will be reconciled to them with promise—if you will comply, to forgive you all thy sins. O grace! O amazing grace! To see a prince entreat a beggar to receive alms would be a strange sight. To see a king entreat the traitor to accept mercy would be a stranger sight than that. But to see God entreat a sinner ... [is greatest!].

APRIL 24

A More Convenient Time

And as he reasoned about righteousness and self-control and the coming judgment, Felix was alarmed and said, "Go away for the present. When I get an opportunity, I will summon you."

ACTS 24:25

God doth not only beseech thee to be reconciled to him but ... [more]. For thy encouragement he hath pronounced, in your hearing, exceeding great and precious promises; "and hath confirmed it by an oath, that by two immutable things, in which it was impossible for God to lie, we might have a strong consolation, who have fled for refuge to lay hold upon the hope set before us."

God's ordinary dealing with sinners when, at first, he ministers conviction to them by his Word, how strangely do they behave themselves! They love not to have their consciences touched. They like not to ponder upon what they have been, what they are, or what is to become of them hereafter. Such thoughts are unmanly, hurtful, disadvantageous. Therefore, "they refused to hearken, and pulled away the shoulder, and stopped their ears, that they should not hear" (Zech. 7, 11). And now they are for anything rather than the Word; an alehouse, a [brothel], a playhouse, sports, pleasures, sleep, the world, and what not so they may stave off the power of the Word of God.

Secondly, when God now comes up closer to them and begins to fasten conviction upon their conscience, [even] though such conviction be the first step to faith and repentance. Yes ... [even] to life eternal, yet what shifts will they have to forget them and wear them off! Yes, although they now begin to see that they must either turn or burn. Yet oftentimes even then they will study to wave [off] a present conversion. They object, they are too young to turn yet. Seven years hence time enough when they are old or come upon a sick bed [they will come].

APRIL 25

The Finger Of God

But if it is by the finger of God that I cast out demons, then the kingdom of God has come upon you.

Luke 11:20

In taking possession of us for his own, in his making of us his house and habitation, so ... the Father and the Son have both gloriously put forth gracious acts in order to our salvation. Yet the Spirit is the first that makes seizure of us (1 Cor. 3:16; 6:19; Eph. 2:21-22). Christ, therefore, when he went away, said not that he would send the Father, but the Spirit, and that he should be in us forever—"If I depart," said Christ, "I will send him, the Spirit of truth, the Comforter" (John 14:16; 16:7, 13).

The Holy Spirit coming into us and dwelling in us, works out many salvations for us now and each of them in order also to our being saved for ever.

1. He saves us from our darkness by illuminating us. Hence, he is called "the Spirit of revelation," because he opens the blind eyes and consequently delivers us from that darkness which else would drown us in the deeps of hell (Eph. 1:17, 19).
2. He it is that convinces us of the evil of our unbelief and shows us the necessity of our believing in Christ; without the conviction of this we should perish.
3. This is that finger of God by which the devil is made to give place unto grace, by whose power else we should be carried headlong to hell.
4. This is he that works faith in our hearts, without which neither the grace of the Father nor the grace of the Son can save us, "For he that believeth not, shall be damned" (Mark 16:16; Rom. 15:13).
5. This is he by whom we are born again. And he that is not so born can neither see nor inherit the kingdom of heaven.

APRIL 26

By My Spirit

Then he said to me, "This is the word of the LORD to Zerubbabel: Not by might, nor by power, but by my Spirit, says the LORD of hosts."

ZECHARIAH 4:6

Now all these things are so necessary to our salvation, that I know not which of them can be wanting; neither can any of them be by any means attained but by this blessed Spirit.

And thus, have I in a few words shown you the grace of the Spirit and how ... [he] puts forth ... [himself] towards the saving of the soul. And truly Sirs, it is necessary that you know these things distinctly—[consider], the grace of the Father, the grace of the Son, and the grace of the Holy Ghost. For it is not the grace of one, but of all these three, that saves him that shall be saved indeed.

The Father's grace saves no man without the grace of the Son. Neither does the Father and the Son save any without the grace of the Spirit. For as the Father loves, the Son must die, and the Spirit must sanctify, or no soul must be saved.

This is he that sets up his kingdom in the heart. And by that means keeps out the devil after he is cast out. Which kingdom of the Spirit, whoever wants, they lie liable to a worse possession of the devil than ever (Matt. 12:43-45; Luke 11:24-25).

By this Spirit we come to see the beauty of Christ, without a sight of which we should never desire him. But should certainly live in the neglect of him and perish (John 16:14; 1 Cor. 2:9-13; Isa. 53:1-2).

By this Spirit we are helped to praise God acceptably, but without it, it is impossible to be heard unto salvation.

By this blessed Spirit the love of God is shed abroad in our hearts, and our hearts are directed into the love of God.

APRIL 27

Who Are Not Saved?

The harvest is past, the summer is ended, and we are not saved.

JEREMIAH 8:20

First. Not the self-righteous, not they that have no need of the physician. "The whole have no need of the physician," saith Christ. "I came not to call the righteous, but sinners to repentance" (Mark 2:17). And again, "He hath filled the hungry with good things, and the rich he hath sent empty away" (Luke 1:53). Now when I say not the self-righteous nor the rich, I mean not that they are utterly excluded. For Paul was such a one. But he was not saved without first [being] awakened ... to see ... [his] need to be saved by grace.

Second. The grace of God saves not him that hath sinned the unpardonable sin. There is nothing left for him "but a certain fearful looking for of judgment, —which shall devour the adversaries" (Heb. 10:27).

Third. That sinner that perseveres in final impenitency and unbelief shall be damned (Rom. 2:2-5; Mark 16:15-16).

Fourth. That sinner whose mind the god of this world has blinded, that the glorious light of the gospel of Christ, who is the image of God, can never shine into him, is lost, and must be damned (2 Cor. 4:3-4).

Fifth. The sinner that makes religion his cloak for wickedness, he is a hypocrite, and continuing so, must certainly be damned (Isa. 33:14; Matt. 24:50-51).

Sixth. In a word, every sinner that perseveres in his wickedness, shall not inherit the kingdom of heaven— "Know ye not that the unrighteous shall not inherit the kingdom of God? Be not deceived: neither fornicators, nor idolaters, nor adulterers, nor effeminate, nor abusers of themselves with mankind, nor thieves, nor covetous, nor drunkards, nor revilers, nor extortioners, shall inherit the kingdom of God" (1 Cor. 6:9-10).

APRIL 28

Who Then Is Saved?

Jesus looked at them and said, "With man it is impossible, but not with God. For all things are possible with God."

Mark 10:27

Those of all these kinds that the Spirit of God shall bring [to] the Father by Jesus Christ. These . . . and none but these can be saved, because else the sinners might be saved without the Father, or without the Son, or without the Spirit.

Now, in all that I have said, I have not in the least suggested that any sinner is rejected because his sins are great. Christ Jesus came into the world to save the chief of sinners. It is not, therefore, the greatness of, but the continuance in sins that indeed damned the sinner. But I always exclude him that hath sinned against the Holy Ghost. That it is not the greatness of sin that excluded the sinner is evident—

It is evident also from the many sinners that we find to be saved, by the revealed will of God. For in the Word, we have mention made of the salvation of great sinners, where their names and their sins stand recorded for our encouragement as:

1. You read of Manasseh, who was an idolater, a witch, a persecutor, yea, a rebel against the Word of God, sent unto him by the prophets; and yet this man was saved (2 Chron. 33:2-13; 2 Kings 21:16).
2. You read of Mary Magdalene, in whom were seven devils; her condition was dreadful, yet she was saved (Luke 8:2).
3. You read of the man that had a legion of devils in him. O how dreadful was his condition! And yet by grace he was saved (Mark 5:1-10).
4. You read of them that murdered the Lord Jesus, and how they were converted and saved (Acts 2:23).
5. You read of the exorcists, how they closed with Christ and were saved by grace (Acts 19:13).

APRIL 29

The Backslider's Hope?

I will heal their backsliding; I will love them freely: for mine anger is turned away from him.

HOSEA 14:4 KJV

Answer:

So was Noah, and yet he found grace in the eyes of the Lord (Gen. 9:21-22). So was Lot, and yet God saved him by grace (Gen. 19:35; 2 Pet. 2:7-9). So was David, yet by grace he was forgiven his iniquities (2 Sam. 12:7-13). So was Solomon, and a great [sinner] ... too. Yet by grace his soul was saved (Ps. 89:28-34). So was Peter and that a dreadful one; yet by grace he was saved (Matt. 26:69-74; Mark 16:7; Acts 15:7-11).

True, these are as bad saved as [the] damned; but to this question: They that are effectually called are saved. They that believe on the Son of God shall be saved. They that are sanctified and preserved in Christ shall be saved. They that take up their cross daily and follow Christ shall be saved.

Take a catalogue of them thus: "Believe on the Lord Jesus Christ, and thou shalt be saved" (Mark 16:16; Acts 16:31). "If thou shalt confess with thy mouth the Lord Jesus, and shalt believe in thine heart that God hath raised him from the dead thou shalt be saved" (Rom. 10:9). Be justified by the blood of Christ, and thou shalt be saved (Rom. 5:9). Be reconciled to God by the death of his Son, and thou shalt be saved by his life (Rom. 5:10). "And it shall come to pass, that whosoever shall call on the name of the Lord shall be saved" (Acts 2:21).

APRIL 30

Why Will You Die?

Say to them, "As I live," declares the LORD *God, "I have no pleasure in the death of the wicked, but that the wicked turn from his way and live; turn back, turn back from your evil ways, for why will you die, O house of Israel?"*

EZEKIEL 33:11

[Caution.] But sinner, if thou would indeed be saved, beware of these four things—

1. Beware of delaying repentance; delays are dangerous and damnable. They are dangerous because they harden the heart. They are damnable because their tendency is to make you outstand the time of grace (Ps. 95:7; Heb. 3-12).
2. Beware of resting in the word of the kingdom without the spirit and power of the kingdom of the gospel. For the gospel coming in word only saves nobody. For the kingdom of God or the gospel where it comes to salvation, is not in word but in power (1 Thess. 1:4-6; 1 Cor. 4:19).
3. Take heed of living in a profession a life that is provoking to God; for that is the way to make him cast thee away in his anger.
4. Take heed that your inside and outside are alike. And both conformable to the Word of his grace. Labour to be like the living creatures which you may read of in the book of the prophet Ezekiel, whose appearance and themselves were one (Ezek. 10:22).

In all this, I have advertised [made known to] you not to be content without the power and Spirit of God in your hearts. For without him you partake of none of the grace of the Father or Son but will certainly miss ... the salvation of the soul.

See some other Scriptures: "He shall save the humble person" (Job 22:29). "Thou wilt save the afflicted people" (Ps. 18:27). "He shall save the children of the needy" (Ps. 72:4). "He shall save the souls of the needy" (Ps. 72:13).

MAY 1

The Strait Gate

Strive to enter in at the strait gate; for many, I say unto you, will seek to enter in, and shall not be able.

LUKE 13:24 KJV

These are the words of our Lord Jesus Christ, and are, therefore, in [an] especial manner to take notice. Besides, the subject matter of the words is the most weighty, in other words; how we should attain salvation and therefore [it is] also to be considered.

The occasion of the words was a question which one that was at this time in the company of the disciples put to Jesus Christ; the question was this, "Lord, are there few that be saved?" (v. 23). A serious question, not such as tended to the subversion of the hearers, as too many now-a-days do. But such as in its own nature tended to the awakening of the company to good, and that called for such an answer that might profit the people also. This question was also well pleasing to Jesus Christ. And he prepared and gave such an answer as was without the least retort or show of distaste. Such an answer ... as carried in it the most full resolve to the question itself and help to the persons questioning. "And he said unto them, strive to enter in." The words are an answer, and an instruction also. First. An answer ... that [is] in the affirmative. The gate is strait—many that seek will not be able therefore, but few shall be saved. Second. The answer is an instruction also; "strive to enter in"—good counsel and instruction. Pray God help me, and my reader, and all that love their own salvation to take it!

MAY 2

Will Few Be Saved?

And someone said to him, "Lord, with those who are saved be few?"

LUKE 13:23

The general scope of the text [to strive to enter in] is to be considered, and that is that great thing—salvation. For these words do immediately look at, point to, and give directions about salvation: "Are there few that be saved?" "Strive to enter in at the strait gate."

The words, I say, are to direct us not only to talk of, or to wish for, but to understand how we shall and to seek that we may be effectually saved. Therefore [this is] of the greatest importance. To be saved! What is like being saved? To be saved from sin, from hell, from the wrath of God, from eternal damnation, what is like it? To be made an heir of God, of his grace, of his kingdom, and eternal glory, what is like it? And yet all this is included in this word saved and in the answer to that question, "Are there few that be saved?" Indeed, this word *saved* is but of little use in the world, ... [except] to them that are heartily afraid of ... [being damned].

O when men are sick of sin and afraid of ... [being damned], what a text is that where this word saved is found! Indeed, what a word of worth, and goodness, and blessedness, is it to him that lies [and] continues upon the wrath of a guilty conscience? "But the whole need not a physician." He, therefore, and him only, knows what saved means—that knows what hell, and death, and damnation means.

MAY 3

Souls Made Perfect

But you have come to Mount Zion and to the city of the living God, the heavenly Jerusalem, and to innumerable angels in festal gathering, and the assembly of the firstborn who are enrolled in heaven, and to God, the judge of all, and the spirits of the righteous made perfect.

HEBREWS 12:22-23

An intimation of the kingdom of heaven; for when he saith, "Strive to enter in," and in such phrases, there is supposed a place or state, or both, to be enjoyed. "Enter in"—enter what, or where, but into a state or place, or both? And therefore, when you read this word, "enter in," you must say there is certainly included in the text that good thing that yet is not expressed. "Enter in"—into heaven, that is the meaning where the saved are, and shall be. Into heaven, that place, that glorious place, where God, and Christ, and angels are and the souls or spirits of just men made perfect. "Enter in"—that thing included though not expressed in the words is called in another place, the Mount Zion, the heavenly Jerusalem, the general assembly, and church of the first-born which are written in heaven. And therefore, the words signify unto us that there is a state most glorious.

And ... when this world is ended and that this place and state are likewise to be enjoyed and inherited by a generation of men forever. Besides, this word, "enter in," signifies that salvation to the full is to be enjoyed only there. There all shall be well to all eternity. Further, all the parts of, and circumstances that attend salvation, are only there to be enjoyed. There is the glory and fullness of joy and everlasting pleasures. There is God and Christ to be enjoyed by open vision, and more. There are angels and saints. Further, there is no death, nor sickness, no sorrow nor sighing forever. There is no pain, nor persecutor, nor darkness, to eclipse our glory. O this Mount Zion! O this heavenly Jerusalem! (2 Cor. 5:1-4, Ps. 16:11, Luke 20:35-36).

MAY 4

Entrance Into Heaven

I am the door, if anyone enters by me, he will be saved and go in and out and find pasture.

JOHN 10:9

It is called a gate. It is set forth by the similitude [likeness] of a gate. A gate, you know, is of double use. It is to open and shut. So, consequently, to let in or to keep out; and to do both these at the [set] season. As he said, "Let not the gates of Jerusalem be opened until the sun be hot." And again, "I commanded that the gates should be shut, and charged that they should not be opened till after the Sabbath" (Neh. 7:3; 13:19-20). And so you find of this gate of heaven, when the five wise virgins came, the gate was opened. But afterwards came the other virgins, and the door was shut (Matt. 25). So then, the entrance into heaven is called a gate, to show there is a time when there may be entrance. And there will come a time when there shall be none. Indeed, this is a chief truth contained in the text—"Strive to enter in at the strait gate; for many, I say unto you, will seek to enter in, and shall not be able." I read in the Scriptures of two gates or doors, through which they that go to heaven must enter.

There is the door of faith, the door which the grace of God has opened to the Gentiles. This door is Jesus Christ as also himself does testify, saying, "I am the door" (John 10:9; Acts 14:27). By this door men enter into God's favor and mercy, and find forgiveness through faith in his blood, and live in hope of eternal life. And therefore, himself also has said, "I am the door; by me if any man enter in, he shall be saved" that is, received to mercy, and inherit eternal life.

MAY 5

Is Not Christ Himself the Gate?

When once the master of the house has risen and shut the door, and you begin to stand outside and to knock at the door saying, "Lord, open to us," then he will answer you, "I do not know where you come from."

LUKE 13:25

It is that gate that lets men into or shuts men out of that place or kingdom where Abraham, and Isaac, and Jacob are. Which place is that paradise where Christ promised the thief that he should be that day that he asked to be with him in his kingdom. It is that place into which Paul said he was caught when he heard words unlawful or impossible for a man to utter (2 Cor. 12:1-6).

Is not Christ the gate?

[It is] ... he without whom no man can get there. Because by his merit's men obtain that world. And because he, as the Father, is the donor and disposer of that kingdom to whom he will. Further, this place is called his house and himself the master of it—"When once the master of the house is risen up, and hath shut to the door" (Luke 13:25) But we used to say that the master of the house is not the door. Men enter heaven, then, by him not as he is the gate, or door, or entrance, into the celestial mansion-house. But as he is the giver and disposer of that kingdom to them whom he shall count worthy because he hath obtained it for them.

That this gate is the very passage into heaven, consider the text hath special reference to the day of judgment. When Christ will have laid aside his mediatory office, which before he exercised for the bringing to the faith his own elect. And will then act, not as one that justifies the ungodly, but as one that will judge sinners. He will now be risen from the throne of grace, and shut up the door against all the impenitent, and will be set upon the throne of judgment, from there to proceed with ungodly sinners.

MAY 6

Behold! Today Is The Day

For he says, "In a favorable time I listened to you, and in a day of salvation I have helped you." Behold, now is the favorable time; behold, now is the day of salvation.

2 Corinthians 6:2

An objection raised that one should strive today:

Christ bids [all to] strive: "Strive" now "to enter in at the strait gate." But if that gate be as you say, the gate or entrance into heaven; then it should seem that we should not strive till the day of judgment for we shall not come at that gate till then.

Answer to the objection:

Christ, by this exhortation [to] strive does not at all admit of, or countenance [any] delays. Or that a man should neglect his own salvation. But puts poor creatures upon preparing for the judgment and counsels them now to get those things that will then give them entrance into glory. This exhortation is much like these: "Therefore be ye also ready, for in such an hour as ye think not the Son of man cometh.—And they that were ready went in with him to the marriage, and the door was shut" (Matt. 24:44, 25:10).

So that when he saith, "Strive to enter in," it is as if he should say, blessed are they that shall be admitted another day to enter into the kingdom of heaven. But they that shall be counted worthy of so unspeakable a favor, must be well prepared and fitted for it beforehand. Now, the time to be fitted is not the day of judgment but the day of grace. Not then, but now. Therefore, strive now for those things that will then give you entrance into the heavenly kingdom.

MAY 7

The Straitness Of The Gate[1]

Or do you not know that the unrighteous will not inherit the kingdom of God?

1 CORINTHIANS 6:9A

The straitness of this gate is not to be understood carnally, but mystically. You are not to understand it, as if the entrance into heaven was some little pinching wicket. No, the straitness of this gate is quite another thing. This gate is wide enough for all them that are the truly gracious and sincere lovers of Jesus Christ. But so strait as that not one of the other [kind] can by any means enter in: "Open to me the gates of righteousness: I will go into them, and I will praise the Lord: this gate of the Lord, into which the righteous shall enter" (Ps. 118:19-20). By this word Christ Jesus has showed unto us that without due qualifications there is no possibility of entering into heaven; the strait gate will keep all others out. When Christ spoke this parable, he had doubtless his eye upon some passage or passages of the Old Testament with which the Jews were well acquainted. I will mention ... [one].

The place by which God turned Adam and his wife out of paradise. Possibly our Lord might have his eye upon that. For though that was wide enough for them to come out at yet it was too strait for them to go in at. But what should be the reason for that? Why, they had sinned; and therefore God "placed at the east of that garden cherubims, and a flaming sword which turned every way, to keep the way of the tree of life" (Gen. 3:24). "Know ye not that the unrighteous shall not inherit the kingdom of God? Be not deceived, neither fornicators, nor idolaters, nor adulterers, nor effeminate, nor abusers of themselves with mankind, nor thieves, nor covetous, nor drunkards, nor revilers, nor extortioners, shall inherit the kingdom of God" (1 Cor. 6:9-10).

---

1 "Straitness" is defined as distress; difficulty; pressure from narrowness of circumstances or necessity of any kind, particularly from poverty; want; scarcity. Bunyan's spelling retained here for emphasis.

MAY 8

Keepers Of The Door

Outside are the dogs and sorcerers and the sexually immoral and murderers and idolaters, and everyone who loves and practices falsehood.

Revelation 22:15

Perhaps our Lord might have his eye upon the gates of the temple when he spoke this word unto the people. For though the gates of the temple were six cubits wide, yet they were so strait, that none that were unclean in anything might enter in thereat (Ezek. 40:48). Because there were placed at these gates, porters, whose office was to look that none but those that had right to enter might go in thither [there]. And so, it is written, Jehoiada set "porters at the gates of the house of the Lord, that none which was unclean in anything should enter in" (2 Chron. 23:19), Souls, God has porters at the gates of the temple [and] at the gate of heaven. Porters, I say, placed there by God, to look that none that are unclean in anything may come in thither. At the gate of the church, none may enter now that are openly profane, and scandalous to religion. No, though they plead they are beloved of God: "What hath my beloved to do in mine house," saith the Lord, "seeing she hath wrought lewdness with many?" (Jer. 11:15).

I say, I am very apt to believe that our Lord Jesus Christ had his thoughts upon these two texts, when he said the gate is strait. And that which confirms me the more in the things is this, a little below the text he saith, "There shall be weeping and gnashing of teeth, when ye shall see Abraham, and Isaac, and Jacob, and all the prophets, in the kingdom of heaven, and you yourselves thrust out" (Luke 13:28). Thrust out, which signifies a violent act, resisting with striving those that would—though unqualified—[to] enter.

MAY 9

Causes Of This Gate's Straitness

Not everyone who says to me, "Lord, Lord," will enter the kingdom of heaven, but the one who does the will of my Father who is in heaven.

MATTHEW 7:21

There is sin, the sin of the profane and the sin of the professor.

The sin of the profane. But this needs not be enlarged upon, because it is concluded upon at all hands, where there is the common belief of the being of God, and the judgment to come, that "the wicked shall be turned into hell, and all the nations that forget God" (Ps. 9:17).

But there is [also] the sin of professors; or take it rather thus, there is a profession that will stand with an unsanctified heart and life. The sin of such will overpoise[1] the salvation of their souls, the sin end being the heaviest end of the scale. I say, that being the heaviest end which hath sin in it, they tilt over. And so are, notwithstanding their glorious profession, drowned in perdition and destruction. For none such has any inheritance in the kingdom of Christ and of God. Therefore "let no man deceive you with vain words; for because of these things cometh the wrath of God upon the children of disobedience." Neither will a profession be able to excuse them (Eph. 5:3-6). The gate will be too strait for such as these to enter in thereat. A man may partake of salvation in part, but not of salvation in whole. God saved the children of Israel out of Egypt but overthrew them in the wilderness:— "I will therefore put you in remembrance, though ye once knew this, how that the Lord, having saved the people out of the land of Egypt, afterward destroyed them that believed not" (Jude 5). So, we see that, notwithstanding their beginning, "they could not enter in, because of unbelief" (Heb. 3:19).

1 "Overpoise" is chiefly figurative, that which outweighs, excessive weight.

MAY 10

Who Are The Unrighteous?

Or do you not know that the unrighteous will not inherit the kingdom of God?

1 Corinthians 6:9a

There is the word of the law and that will make the gate strait also. None must go in thereat but those that can go in by the ... [way] of the law. For though no man be, or can be, justified by the works of the law. Yet unless the righteousness and holiness by which they attempt to enter this kingdom be justified by the law, it is in vain once to think of entering in at this strait gate. Now the law justifies not, but upon the account of Christ's righteousness. If therefore you be not indeed found in that righteousness, you will find the law lies just in the passage into heaven to keep thee out. Every man's work must be tried by fire that it may be manifest of what sort it is. There are two errors in the world about the law: One is, when men think to enter in at the strait gate by the righteousness of the law. The other is, when men think they may enter into heaven without the leave of the law.

When the apostle had told the Corinthians that "the unrighteous should not inherit the kingdom of God," and that such were some of them, he adds: "But ye are washed, but ye are sanctified, but ye are justified, in the name of the Lord Jesus, and by the Spirit of our God" (1 Cor. 6:9-11). Closely concluding, that had they not been washed, and sanctified, and justified, in the name of the Lord Jesus, the law, for their transgressions, would have kept them out; it would have made the gate too strait for them to enter in.

MAY 11

Angels: Christ's Gate Keepers

So, it will be at the end of the age. The angels will come out and separate the evil from the righteous.

MATTHEW 13:49

"But ye are washed, but ye are sanctified, but ye are justified, in the name of the Lord Jesus, and by the Spirit of our God" (1 Cor. 6:9-11). Closely concluding, that had they not been washed, and sanctified, and justified, in the name of the Lord Jesus, the law, for their transgressions, would have kept them out. It would have made the gate too strait for them to enter in.

There are also the angels of God, and by reason of them the gate is strait. The Lord Jesus called the end of the world his harvest. And saith ... that the angels are his reapers. These angels are therefore to gather his wheat into his barn, but to gather the ungodly into bundles to burn them (Matt. 13:39, 41, 49). Unless therefore, the man that is unsanctified can master the law, and conquer angels. Unless he can ... pull them out of the gateway of heaven, himself is not to come thither forever. No man goes to heaven but by the help of the angels—I mean at the day of judgment. For the Son of man "shall send his angels with a great sound of a trumpet, and they shall gather together his elect from the four winds, from one end of heaven to the other." (Matt. 24:31) If those that shall enter in at the strait gate shall enter in thither [there] by the conduct of the holy angels, pray when you do think those men will enter in thither. [Consider] ... whom the angels are commanded to gather [to] them, to "bind them in bundles to burn them?" This, therefore, is a ... [great] difficulty. The angels will make this entrance strait. Yea, too strait for the unjustified and unsanctified to enter in thither.

MAY 12

What Does The Word Strive Import?[1]

Only let your manner of life be worthy of the Gospel of Christ, so that whether I come and see you or am absent, I may hear of you that you are standing firm in one spirit, with one mind striving side by side for the faith of the gospel.

PHILIPPIANS 1:27

"Strive to enter in at the strait gate." These words are fitly added; for since the gate is strait, it follows that they that will enter must strive.

"Strive." This word strive supposes that great idleness is natural to professors.[2] They think to get to heaven by lying, as it were, on their elbows. It also suggests that many will be many difficulties that professors will meet before they get to heaven. It also concludes that only the labouring Christian, man, or woman, will get in thither [there].

How should we strive?

When he saith, Strive, it is as much as to say, Bend yourselves to the work with all your might. "Whatsoever thy hand findeth to do, do it with thy might; for there is no work, nor device, nor knowledge, nor wisdom in the grave, where you are going" (Eccles. 9:10). Thus, Samson did when he set himself to destroy the Philistines; "He bowed himself with all his might" (Judg. 16:30). Thus, David did also, when he made provision for the building and beautifying of the temple of God (1 Chron. 29:2). And thus, must you do, if ever you would enter into heaven.

When he saith, Strive, he calls for the mind and will, that they should be on his side, and on the side of the things of his kingdom. For none strive indeed, but such as have given the Son of God their heart; of which the mind and will are a principal part. For saving conversion lies more in the turning of the mind and will to Christ, and to the love of his heavenly things, than in all knowledge and judgment. The apostle confirms this, "Stand fast in one spirit, with one mind striving" (Phil. 1:27).

1 "Import" is a synonym for "what something means."

2 "Professors" are those who have professed Christ as Saviour publicly.

MAY 13

We Must Strive Lawfully!

An athlete is not crowned unless he competes according to the rules.

2 TIMOTHY 2:5

The answer in general is you must strive lawfully, "and if a man also strive for masteries [compete],[1] yet is he not crowned, except he strive lawfully." (2 Tim. 2:5) But you will say, what is it to strive lawfully? Answer—

To strive against the things which are abhorred by the Lord Jesus. Yea, to resist to the spilling of your blood striving against sin (Heb. 12:4). To ... [strive against] all those things that are condemned by the Word. Yea, though they [should] be your own right hand, right eye, or right foot, in abomination and to seek by all godly means the utter suppressing of them (Mark 9:43, 45, 47).

To strive lawfully is to strive for those things that are commanded in the Word.—"But thou, O man of God, flee the world, and follow after," that is [to] strive for "righteousness, godliness, faith, love, patience, meekness; fight the good fight of faith, lay hold on eternal life" (1 Tim. 6:11-12).

He that strives lawfully, must be therefore very temperate in all the good and lawful things of this life. "And every man that strives for the mastery is temperate in all things. Now they do it to obtain a corruptible crown; but we an incorruptible" (1 Cor. 9:25). Most professors give leave to the world and the vanity of their hearts, to close with them, and to hang about their necks, and make their striving to stand rather in an outcry of words, than a hearty labour against the lusts and love of the world, and their own corruptions. But this kind of striving is but a beating of the air and will come to just nothing at last (1 Cor. 9:26).

1 "Masteries" is to compete in an athletic event.

MAY 14

The Particulars Of Lawful Striving

For we are his workmanship, created in Christ Jesus for good works,...

Ephesians 2:10

He that strives lawfully, must take God and Christ along with him to ... [his] work, otherwise he will certainly be undone. "Whereunto," said Paul, "I also labour, striving according to his working, which worketh in me mightily." (Col. 1:29) And for the right performing of this, he must observe these following particulars: —

1. He must take heed that he does not strive about things, or words, to no profit. For God will not then be with him. "Of these things," saith the apostle, "put them in remembrance; charging them before the Lord, that they strive not about words to no profit, but to the subverting of the hearers" (2 Tim. 2:14).

2. He must take heed that while he strives against one sin, he does not harbor and shelter another. Or that while he cries out against other men's sin, he does not countenance [tolerate] his own.

3. In the striving, strive to believe, strive for the faith of the gospel. For the more we believe the gospel and the reality of the things of the world to come with the more stomach [intestinal fortitude] and courage shall we labour to possess the blessedness (Phil. 1:27).

4. As we should strive for and by faith. So, we should strive by prayer, by fervent and effectual prayer. (Rom. 15:30) O the swarms of our prayerless professors! But what striving by prayer was there then among Christians for the thing that gives admittance into this kingdom, over [what] there is in these latter days!

(5.) We should also mortify our members that are upon the earth. "I therefore so run," said Paul [that] "... I keep under my body and bring it into subjection [daily]" (1 Cor. 9:26-27).

MAY 15

But Why Should We Strive?

Therefore, my beloved, as you have always obeyed, so now, not only as in my presence but much more in my absence, work out your own salvation with fear and trembling,...

PHILIPPIANS 2:12

Answer[s]—

1. Because the thing for which you are here exhorted to strive, it is worth striving for. It is for not less than for a whole heaven, and an eternity of felicity there. How will men that have before them a little honor, a little profit, a little pleasure, strive? I say again, how will they strive for this? Now they do it for a corruptible crown, but we an incorruptible. For what is there again either in heaven or earth like them to provoke a man to strive?

2. Strive, because otherwise the devil and hell will assuredly have thee. He goes about like a roaring lion, seeking whom he may devour (1 Pet. 5:8). These fallen angels, they are always watchful, diligent, unwearied. They are also mighty, subtle, and malicious, seeking nothing more than the damnation of your soul. O thou that art like the artless dove, strive!

3. Strive, because every lust strives and wars against your soul. "Dearly beloved, I beseech you," said Peter, "as strangers and pilgrims, abstain from fleshly lusts, which war against the soul" (1 Pet. 2:11). It is a rare thing to see or find out a Christian that indeed can bridle his lusts.

4. Strive, because you have a whole world against you. The world hates you if you are a Christian. The men of the world hate you; the things of the world are snares for you, even thy bed and table, thy wife and husband. Yes, even your most lawful enjoyments have that in them that will certainly sink your soul to hell, if thou dost not strive against the snares that are in them (Rom. 11:9).

MAY 16

What Bars You From The Strait Gate?

For the weapons of our warfare are not of the flesh but have divine power to destroy strongholds. We destroy arguments and every lofty opinion raised against the knowledge of God, and take every thought captive to obey Christ.

2 CORINTHIANS 10:4-5

The world will seek to keep you out of heaven with mocks, flouts, taunts, threatenings, jails, gibbets [gallows], halters, burnings, and a thousand deaths; therefore strive! Again, if it cannot overcome you with these, it will flatter, promise, allure, entice, entreat, and use a thousand tricks on this hand to destroy you. And observe, many that have been stout against the threats of the world have yet been overcome with the bewitching flatteries of the same.

There ever was enmity betwixt [between] the devil and the church, and betwixt his seed and her seed too. ... There hath been great desires and endeavors among men to reconcile these two in one, to wit, the seed of the serpent and the seed of the woman. But it could never yet be accomplished. The world says they will never come over to us. And we again say, by God's grace, we will never come over to them.

But the business hath not ended in words; both they and we have also added our endeavors to make each other submit, but endeavors have proved ineffectual too. They, for their part, have devised all manner of cruel torments to make us submit, as slaying with the sword, stoning, sawing asunder, flames, wild beasts, banishments, hunger, and a thousand miseries. We again, on the other side, have laboured by prayers and tears, by patience and long-suffering, by gentleness and love, by sound doctrine and faithful witness-bearing against their enormities, to bring them over to us. But the enmity remains. So that they must conquer us or we must conquer them. One side must be overcome; but the weapons of our warfare are not carnal, but mighty through God.

MAY 17

We Are Commanded To Strive!

And he said to all, "If anyone would come after me, let him deny himself and take up his cross daily and follow me."

LUKE 9:23

"Strive to enter in"[!] I think the words, at the first reading, do intimate to us that the Christian in all that ever he does in this world should carefully heed and regard his soul—I say, in all that ever he does. Many are for their souls by fits and starts. But a Christian indeed, in all his doing and designs which he contrives and manages in this world should have a special eye to his own future and everlasting good. In all his labours he should strive to enter in: "Wisdom [Christ] is the principal thing; therefore, get wisdom: and with all thy getting get understanding" (Prov. 4:7). Get nothing, if you cannot get Christ and grace, and further hopes of heaven in that getting. Get nothing with a bad conscience, with the hazard of your peace with God, and that in getting it you weaken your graces which God hath given you. Add grace to grace, both by religious and worldly duties: "For so an entrance shall be ministered unto you abundantly into the everlasting kingdom of our Lord and Saviour Jesus Christ" (2 Pet. 1:11).

You may help your faith and thy hope in the godly management of your calling and may get further footing in eternal life, by studying the glory of God in all your worldly employment. I am speaking now to Christians that are justified freely by grace and am encouraging; rather counselling of them to strive to enter in. For there is an entering in by faith and good conscience now, as well as our entering in body and soul hereafter. And I must add that the more common it is to your soul to enter in now by faith. The more steadfast hope shalt you have of entering in hereafter in body and soul.

MAY 18

Hot Or Cold?

I know your work: you are neither cold nor hot. Would that you were either cold or hot.

REVELATION 3:15

"Strive to enter in." By these words ... the Lord Jesus gives sharp rebuke to those professors that have not eternal glory but temporal things in their eye—by all the bustle that they make in the world about religion. Some there are that make a stir, what a noise and clamor, with their notions and forms. And yet perhaps all is for the loaves; because they have eaten of the loaves and are filled (See John 6:26). These strive indeed to enter, but it is not into heaven. They find [their] religion hath a good trade at the end of it.

"Strive to enter in." These words also sharply rebuke them who content themselves as the angel of the church of Sardis, did, to wit; "to have a name to live, and be dead" (Rev. 3:1). [Consider] ... the Laodiceans, who took their religion upon trust, and were content with a poor, wretched, lukewarm profession. For such as these do altogether unlike to the exhortation in the text, that says: Strive, and they sit and sleep. That [text] says, strive to enter in, and they content themselves with a profession that is never like to bring them ... [there to the gate].

"Strive to enter in." Further, these words put us upon proving the truth of our graces now. For if the strait gate be the gate of heaven and yet we are to strive to enter ... it now; even while we live and before we come ... [there], then doubtless Christ means by this exhortation that we should use all lawful means to prove our graces in this world whether they will stand in the judgment or no[t]. Strive to enter in; get those graces now that will prove true graces then (Rev. 3:18).

MAY 19

Seek the Eternal City

For here we have no lasting city, but we seek the city that is to come.

HEBREWS 13:14

"Strive to enter in." The reason why Christ added these words, "to enter in," is obvious. To wit, because there is no true and lasting happiness on this side of heaven. I say, none that is both true and lasting, I mean, as to our sense and feeling as there shall [be]; "For here have we no continuing city, but we seek one to come" (Heb. 13:14). The heaven is within, strive therefore to enter in. Glory is within, strive therefore to enter in. Mount Zion is within, strive therefore to enter in. And to make up all, the God and Father of our Lord Jesus Christ, and that glorious Redeemer, is within, strive therefore to enter in.

"Strive to enter in." "For without are dogs, and sorcerers, and whoremongers, and murderers, and idolaters, and whosoever loveth and maketh a lie." Without are also the devils, and hell, and death, and all damned souls. Without is howling, weeping, wailing, and gnashing of teeth; yea, without are all the miseries, sorrows, and plagues that an infinite God can in justice and power inflict upon an evil and wicked generation.

But you ... [might ask], "[S]hould we try our graces [to strive]?" Would you have us run into temptation, to try if they be sound or rotten? Answer. You need not run into [toward] trials. God hath ordained that enough of them shall overtake you to prove your graces either rotten or sound before the day of your death, if you have a sufficiency of grace to withstand. I say, you shall have trials enough [to] overtake you, to prove your grace sound or rotten. To wit, whether your graces be such as will carry thee in at the gates of heaven or no.

MAY 20

Motive To Strive To Enter Into This Gate

Not everyone who says to me, "Lord, Lord," will enter the kingdom of heaven.

Mattew 7:21a

We come now to the motive which our Lord urges to enforce his exhortation. [Jesus] ... told us before that the gate was strait. He also exhorted us to strive to enter in thereat, or to get those things now that will further our entrance then, and to set ourselves against those things that will hinder our entering in.

In this motive there are five things to be minded.

1. That there will be a disappointment to some at the day of judgment; they will seek to enter in, and shall not be able.
2. That not a few, but many, will meet with this disappointment; "For many will seek to enter in, and shall not be able."
3. This doctrine of the miscarriage [breakdown] of many then, it stands upon the validity of the Word of Christ; "For many, I say, will seek to enter in, and shall not be able."
4. Professors shall make a great heap among the many that shall fall short of heaven; "For many, I say unto you, will seek to enter in, and shall not be able."
5. Where grace and striving are wanting now, seeking, and contending to enter in will be unprofitable then; "For many, I say unto you, will seek to enter in, and shall not be able."

[Remember these words of Christ the Lord:] "Strive to enter in at the strait gate; for many, I say unto you, will seek to enter in, and shall not be able."

MAY 21

Who Are The "Many?"

On that day many will say to me, "Lord, Lord, did we not prophesy in your name, and cast out demons in your name, and do many mighty works in your name?"

MATTHEW 7:22

Various applications of the word *many*:

1. Sometimes ... *[many]* intends the open profane, the wicked and ungodly world, as where Christ said, "Wide is the gate, and broad is the way, that leadeth to destruction, and many there be which go in thereat" (Matt. 7:1-3). I say, by the *many* here, he intends those chiefly that go on in the broad way of sin and profaneness, bearing the "tokens" of their damnation in their foreheads, those whose daily practice proclaims that their "feet go down to death, and their steps take hold on hell" (Job 21:29-30; Isa. 3:9; Prov. 4).

2. Sometimes this word *many* intends those that cleave to the people of God deceitfully, and in hypocrisy or as Daniel has it: "Many shall cleave to them with flatteries" (Dan. 11:34). The word *many* in this text includes all those who feign themselves better than they are in religion. It includes, I say, those that have religion only for a holiday suit to set them out at certain times and when they come among suitable company.

3. Sometimes this word *many* intended them that apostatize from Christ, such as for a while believe, and in time of temptation fall away. As John said of some of Christ's disciples: "From that time *many* of his disciples went back and walked no more with him" (John 6:66).

4. Sometimes this word *many* intends those poor, ignorant, deluded souls that are led away with every wind of doctrine; those who are caught with the cunning and crafty deceiver, who lieth in wait to beguile unstable souls: "And many shall follow their pernicious ways, by reason of whom the way of truth shall be evil spoken of" (2 Pet. 2:2).

MAY 22

Import of the Words "I Say Unto You"

But I say unto you ...

MATTHEW 5:39

"For many, I say unto you." These latter words carry in them an [important] argument to prove the truth asserted before: First, in that he directly points at his followers: "I say unto you": Many, I say unto you, even to you that are my disciples, to you that have eat and drunk in my presence. I know that sometimes Christ has directed his speech to his disciples, not so much upon their accounts as upon the accounts of others. But here it is not so; the "I say unto you," in this place, it immediately concerned some of themselves: I say unto you, you shall begin to stand without, and to knock, "saying, Lord, Lord, open unto us, and he shall answer and say unto you, I know you not whence ye are; then shall ye begin to say, We have eaten and drunk in thy presence, and thou hast taught in our streets. But he shall say, I tell you, I know you not whence ye are; depart from me, all ye workers of iniquity": It is you, you, YOU, that I mean! "I say unto you." It is common with a professing people when they hear a smart and a thundering sermon, to say: Now has the preacher paid off [bought off] the drunkard, the swearer, the liar, the covetous, and adulterer; forgetting that these sins may be committed in a spiritual and mystical way. There is spiritual drunkenness, spiritual adultery, and a man may be a liar that calls God his Father when he is not, or that calls himself a Christian, and is not.

"I say unto you!" Jesus said, "For many, I say unto YOU, shall seek to enter in, and shall not be able."

MAY 23

Use An Application Of The Whole[1]

Examine yourselves, to see whether you are in the faith ...
2 CORINTHIANS 13:5A

I come now to make some brief use and application of the whole.

My first word shall be to the open profane. Poor sinner, you who read here that but a few will be saved; that many that expect heaven will go without heaven. What do you say to this, poor sinner? Let me say it over again. There are but [a] few to be saved, but very few. Let me add, but few professors—but few eminent professors. What do you say now, sinner? If judgment begins at the house of God, what will the end of them be that obey not the gospel of God? This is Peter's question. Can you answer it, sinner? Yea, I say again, if judgment must begin at them, will it not make you think, what shall become of me? And I add, when thou shalt see the stars of heaven tumble down to hell, can you think that such a muckheap [dung] of sin as you shall be lifted up to heaven? Peter asks you another question, to wit, "If the righteous scarcely be saved, where shall the ungodly and the sinner appear?" (1 Pet. 4:18). Can you answer this question, sinner? Stand among the righteous you may not: "The ungodly shall not stand in the judgment, nor sinners in the congregation of the righteous" (Ps. 1:5). Stand among the wicked you then will not dare to do. Where will you appear, sinner? To stand among the hypocrites will avail you of nothing. The hypocrite "shall not come before him," that is, with acceptance, but shall perish (Job 13:16). Because it concerns thee much, let me over with it again! When thou shalt see less sinners than thou art, bound up by angels in bundles, to burn them, where wilt thou appear, sinner?

---

1 That is, applications for the whole book of *The Strait Gate: Or, Great Difficulty of Going to Heaven: Plainly Proving, by the Scriptures, That Not Only The Rude and Profane, But Many Great Professors, Will Come Short of that Kingdom.*

MAY 24

The Potter's Wheel

So I went down to the potter's house, and there he was working at his wheel. And the vessel he was making of clay was spoiled in the potter's hand, and he reworked it into another vessel, as it seemed good to the potter to do.

JERMIAH 18:3-4

My second word is to them that are upon the potter's wheel; concerning whom we know not yet whether their convictions and awakenings will end in conversion or not. [These] ... things I shall say to you, both to further your convictions, and to caution you from staying anywhere below or short of saving grace.

1. Remember that but few shall be saved; and if God should count thee worthy to be one of that few, what a mercy would that be!

2. Be thankful, therefore, for convictions. Conversion begins at conviction, though all conviction doth not end in conversion. It is a great mercy to be convinced that we are sinners, and that we need a Saviour. Count it therefore a mercy, and that their convictions may end in conversion. Do you take heed of stifling them. It is the way for poor sinners to look upon convictions as things that are hurtful. And therefore, they used to shun the awakening ministry, and to check a convincing conscience. Such poor sinners are much like the wanton boy that stands at the maid's elbow, to blow out her candle as fast as she lights it at the fire. Convinced sinner, God lights your candle, and you put it out. God lights it again, and you put it out ... And then, like the Egyptians, you dwell all your days in darkness, and never see more light. But by the light of hellfire; wherefore give glory to God, and if he awakens thy conscience, quench not your convictions. Do it, said the prophet, "before he causes darkness, and before your feet stumble upon the dark mountains, and he turn" your convictions "into the shadow of death, and make them gross darkness" (Jer. 13:16).

MAY 25

Covetousness Is Idolatry

Put to death therefore what is earthly in you: sexual immorality, impurity, passion, evil desires, and covetousness, which is idolatry.

COLOSSIANS 3:5

My third word is to professors. Sirs, give me leave to set my trumpet to your ears again a little. When every man has put in all the claim they can for heaven but few will have it for their inheritance.

1. I begin with you whose religion lies only in your tongues. I mean you who are little or nothing known from the rest of the rabble of the world, only you can talk better than they. Hear me a word or two. If "I speak with the tongues of men and of angels, and have not charity," that is, love to God, and Christ, and saints, and holiness, "I am nothing". [You are] ... no child of God and so have nothing to do with heaven. (1 Cor. 13:1-2) A prating tongue will not unlock the gates of heaven, nor blind the eyes of the Judge. [See] ... to it. "The wise in heart will receive commandments; but a prating fool shall fall" (Prov. 10:8).

2. Covetous professor, thou that make a gain of religion, that uses your profession to bring grist to thy mill, look to it also. Gain is not godliness. Judas' religion lay much in the bag but his soul is now burning in hell. All covetousness is idolatry. But what is that, or what will you call it, when men are religious for filthy lucre's [money's] sake? (Ezek. 33:31).

3. Wanton professors, I have a word for you. I mean you that can tell how to misplead Scripture, to maintain your pride, your banqueting, and abominable idolatry. Read what Peter says. You are the snare and damnation of others. You "allure through the lust of the flesh, through much wantonness, those that were clean escaped from them who live in error" (2 Pet. 2:18).

MAY 26

Strive To Enter His Rest

Let us therefore strive to enter that rest, so that no one may fall by the same sort of disobedience.

HEBREWS 4:11

[Fourth,] ... what a strange disappointment will many professors meet with at the day of judgment! I speak not now to the open[ly] profane. Everybody, as I have said, that has but [a] common understanding between good and evil knows that they are in the broad way to hell and damnation. And they must needs come thither. Nothing can hinder it but repentance unto salvation.

Neither is it amiss, if we take notice of the examples that are briefly mentioned in the Scriptures, concerning professors that have miscarried.

1. Judas perished from among the apostles (Acts 1).
2. Demas, as I think, perished from among the evangelists (2 Tim. 4:10).
3. Diotrephes from among the ministers, or them in office in the church (3 John 9).
4. And as for Christian professors, they have fallen by heaps, and almost by whole churches (2 Tim. 1:15; Rev. 3:4, 15-17).
5. Let us add to these, that the things mentioned in the Scriptures about these matters, are but brief hints and items of what is afterwards to happen. As the apostle said, "Some men's sins are open beforehand, going before to judgment; and some men they follow after" (1 Tim. 5:24).

So ... fellow-professors, let us fear ... [unless] a promise being left us of entering into this rest, any of us should seem to come short of it. O! to come short! nothing kills like it, nothing will burn like it. I intend not to be discouragements, but awakenings. The churches have a need of awakening, and so have all professors. Do not despise me, therefore, but hear me over again. What a strange disappointment will many professors meet with at the day of God Almighty!

MAY 27

Amazed By Their Disappointment

It is a fearful thing to fall into the hands of the living God.
HEBREWS 10:31

[Fifth, the professor's] ... disappointment will be fearful, so certainly it will be very full of amazement.

1. Will it not amaze them to be unexpectedly excluded from life and salvation?

2. Will it not be amazing to them to see their own madness and folly, while they consider how they have dallied with their own souls. And [they] took lightly for granted that they had that grace that would save them, but have left them in a damnable state?

3. Will they not also be amazed one at another, while they remember how in their lifetime, they counted themselves fellow heirs of life? To allude to that of the prophet, "They shall be amazed one at another, their faces shall be as flames" (Isa. 13:8).

4. Will it not be amazing to some of the damned themselves, to see some come to hell that then they shall see come ... [there]? To see preachers of the Word, professors of the Word, practitioners in the Word, to come ... [there]. What wondering was there among them at the fall of the king of Babylon since he thought to have swallowed up all because he was run down by the Medes and Persians! "How art thou fallen from heaven, O Lucifer, son of the morning! How art thou cut down to the ground which didst weaken the nations!" If such a thing as this will with amazement surprise the damned, what an amazement will it be to them to see such a one as he whose head reached to the clouds, to see him come down to the pit and perish forever like his own dung. "Hell from beneath is moved for thee, to meet thee at thy coming; it stirs up the dead for thee, even all the chief ones of the earth" (Isa. 14:9).

MAY 28

Do You Compare Yourself?

Not that we dare to classify or compare ourselves with some of those who ae commending themselves. But when they measure themselves by one another and compare themselves with one another, they are without understanding.

2 CORINTHIANS 10:12

We will add to all these, the professor that would prove himself a Christian, by comparing himself with others, instead of comparing himself with the Word of God. This man comforts himself because he is as holy as such and such [a person]. He also knows as much as that old professor, and then concludes he shall go to heaven: As if he certainly knew, that those with whom he compares himself would be undoubtedly saved. No, may they not both fall short? But to be sure he is in the wrong that hath made the comparison; and a wrong foundation will not stand in the day of judgment.

Yet again, [a sixth] ... word, if I may awaken professors. Consider, though the poor carnal world shall certainly perish. Yet they will want these things to aggravate their sorrow, which you will meet with in every thought that you will have of the condition you were in when you were in the world.

1. They will not have a profession, to bite them when they come there.
2. They will not have a taste of a lost heaven, to bite them when they come there.
3. They will not have the thoughts of, "I was almost at heaven," to bite them when they come there.
4. They will not have thoughts of how they cheated saints, ministers, churches, to bite them when they come there.
5. They will not have the dying thoughts of false faith, false hope, false repentance, and false holiness, to bite them when they come thither. I was at the gates of heaven, I looked into heaven, I thought I should have entered into heaven.

MAY 29

A Word Of Warning

Therefore be careful lest the light in you be darkness.

LUKE 11:35

[Seventh,]—give me leave now in a word to give you a little advice.

First:

1. Do you love your own soul? Then pray to Jesus Christ for an awakened heart. For a heart so awakened with all the things of another world, that you may be allured to Jesus Christ.
2. When you come there, beg again for more awakenings about sin, hell, grace, and about the righteousness of Christ.
3. Cry also for a spirit of discernment that you may know that which is saving grace indeed.
4. Above all studies apply yourself to the study of those things that show you the evil of sin, the shortness of man's life, and which is the way to be saved.
5. Keep company with the most godly among professors.
6. When you hear what the nature of true grace is, defer not to ask your own heart if this grace be there. And here take heed—

Secondly:

1. That the preacher himself be sound, and of good life.
2. That you take not seeming graces for real ones, nor seeming fruits for real fruits.
3. Take heed that a sin in your life goes not unrepented of. For that will make a flaw in your evidence, a wound in your conscience, and a breach in your peace. If [all this] at last it does not drive all the grace in you into so dark a corner of your heart, that you shall not be able, for a time, by all the torches that are burning in the gospel; to find it out to your own comfort and consolation.

MAY 30

The Letter Kills but the Spirit Gives Life

... who has made us sufficient to be ministers of a new covenant, not of the letter but of the Spirit. For the letter kills, but the Spirit gives life.

2 CORINTHIANS 3:6

There is the word of the law, and that will make the gate strait also. None must go in there but those that can go in by the leave of the law. For though no man be, or can be, justified by the works of the law, yet unless the righteousness and holiness by which they attempt to enter this kingdom be justified by the law. It is in vain once to think of entering in at this strait gate. Now the law justifieth not, but upon the account of Christ's righteousness. If therefore thou be not indeed found in that righteousness, thou wilt find the law lie just in the passage into heaven to keep thee out. Every man's work must be tried by fire, that it may be manifest of what sort it is. There are two errors in the world about the law: one is, when men think to enter in at the strait gate by the righteousness of the law; the other is, when men think they may enter into heaven without the leave of the law. Both these, I say, are errors; for as by the works of the law no flesh shall be justified; so, without the consent of the law, no flesh shall be saved. "Heaven and earth shall pass away, before one jot or tittle of the law shall fail, till all be fulfilled." He therefore must be damned that cannot be saved by the consent of the law. And, indeed, this law is the flaming sword that turneth all away. Yea, that lieth to this day in the way to heaven, for a bar to all unbelievers and unsanctified professors. For it is taken out of the way for the truly gracious only.

MAY 31

A Warning, A Prayer, An Invitation[1]

The Spirit and the Bride say, "Come." And let the one who hears say, "Come." And let the one who is thirsty come; let the one who desires take of the water of life without price.

REVELATION 22:17

God, I hope, hath put it into my heart to write to you another time, and that about matters of greatest moment—for now we discourse not about things controverted among the godly. But directly about the saving or damning of the soul. Yea, moreover, this discourse is about the fewness of them that shall be saved, and it proves that many a high professor will come short of eternal life. Wherefore the matter must needs be sharp, and so disliked by some, but let it not be rejected by you. The text calls for sharpness, so do the times, yea, the faithful discharge of my duty towards you hath put me upon it.

And it will be well for you if you can graciously lament (Matt. 11:17). Some, they say, make the gate of heaven too wide and some make it too narrow. For my part, I have here presented you with as true a measure of it as by the Word of God I can. If there be need and it wounds, get healing by [Christ's] blood. If it disquiets [you] get peace by [His] blood. If it takes away all you have, because it was naught [nothing], (for this book is not prepared to take away true grace from any). Then buy of Christ "gold tried in the fire, that thou mayest be rich, and white raiment, that thou mayest be clothed, and that the shame of thy nakedness do not appear, and anoint thine eyes with eye-salve, that thou mayest see" (Rev. 3:18). The Lord give you a heart to judge right of yourself, right [out] of this book, and so to prepare [you] for eternity, that you may not only expect entrance, but be received into the kingdom of Christ and of God. Amen.

So prays thy Friend [John Bunyan].

1 This was written by George Offor in his "Introduction" to John Bunyan's *The Strait Gate.*

JUNE 1

A Proposition

For all who rely on works of the law are under a curse; for it is written, "Cursed be everyone who does not abide by all things written in the Book of the Law, and do them."

GALATIANS 3:10

The terms of this proposition are easy. Yet if it will help, I will speak a word or two for explication.

First. By a sinner, I mean one that has transgressed the law; "for sin is the transgression of the law" (1 John 3:4).

Second. By the curse of the law, I mean that sentence, judgment, or condemnation which the law pronounces against the transgressor (Gal. 3:10).

Third. By justifying righteousness, I mean that which stands in the doing and suffering of Christ when he was in the world (Rom. 5:19).

Fourth. By the residing of this righteousness in Christ's person, I mean it still abides with him as to the action, though the benefit is bestowed upon those that are his.

Fifth. By the imputation of it to us, I mean God's making of it ours by an act of his grace. That we by it might be secured from the curse of the law.

Sixth. When I say there is no other way to be justified. I cast away TO THAT END the law, and all the works of the law as done by us. ...

Mark, the righteousness is ... "in him," not "in us," even then when we are made partakers ... [and] benefit of it. Even as the wing and feathers still abide in the hen when the chickens are covered, kept, and warmed thereby.

JUNE 2

Christ Our Righteousness

For as by the one man's disobedience the many were made sinners, so by the one man's obedience the many will be made righteous.

ROMANS 5:19

Now—to wit, what sin and the curse is—stand clear in all men's sight, unless they be atheists or desperately heretical. I shall, therefore, in [a] few words ... [declare].

Therefore, justifying righteousness is the doing and suffering of Christ when he was in the world. This is clear, because we are said to be "justified by his obedience," by his obedience to the law (Rom. 5:19). Hence, he is said again to be the end of the law for that very thing—"Christ is the end of the law for righteousness" (Rom. 10:4). What is that [end]? Why, the requirement or demand of the law. But what are they? Why, righteousness [even a] perfect righteousness (Gal. 3:10). Perfect righteousness, what [are we] to do? That the soul concerned might stand spotless in the sight of God (Rev. 1:5).

Now this lies only in the doings and sufferings of Christ. For "by his obedience many are made righteous." Wherefore as to this, Christ is the end of the law that being found in that obedience. [This] ... becomes to us sufficient for our justification. Hence, we are said to be made righteous by his obedience; yea, and to be washed, purged, and justified by his blood (Heb. 9:14; Rom. 5:18-19).

That this righteousness still resides in and with the person of Christ; even then when we stand just before God thereby is clear, for that we are said when justified to be justified "in him." "In the Lord shall all the seed of Israel be justified." And again, "Surely, shall one say, In the Lord have I righteousness" (Isa. 45:24-25). And again, "But of him are ye in Christ Jesus, who of God is made unto us—righteousness" (1 Cor. 1:30).

JUNE 3

He Was Made Sin For Us

For he hath made him to be sin for us, who knew no sin; that we might be made the righteousness of God in him.

2 CORINTHIANS 5:21 KJV

Mark, the righteousness is still "in him," not "in us," even then when we are made partakers of the benefit of it, even as the wing and feathers still abide in the hen when the chickens are covered, kept, and warmed thereby.

For as my doings, though my children are fed and clothed thereby, are still my doings, not theirs. So, the righteousness wherewith we stand just before God from the curse, still resides in Christ, not in us. Our sins, when laid upon Christ, were yet personally ours, not his. So, his righteousness, when put upon us, is yet personally his, not ours. What is it, then? Why, "he was made to be sin for us, who knew no sin; that we might be made the righteousness of God in him" (2 Cor. 5:21).

It is, therefore, of a justifying virtue, only by imputation, or as God reckons it to us. Even as our sins made the Lord Jesus a sinner—nay, "sin," by God's reckoning of them to him.[1]

It is necessary that this be known ... [by] us. For if the understanding, be muddy as to this, it is impossible that such should be sound in the faith. Also in temptation, that man will be at a loss that looks for a righteousness for justification in himself, when it is to be found nowhere but in Jesus Christ. The apostle, who was his crafts master as to this, was always "looking to Jesus," that he "might be found in him," knowing that nowhere else could peace or safety be had (Phil. 3:6-9). And, indeed, this is one of the greatest mysteries in the world. Namely, that a righteousness that resides with a person in heaven should justify me, a sinner, on earth!

1 The reformational doctrine of "Double Imputation" is here alluded to by Bunyan. Whereby, God puts all of our sins on Christ and puts all of Christ's righteousness on us; that is our accounts.

JUNE 4

No Other Name

Neither is there salvation in any other: for there is none other name under heaven given among men, whereby we must be saved.

ACTS 4:12 KJV

Therefore, the law and the works thereof, as to this must by us be cast away. Not only because they here are useless, but also, they being retained are a hindrance. That they are useless is evident, for that salvation comes by another name (Acts 4:12). And that they are a hindrance it is clear. For the very adhering to the law, though it be but a little, or in a little part, prevents justification by the righteousness of Christ (Rom. 9:31-32).

What shall I say? As to this, the moral law is rejected, the ceremonial law is rejected, and man's righteousness is rejected. For that they are here both weak and unprofitable (Rom. 8:2-3; Gal. 3:21; Heb. 10:1-12). Now if all these and their works as to our justification are rejected, where, but in Christ is righteousness to be found?

Thus much, therefore, for the explication of the proposition—namely, that there is no other way for sinners to be justified from the curse of the law in the sight of God, than by the imputation of that righteousness long ago performed by, and still residing with, the person of Jesus Christ ...

I ... show you that a man may be justified even then when his action is condemned. Also, that a man may be in a state of condemnation when his action may be justified. But with these distinctions I will not take up time, my intention being to treat of justification as it sets a man free or quit from sin, the curse and condemnation of the law in the sight of God, to eternal salvation.[1]

1 Editor: This paragraph of George Offor added to Bunyan's here for clarity.

JUNE 5

God's Foolishness Is Wiser Than Men

For the foolishness of God is wiser than men, and the weakness of God is stronger than men.

1 CORINTHIANS 1:25

That he suffered as a common person is true. By common I mean a public person, or one that presents the body of mankind in himself. [There is] ... a multitude of Scriptures [that] bear witness to [this], especially that fifth chapter of the Romans. Where ... he is set before us as the head of all the elect, even as Adam was once head of all the world. Thus, he lived, and thus he died; and this was a mysterious act. And that he should die as a sinner, when yet himself did "no sin," nor had any "guile found in his mouth," made this act more mysterious (1 Pet. 1:19, 2:22, 3:18). That he died as a sinner is plain—"He hath made him to be sin." (2 Cor 5:21) "And the Lord laid upon him the iniquity of us all" (Isa. 53:6). That ... as to his own person he was completely sinless is also as truly manifest, and that by a multitude of Scriptures. Now ... that Christ Jesus should be thus considered and thus die was the great mystery of God. Hence Paul tells us, that when he preached "Christ crucified," he preached not only the "wisdom of God," but the "wisdom of God in a mystery," even his "hidden wisdom." (1 Cor. 1:24, 2:7-8; Job 28:20-21).

It is also so mysterious that it goes beyond the reach of all men, except those to whom an understanding is given of God to apprehend it. That one particular man should represent all the elect in himself and that the most righteous should die as a sinner, yea, as a sinner by the hand of a just and holy God—is a mystery of the greatest depth!

JUNE 6

The Seed Of Abraham

For surely it is not angels that he helps, but he helps the offspring of Abraham.

HEBREWS 2:16

Now, then, we will speak of this first, as to how Christ prepared himself ... mysteriously to act. He took hold of our nature. I say, he took hold of us, by taking upon him flesh and blood. The Son of God ... took not upon him a particular person, though he took to him a human body and soul. But that which he took was, as I may call it, a lump of the common nature of man. And by that, hold of the whole elect seed of Abraham; "For verily he took not on him the nature of angels, but he took on him the seed of Abraham" (Heb. 2:16). Hence, he, in a mystery, became us, and was counted as all the men that were or should be saved.

Indeed, Jesus Christ fulfilled the righteousness of the law ... because indeed fulfilled [it] in our nature: "For what the law could not do, in that it was weak through the flesh, God sending his own Son in the likeness of sinful flesh, and for sin, condemned sin in the flesh, that the righteousness of the law might be fulfilled in us" (Rom. 8:3-4). But because none should appropriate this unto themselves that have not had passed upon them a work of conversion. Therefore, he adds, "Who walk not after the flesh, but after the Spirit" (v. 4).

The reason of all this is, because we are said to be in him in his doing, in him by our flesh, and by the election of God. So, then, as all men sinned when Adam fell, so all the elect did righteousness when Christ wrought and fulfilled the law; "for as in Adam all die, even so in Christ shall all be made alive" (1 Cor. 15:22).

JUNE 7

We Suffer With Christ

We know that our old self was crucified with him in order that the body of sin might be brought to nothing, so that we would no longer be enslaved to sin.

ROMANS 6:6

As we are said to do by Christ, so we are said to suffer by him, to suffer with him. "I am crucified with Christ," said Paul. And again, "Forasmuch then as Christ hath suffered for us in the flesh, arm yourselves likewise with the same mind; for he that hath suffered in the flesh hath ceased from sin" (1 Pet. 4:1). Mark how the apostle seems to change the person. First, he says, it is Christ that suffered and that is true. But then he insinuates that it is us that suffered. For the exhortation is to believers, to "walk in newness of life" (Rom. 6:4). And the argument is because they have suffered in the flesh, "For he that hath suffered in the flesh hath ceased from sin; that he no longer should live the rest of his time in the flesh to the lusts of men, but to the will of God" (1 Pet. 4:1-2). We then suffered when Christ suffered; we then suffered in his flesh, and our "old man was crucified with him" (Rom. 6:6). That is, in his crucifixion: for when he hanged on the cross all the elect hanged there in their common flesh which he assumed and because he suffered there as a public man.

As we are said to suffer with him, so we are said to die, to be dead with him. With him, that is, by the dying of his body. "Now, if we be dead with Christ, we believe that we shall also live with him" (Rom. 6:8). Wherefore he said in other places, "Brethren, ye are become dead to the law by the body of Christ"; for indeed we died then to it by him.

JUNE 8

We Are Quickened Together With Him

And you, who were dead in your trespasses and the uncircumcision of your flesh, God made alive together with him, having forgiven us all our trespasses.

COLOSSIANS 2:13

As we are said thus to be dead, so we are said also to rise again by him—"Thy dead men," he said to the Father, "shall live, together with my dead body shall they arise" (Isa. 26:19). And again, "After two days he will revive us; in the third day—we shall live in his sight" (Hosea 6:2).

Both these Scriptures speak of the resurrection of Christ, of the resurrection of his body on the third day. But behold, as we were said before to suffer and be dead with him, so now we are said also to rise and live in God's sight by the resurrection of his body. For, as was said, the flesh was ours. [Christ] ... took part of our flesh when he came into the world and in it he suffered, died, and rose again (Heb. 2:14). We also were therefore counted by God, in that God-man, when he did this. Yea, he suffered, died, and rose as ... [our] common head.

Hence also the New Testament is full of this, saying: "If ye be dead with Christ" (Col. 2:20). "If ye be risen with Christ" (3:1). And again, "He hath quickened us together with him" (2:13). The apostle has words that cannot easily be shifted or evaded. Christ then was quickened when he was raised from the dead. Nor is it proper to say that he was ever quickened either before or since. ... [W]e also are quickened personally by grace the day in which we are born unto God by the gospel. Yet ... [before] that, we are quickened in our head; quickened when he was raised from the dead, quickened together with him.

JUNE 9

Delivered For Our Trespasses

[Christ] ... who was delivered up for our trespasses and raised for our justification.

ROMANS 4:25

We received, by our thus being counted in him, that benefit which did precede his rising from the dead; and what was that but the forgiveness of sins? For this stands clear to reason, that if Christ had our sins charged upon him at his death, he then must be discharged of them to his resurrection. Now, though it is not proper to say they were forgiven to him, because they were purged from him by [his] merit. Yet they may be said to be forgiven us, because we receive this benefit by grace. And this, I say, was done precedent to his resurrection from the dead. "He hath quickened us together with him, HAVING forgiven us all trespasses." He could not be "quickened" till we were "discharged." Because it was not for himself, but for us, that he died. Hence, we are said to be at that time, as to our own personal estate, dead in our sins, even when we are "quickened together with him" (Col. 2:13).

Therefore, both the "quickening" and "forgiveness" too, so far as we are in this text concerned, is to him, as we are considered in him, or to him, with respect to us. "Having forgiven you ALL trespasses." For necessity ... [it is] required; because how else was it possible that the pains of death should be loosed in his rising. A full discharge therefore was, in and by Christ, received of God of all our sins afore he rose from the dead. As his resurrection [was] truly declared: For he "was delivered for our offences and was raised again for our justification" (Rom. 4:25). This therefore is one of the privileges we receive by the rising again of our Lord, for that we were in his flesh considered, yea, and in his death and suffering too.

JUNE 10

Sharers In His Resurrection

So you also must consider yourselves dead to sin and alive to God in Christ Jesus.

ROMANS 6:11

By this ... we have now escaped death. "Knowing that Christ being raised from the dead dies no more; death hath no more dominion over him. For in that he died, he died unto," or for, "sin once; but in that he lives, he lives unto God" (Rom. 6:9-10). Now in all this ... we that are of the elect are privileged. For that we also are raised up by the rising of the body of Christ from the dead. And thus, the apostle bids us reckon: "Likewise reckon ... also yourselves to be dead indeed unto sin, but alive unto God through Jesus Christ" (Romans 6:11). He says, "I am the resurrection and the life." For all his are safe in him ... [by his] suffering, dying, and rising. He is the life, "our life." Yea ... that by him the elect do live before God, even ... when as to themselves they yet are dead in their sins. Wherefore ... it is that in time they partake of quickening grace from their Head to the making of them, also live by faith to their living hereafter with him in glory. For if Christ lives, they cannot die that were sharers with him in his resurrection. Hence, they are said to "live," being "quickened together with him." [And] ... from that day to this, all that ... were in him at his death and resurrection, are already in the "dispensation of the fulness of times," daily "gathering to him." For this he hath purposed [and] none can disannul—"In the dispensation of the fullness of times he might gather together in one all things in Christ, both which are in heaven and which are in earth; even in him"(Eph. 1:10).

JUNE 11

To Know Him

That I may know him, and the power of his resurrection, and the fellowship of his sufferings, being made conformable unto his death.

PHILIPPIANS 3:10 KJV

Nor does this doctrine of justification by imputed righteousness hinder the doctrine of regeneration or conversion. Nay, it lays a foundation for it. For by this doctrine, we gather assurance that Christ will have his own. For if already they live in their head [Christ], what is that but a pledge that they shall live in their persons with him? And consequently, ... to that end they shall, in the times allotted for that end, be called to a state of faith. [A state] ... which God has ordained shall precede and go before their personal enjoyment of glory. Nor does this hinder their partaking of the symbol of regeneration and of their other privileges to which they are called in the day of grace. Yea, it lays a foundation for all these things. For if I am dead with Christ, let me be like one dead with him, even to all things to which Christ died when he hanged on the tree. And then he died to sin, to the law and to the rudiments of this world (Rom. 6:10, 7:4; Col. 2:20). And if I be risen with Christ; [then] let me live like one born from the dead in newness of life, and having my mind and affections on the things where Christ now sits on the right hand of God. And indeed, he professes in vain that talks of these things and cares not to have them also answered in himself. This was the apostle's way. Namely, to covet to "know him, and the power of his resurrection, and the fellowship of his sufferings, being made conformable unto his death" (Phil. 3:10).

JUNE 12

We Are All An Unclean Thing

... all our righteous deeds are like a polluted garment.

Isaiah 64:6

We will now come to the present state and condition of those that are justified. I mean with respect to their own qualifications and so prove the truth of this our great position. And this I will do, by giving of you plain texts that discover it and that consequently prove our point. And after that by giving of you reasons drawn from the texts.

[Consider] ... "Speak not thou in thine heart," no, not in your heart, "after that the Lord thy God hath cast them out [their enemies] before you, saying, For my righteousness—do I possess this land.—Not for thy righteousness or for the uprightness of your heart do you go to possess their land.—Understand, therefore, that the Lord your God gave you not this good land to possess it for your righteousness; for you are a stiff-necked people (Deut. 9:4-6).

In these words, very pat for our purpose, two things are worthy of our consideration.

1. The people here spoken to were the people of God; and so by God himself are they here twice acknowledged to be—"The Lord thy God, the Lord thy God." So then, the righteousness here intended is not the righteousness that is in the world but that which the people of God perform.
2. The righteousness here intended is not some, but all and every whit [small part] of that the church performs to God: Say not in your heart, after the Lord has brought you in, it was for my righteousness. No, all your righteousness, from Egypt to Canaan will not purchase Canaan for you.

Say: "But we are all as an unclean thing, and all our righteousnesses are as filthy rags; and we all do fade as a leaf; and our iniquities, like the wind, have taken us away" (Isa. 64:6).

JUNE 13

All Our Righteousnesses Are As Filthy Rags

As it is written: "one is righteous, no, not one."
ROMANS 3:10

But we are all as an unclean thing, and all our righteousnesses are as filthy rags; and we all do fade as a leaf; and our iniquities, like the wind, have taken us away.
ISAIAH 64:6 KJV

In these words we have a relation both of persons and things.

1. Of persons. And they are a righteous people, a righteous people put all together—"We, we all are."
2. The condition of this people, even of ALL of them, take them at the best, are, and that by their own confession, "as an unclean thing."
3. Again; the things here attending this people are their good things, put down under this large character, "Righteousnesses, ALL our righteousnesses."

These expressions therefore comprehend all their religious duties, both before and after faith too. But what are all these righteousnesses? Why, they are all as "filthy rags" when set before the justice of the law. Yea, it is also confessed and that by these people that their iniquities, notwithstanding all their righteousnesses, like the wind, if grace prevent not, would "carry them away." This being so, how is it possible for one that is in his sins, to work himself into a spotless condition by works done before faith, by works done by natural abilities? Or to perform a righteousness which can look God in the face, his law in the face, and to demand and obtain the forgiveness of sins, and the life that is eternal? It cannot be: "men must therefore be justified from the curse, in the sight of God while sinners in themselves," or not at all.

JUNE 14

No One Is Good

Surely there is not a righteous man on earth who does good and never sins.

ECCLESIASTES 7:20

Although the words before are large, yet these seem far larger. There is not a man, not a just man, not a just man upon the earth, that doeth good and sins not. Now, if no good man, if no good man upon earth doth good and sins not; then no good man upon earth can set himself by his own actions justified in the sight of God. For he has sin mixed with his good. How then shall a bad man, any bad man, the best bad man upon earth, think to set himself by his best things just in the sight of God? And if the tree makes the fruit either good or evil, then a bad tree—and a bad man is a bad tree—can bring forth no good fruit. How then shall such a one do that that shall "cleanse him from his sin," and set him as "spotless before the face of God"?

"Hearken unto me, ye stout-hearted, that are far from righteousness: I bring near my righteousness" (Isa. 46:12-13).

1. This call is general, and so proves, whatever men think of themselves, that in the judgment of God there is none at all righteous. Men, as men, are far from being so.
2. This general offer of righteousness, of the righteousness of God, declares that it is in vain for men to think to be set just and righteous before God by any other means.
3. There is here also insinuated, that for him that thinks himself the worst, God has prepared a righteousness, and therefore would not have him despair of life that sees himself far from righteousness. From all the Scriptures, therefore, it is manifest, "that men must be justified from the curse of the law, in the sight of God, while sinners in themselves."

JUNE 15

The General Call

Listen to me, you stubborn of heart, you who are far from righteous: I bring near my righteousness; it is not far off, and my salvation will not delay.

ISAIAH 46:12-13A

1. This call is general and so proves whatever men think of themselves, that in the judgment of God there is none at all righteous. Men, as men, are far from being so.

2. This general offer of righteousness, of the righteousness of God, declares that it is in vain for men to think to be set just and righteous before God by any other means.

3. There is here also insinuated that for him that thinks himself the worst, God has prepared a righteousness. Therefore, would not have him despair of life that sees himself far from righteousness. From all these Scriptures ... it is manifest, "that men must be justified from the curse of the law, in the sight of God, while sinners in themselves."

"Come unto me, all ye that labour and are heavy laden, and I will give you rest" (Matt. 11:28).

Here we have a labouring people, a people labouring for life; but by all their labour, you see, they cannot ease themselves. Their burden remains upon them; they are yet heavily laden. The load here is, doubtless, guilt of sin, such as David had when he said by reason thereof, he was not able to look up (Ps. 38:3-5). Therefore, you have an experiment set before you of those that are trying what they can do for life. But behold, the more they stir, the more they sink under the weight of the burden that lies upon them. And the conclusion—to wit, Christ's call to them to come to him for rest—declares that, in his judgment, rest was not to be had elsewhere.

JUNE 16

None Understand

As it is written: "None is righteous, no not one; no one understands; no one seeks for God. All have turned aside; together they have become worthless; no one does good, not even one."

ROMANS 3:10-12

These words have respect to a righteousness which is justified by the law; and they conclude that none by his own performances is righteous with such a righteousness; and it is concluded from five reasons—

1. Because they are not good; for a man must be good before he does good, and perfectly good before he does good and sins not.

2. Because they understand not. How then should they do good? For a man must know before he does, else how should he divert himself to do?

3. Because they want a heart; they seek not after God according to the way of his own appointment.

4. They are all gone out of the way; how then can they walk therein?

5. They are altogether become unprofitable. What worth or value then can there be in any of their doings? These are the reasons by which he proves that there is "none righteous, no, not one."

JUNE 17

Feet Swift To Shed Blood

Their feet are swift to shed blood ...

ROMANS 3:15

And yet this is not all. [Paul] ... also proves, and that by five more reasons, that it is not possible they should do good—

1. "Their feet are swift to shed blood" (Rom. 3:15). This implies an inclination, an inward inclination to evil courses; a quickness of motion to do evil, but a backwardness to do good.

2. "Destruction and misery are in their ways" (v. 16). Take "ways" for their "doings," and in the best of them destruction lurks, and misery yet follows them at the heels.

3. "The way of peace have they not known"; that is far above out of their sight (v. 17). Wherefore the labour of these foolish ones will weary every one of them, because they know not the way that goes to the city (Eccles. 10:15).

4. "There is no fear of God before their eyes" (v. 18). How then can they do anything with that godly reverence of his Holy Majesty that is and must be essential to every good work? For to do things, but not in God's fear, to what will it amount? Will it avail [for them]?

5. All this while they are under a law that calls for works that are perfectly good. That will accept of none but what are perfectly good. And that will certainly condemn them because they neither are nor can be perfectly good. "For what things soever the law saith, it saith it to them who are under the law; that every mouth may be stopped, and all the world may become guilty before God" (v. 19).

Thus, ... by [five] reasons, that none are nor can be, righteous before God by works that they can do. Therefore "men must be justified from the curse, in the sight of God, while sinners in themselves."

JUNE 18

Two Kinds Of Righteousness[1]

But now the righteousness of God has been manifested apart from the law, although the Law and the Prophets bear witness to it—.

ROMANS 3:21

This text utterly excludes the law—what law? The law of works, the moral law, (Rom. 3:27)—and makes mention of another righteousness—even a righteousness of God. For the righteousness of the law is the righteousness of men, men's "own righteousness" (Phil. 3:9). Now, if the law, as to a justifying righteousness, is rejected; then the very matter upon and by which man should work is rejected. And if so, then he must be justified by the righteousness of God—or not at all[!] For he must be justified by a righteousness that is without the law—to wit, the righteousness of God. Now, this righteousness of God, whatever it is, to be sure it is not a righteousness that flows from men. For that, as I said, is rejected, and the righteousness of God opposed unto it, being called a righteousness that is without the law, without our personal obedience to it. The righteousness of God, or a righteousness of God's completing, a righteousness of God's bestowing, a righteousness that God also gives unto, and puts upon all them that believe (Rom. 3:22). [It is] ... a righteousness that stands in the works of Christ, and that is imputed both by the grace and justice of God (vv. 24-26). Where, now, is room for man's righteousness, either in the whole, or as to any part thereof? I say, where, as to justification with God?

1 Theological note: There is a theological conundrum here. One can be made righteous by keeping the law of God. But it must be kept impeccably both internally and externally and thus perfectly, which individuals cannot do and stand holy before God. The other "law" or righteousness is the law of faith. "Abraham believed God and it was imputed to him for righteousness" (Gen. 15:6).

JUNE 19

Father Abraham

What then shall we say was gained by Abraham, our forefather according to the flesh?

ROMANS 4:1

Now, the apostle is at the root of the matter. For Abraham is counted the father of the faithful. Consequently, the man whose way of attaining justification must needs be exemplary to all the children of Abraham. Now, the question is, how did Abraham find it? How he found that which some of his children sought and missed (Rom. 9:32)? That is, how he found justifying righteousness. For it was that which Israel sought and attained not unto (11:7). "Did he find it," said Paul, "by the flesh?" Or, as he was in the flesh? Or, by acts and works of the flesh? But what are they? Why, the next verse tells you "they are the works of the law" (Rom. 4).

"If Abraham was justified by works;" that is, as pertaining to the flesh, for the works of the law are none other but the best sort of the works of the flesh. And so, Paul calls all they that he had before his conversion to Christ: "If any other man," saith he, "thinketh he hath whereof he might trust in the flesh, I more." And then he counts several of his privileges. To which he at last adjoined the righteousness of the moral law, saying, "Touching the righteousness which is in the law, [I was] blameless" (Phil. 3:4-6). And it is proper to call the righteousness of the law the work of the flesh. Because it is the work of a man, of a man in the flesh. For the Holy Ghost does not attend the law, or the work thereof, as to this, in man, as man; that has [been] confined itself to another ministration, whose glorious name it bears (2 Cor. 3:8).

JUNE 20

Grace Excludes Works

Now to the one who works, his wages are not counted as a gift but as his due.

ROMANS 4:4

These words do not only back what went before, as to the rejection of the law for righteousness as to justification with God; but supposing the law was of force to justify. Life must not be allowed to come that way because of the evil consequences that will unavoidably flow from it.

1. By this means, grace and justification by grace, would be rejected; and that would be a foul business. It would not be reckoned of grace.
2. By this, God would become the debtor and so the underling; and so, we in this the more honorable.

It would not be reckoned of grace, but of debt; and what would follow from hence?

1. By this we should frustrate the design of heaven, which is, to justify us freely by grace, through a redemption brought in by Christ (Rom. 3:24-26; Eph. 2:8-13).
2. By this we should make ourselves the Saviours, and jostle Christ quite out of doors (Gal. 5:2-4).
3. We should have heaven at our own dispose, as a debt, not by promise, and so not be beholden to God for it (Gal. 3:18). It must, then, be of grace not of works for the prevention of these evils.

JUNE 21

Faith Casts Out Works

But the law is not of faith ...

GALATIANS 3:12

Again, it must not be of works, because if it should, then God would be the debtor, and we the creditor. Now, much blasphemy would flow from this:

1. God himself would not be his own to dispose of; for the inheritance being God, as well as his kingdom (for so it is written, 'heirs of God' (Rom. 8:17)). [He] himself, I say, must needs be our purchase.
2. If so, then we have right to dispose of him, of his kingdom and glory, and all—"Be astonished, O heavens, at this!"— For if he be ours by works, then he is ours of debt. If he is ours in debt, then he is ours by purchase. And then again, if so, he is no longer his own, but ours, and at our disposal.

So then, "men are justified from the curse, in the sight of God, while sinners in themselves.""But to him that worketh not, but believeth on him that justifies the ungodly, his faith is counted for righteousness" (Rom. 4:5).

These words show how we must stand just in the sight of God from the curse of the law. Both as it respects justification itself, [it is] also the instrument or means that receives that righteousness which justifies.

1. As for that righteousness that justifies, it is not personal performances in us. For the person here justified stands, in that respect, as one that works not as one that is ungodly.
2. As it respects the instrument that receives it, that faith, as in the point of justifying righteousness, will not work, but believe. But receive the works and righteousness of another; for works and faith in this are set in opposition. (Gal. 3:12).

JUNE 22

Saving Faith Is Not Of The Law

For by grace you have been saved through faith. And this is not your own doing; it is the gift of God, not a result of works, so that no one may boast.

EPHESIANS 2:8-9

But to him that worketh not, but believeth on him that justifieth the ungodly, his faith is counted for righteousness.

ROMANS 4:5 KJV

These words show how we must stand just in the sight of God from the curse of the law. Both as it respects justification itself, as also the instrument or means that receives that righteousness which justifies.

[First] As for that righteousness that justifies; it is not personal performances in us. For the person here justified stands, in that respect, as one that worketh not, as one that is ungodly.

[Second] As it respects the instrument that receives it: That faith as in the point of justifying righteousness will not work but believe. But [he will] receive the works and righteousness of another; for works and faith in this are set in opposition. He does not work—he does believe (Gal. 3:12). He works not but believes on him who justifies us [who are] ungodly. As Paul also said in another place: The law is not of faith (Rom. 10:5-6).

And again, works ... [and] faith ... [are] far different. The law says, "Do this and live." But the doctrine of faith says, "If thou shalt confess with thy mouth the Lord Jesus, and shalt believe in thine heart that God hath raised him from the dead, thou shalt be saved. For with the heart man believeth unto righteousness" (Rom. 10:9-10).

[And] again; faith when it hath received the Lord Jesus, it has done that which pleases God. Therefore, the very act of believing is the most noble in the world. Believing sets the crown upon the head of grace; it seals to the truth of the sufficiency of the righteousness of Christ, and gives all the glory to God (John 3:33).

JUNE 23

The Blest Man

Even as David also describes the blessedness of the man to whom God imputes righteousness without works.

ROMANS 4:6 KJV

Did our adversaries[1] understand this one text, they would not so boldly affirm ... that the words, "impute, imputed, imputeth, imputing,"[2] are not used in Scripture. For men ... [do] not really and personally [have] faith. Yet faith is imputed to men. Nay, they are not really and personally sin, nor really and personally righteousness. Yet these are imputed to men: so, then, both good things and bad ... [are] imputed to men. Yet themselves be really and personally neither. But to come to the point: What righteousness hath that man that hath no works? Doubtless none of his own. Yet God imputes righteousness to him. Yea, what works of that man doth God impute to him that he yet justifies as ungodly?

Further, He that hath works as to justification from the curse before God, not one of them is regarded of God. So, then, it matters not whether you have righteousness of thine own or none. "Blessed is the man to whom the Lord imputeth righteousness without works." Man's blessedness—the blessedness of justification from the curse in the sight of God, lies not in good works done by us. Either before or after faith receives [it], but in a righteousness which God imputes without works; as we "work not" as we "are ungodly."

Therefore ... where sin is real, there can be no perfect righteousness; but the way of justification must be through perfect righteousness, therefore by another than our own, "Blessed is the man to whom the Lord will not impute sin" (v. 8).

---

1 Those who believe one can be made righteous before God by keeping the Law.

2 "Impute" and its cognates here mean "to put on one's account." It is a book-keeping term.

JUNE 24

The LORD God As Clothier

And the LORD God made for Adam and his wife garments of skins and clothed them.

GENESIS 3:21

[Consider an Old Testament example of justification by imputed righteousness.] In the beginning of this chapter, you find these two persons reasoning with the serpent, the effect of which discourse was [that] they take of the forbidden fruit and so break the command of God (vv. 7-15). This done, they hide themselves and cover their nakedness with aprons. But God finds out their sin, from the highest branch even to the roots thereof. What followed? Not one precept by which they should by works obtain the favor of God. But the promise of a Saviour; of which promise this twenty-first verse is a mystical interpretation: "The Lord God made them coats of skins and clothed them."

Observe—

1. That these coats were made, not before, but after they had made themselves aprons; a plain proof their aprons were not sufficient to hide their shame from the sight of God.
2. These coats were made not of Adam's inherent righteousness. For that was lost before by sin, but of the skins of the slain. [This was a] type of the death of Christ and of the righteousness brought in thereby—"By whose stripes we are healed" (Isa. 53:5).
3. This is further manifest for the coats, [for] God made them. And for the persons God clothed them therewith: To show that as the righteousness by which we must stand just before God from the curse is a righteousness of Christ's performing, not of theirs. So, he, not they, must put it on them also—for of God we are in Christ and of God his righteousness is made ours (1 Cor. 1:30).

JUNE 25

Faith Offers Sacrifice

... Abel also brought of the firstborn of his flock and of their fat portions. And the LORD had regard for Abel and his offering.

GENESIS 4:4

"By faith he offered." Wherefore faith was precedent or before he offered. Now faith hath to do with God through Christ; not with him through our works of righteousness. Besides, Abel was righteous before he offered, before he did do good; otherwise, God would not have testified of his gift. "By faith he obtained witness that he was righteous," for God approved of his gifts. Now faith ... before the Father respects the promise of forgiveness of sins through the undertaking of the Lord Jesus. Wherefore Abel's faith as to justifying righteousness before God looked not forward to what should be done by himself, but [looked] back to the promise of the seed of the woman that was to destroy the power of hell, and "to redeem them that were under the law" (Gen. 3:15; Gal. 4:4-5). By this faith he shrouds himself under the promise of victory, and the merits of the Lord Jesus. ... God finds him righteous; and being righteous "he offered to God a more excellent sacrifice than his brother." For Cain's person was not first accepted through the righteousness of faith going before, although he seemed foremost as to personal acts of righteousness (Gen. 4). Abel therefore was righteous before he did good works. But that could not be but alone through that respect God had to him for the sake of the Messias [Christ] promised before ([Gen.] 3:15). But the Lord's so respecting Abel presupposed that at that time he stood in himself by the law a sinner, otherwise he needed not to be respected for and upon the account of another.

Abel ... as he acted [in] faith before he offered sacrifice, must thereby entirely respect the promise, which promise was not grounded upon a condition of works to be found in Abel.

JUNE 26

Jacob I Loved

And the LORD said to her, ... "The one shall be stronger than the other, the older shall serve the younger."

GENESIS 25:23

As it is written, "Jacob I loved, but Esau I hated"

ROMANS 9:13

[Consider other Old Testament examples of justification by imputed righteousness.] These words, after Paul's exposition [above], are to be understood of justification in the sight of God, according to the purpose and decree of electing love which had so determined long before. That one of these children should be received to eternal grace; ... not by works of righteousness which they should do but "before they had done either good or evil." Otherwise "the purpose of God according to election" not of works, but of him that calleth, "could not stand," but fall in pieces (Rom. 9:10-12). But none are received into eternal mercy but such as are just before the Lord by a righteousness that is complete. And Jacob, having done no good could by no means have that of his own. Therefore, it must be by some other righteousness, "and so himself be justified from the curse, in the sight of God, while a sinner in himself."

The same may be said concerning Solomon whom the Lord loved with special love. As soon as born into the world, he also confirmed with signal characters. "He sent," said the Holy Ghost, "by the hand of Nathan the prophet, and he called his name Jedidiah, because the Lord loved him (2 Sam. 12:24-25). Was this love of God extended to him because of his personal virtues? No[!] ... for he was yet an infant. He was justified then in the sight of God from the curse by another than his own righteousness.

JUNE 27

God Pitied Orphaned Israel

And when I passed by you and saw you wallowing in your blood, I said to you in your blood, "Live!" I said to you in your blood, "Live!"

EZEKIEL 16:6

[The LORD pitied Israel.] The state of this people you have in the ... verses described, both as to their rise and practice in the world (vv. 1-5).

1. As to their rise. Their original was the same with Canaan, the men of God's curse (Gen. 9:25). "Thy birth and thy nativity is of the land of Canaan"; the same with other carnal men (Rom. 3:9). "Thy father was an Amorite, and thy mother a Hittite" (Ezek. 16:3). Their condition, that has showed us by this emblem—

    1. They had not been washed in water.
    2. They had not been swaddled.
    3. They had not been salted.
    4. They brought filth with them into the world.
    5. They lay stinking in their cradle.
    6. They were without strength to help themselves. Thus, they appear and come by generation.

2. Again, as to their practice—

    1. They polluted themselves in their own blood.
    2. They so continued till God passed by— "And when I passed by thee and saw thee polluted in thine own blood"; —"in thy blood, in thy blood"; it is doubled. Thus, we see they were polluted born, they continued in their blood till the day that the Lord [God] looked upon them; polluted, I say, to the loathing of their persons. Now this was the time of love—"And when I passed by thee, and saw thee polluted in thine own blood, I said unto thee when thou wast in thy blood, Live; yea, I said unto thee when thou wast in thy blood, Live" (Ezek. 16:6)[!]

JUNE 28

God's Initiative

Then I bathed you with water and washed off your blood from you and anointed you with oil.

EZEKIEL 16:9

Question: But how could a holy God say "Live" to such a sinful people?

Answer: Though they had nought but sin, yet he had love and righteousness [for them]. He had love to pity them; righteousness to cover them—"Now when I passed by thee, and looked upon thee, behold, thy time was the time of love" (Ezek. 16:8). What follows?

1. "I spread my skirt over thee"; and
2. "Covered thy nakedness", yea,
3. "I sware unto thee"; and
4. "Entered into covenant with thee"; and
5. "Thou becamest mine." My love pitied thee; my skirt covered thee. Thus, God delivered them from the curse in his sight. "Then I washed thee with water, after thou wast justified; yea, I thoroughly washed away thy blood from thee, and anointed thee with oil" (v. 9).

Sanctification, then, is consequential; justification goes before. The Holy Ghost by this Scripture sets forth to the life, free grace to the sons of men, while they themselves are sinners. I say, while they are unwashed, unswaddled, unsalted, but bloody sinners, for by these words. [They were] "not washed, not salted, not swaddled," he set forth their unsanctified state. Yea, they were not only unsanctified, but also cast out, without pity, to the loathing of their persons. Yea, "no eye pitied them, to do any of these things for them"; no eye but his, whose glorious grace is unsearchable. No eye but his, who could look and love. And blessed be God for the skirt of his glorious righteousness wherewith he covered us when we lay before him naked in blood. It was when we were in our blood that he loved us; when we were in our blood he said, Live[!]

JUNE 29

A Change Of Clothes

Now Joshua was standing before the angel, clothed with filthy garments.

ZECHARIAH 3:3

Joshua is here as men stood who were arraigned before a judge. "Joshua stood before the angel of the Lord, and Satan standing at his right hand to resist him" (v. 1). The same posture as Judas stood in when he was to be condemned. "Set thou," said David, "a wicked man over him; and let Satan stand at his right hand" (Ps. 109: 6). Joshua was clothed ... with filthy rags! Sin upon him, Satan by him, and this before the angel! What must he do now? Go away? No; there he must stand! Can he speak for himself? Not a word; guilt had made him dumb! (Isa. 53:12). Had he no place clean? No; he was clothed with filthy garments! But his lot was to stand before Jesus Christ, that makes intercession for transgressors. "And the Lord said unto Satan, 'The Lord rebuke thee, O Satan; even the Lord that hath chosen Jerusalem, rebuke thee'" (Zech. 3:2). Christ saves from present condemnation those that be still in their sin and blood.

But is he now quit? No; he stands yet in filthy garments. Neither can he, by any that is in him, or done by him, clear himself from him. How then? Why, the Lord clothes him with [a] change of raiment. The iniquities were his own, the raiment was the Lord's. "This is the heritage of the servants of the Lord, and their righteousness is of me, saith the Lord" (Isa. 54:17). "Now Joshua was clothed with filthy garments and stood before the angel. And he answered and spoke unto those that stood before him, saying, 'Take away the filthy garments from him.' And unto him he said, 'Behold, I have caused thine iniquity to pass from thee, and I will clothe thee with change of raiment'" (Zech. 3:3-4).

JUNE 30

A Demon And A Debt

But ... [Jesus] said to him, "Go home to your friends and tell them how much the Lord has done for you, and how he has had mercy on you."

Mark 5:19

A demon: "And when he came into the ship, he that had been possessed with the devil prayed him that he might be with him. Jesus ... saith unto him, 'Go home to thy friends, and tell them how great things God hath done for thee, and hath had compassion on thee'" (Mark 5:18-19).

The present state of this man[:]

1. He was possessed with a devil; with devils, with many; with a whole legion (Matt. 8).
2. These devils had so the mastery of him as to drive him from place to place into the wilderness among the mountains, and so to dwell in the tombs among the dead (Luke 8).
3. He was out of his wits; he would cut his flesh, break his chains. Nay, "no man could tame him" (Mark 5:4-5)[!]
4. When he saw Jesus, the devil in him, as being lord and governor there, cried out against the Lord Jesus (v. 7).

What qualification shows itself as precedent to justification? None but such as devil's work, or as rank bedlams have. Yet this poor man was dispossessed, taken into God's compassion, and was bid to show it to the world.

A debt: "And when they had nothing to pay, he frankly forgave them both" (Luke 7:42).

The occasion of these words was, for that the Pharisee murmured against the woman that washed Jesus' feet, because "she was a sinner." So said the Pharisee, and so saith the Holy Ghost (Luke 7:37). But saith Christ, Simon, I will ask thee a question, "A certain man had two debtors: the one owed him five hundred pence, and the other fifty. And when they had nothing to pay, he frankly forgave them both" (Luke 7:41).

JULY 1

Who Loves Most?

When they could not pay, he cancelled the debt of both. Now which of them will love him more?

LUKE 7:42

The occasion of these words was, for that the Pharisee murmured against the woman that washed Jesus' feet, because "she was a sinner." For so said the Pharisee, and so saith the Holy Ghost[1] (v. 39). But, Christ said, Simon, I will ask thee a question, "A certain man had two debtors: the one owed him five hundred pence, and the other fifty. And when they had nothing to pay, he frankly forgave them both" (v. 41). ["Tell me therefore, which of them will love him most?"] (Luke 7:42b).

Hence, I gather these conclusions—

1. That men that are wedded to their own righteousness understand not the doctrine of the forgiveness of sins. This is manifested by the poor Pharisee; he objected against the woman because she was a sinner.

2. Let Pharisees murmur still, yet Christ has pity and mercy for sinners.

3. Yet Jesus does not usually manifest mercy until the sinner has nothing to pay. "And when they had nothing to pay, he frankly," or freely, or heartily, "forgave them both." If they had nothing to pay, then they were sinners; but he forgives no man but [only] with respect to a righteousness. Therefore, that righteousness must be another's; for in the very act of mercy they are found sinners. They had nothing but debt, nothing but sin, nothing to pay [with]. Then they were "justified freely by his grace, through the redemption that is in Christ Jesus." So, then, "men are justified from the curse, in the sight of God, while sinners in themselves."

1 When Bunyan says "so saith the Holy Ghost," he means that the Holy Spirit is ultimately the author of Scripture.

JULY 2

Your Sins Are Forgiven

And when he saw their faith, he said, "Man, your sins are forgiven you."

LUKE 5:20

This man had not righteousness to stand just[ified] before God withal, for his sins yet remained unforgiven. Wherefore, seeing guilt remained until Christ remitted hi[s sins], he was discharged while ungodly. And [also] observe, his faith here mentioned is not to be reckoned so much the man's as the faith of them that brought him [to Jesus]. Neither did it reach to the forgiveness of sins, but to the miracle of healing. Yet this man, in this condition had his sins forgiven him.

But again, that set the case, the faith was only his as it was not, and that it reached the doctrine of forgiveness. Yet it did it without respect for righteousness in himself. For guilt lay still upon him, he had now his sins forgiven him. But this act of grace was a surprisal; it was ... [unexpected!]. "I am found of them that sought me not" (Isa. 65:1) [saith the Scriptures in another place]. They came for one thing, he gave them another. They came for a cure upon his body, but, to their amazement, he cured first his soul. "Thy sins are forgiven thee." Besides, to have his sins forgiven betokened [a sign of] an act of grace. But grace and works as to this are opposite (Rom. 11:6). Therefore "men are justified from the curse, in the sight of God, while sinners in themselves."

JULY 3

The Justified Prodigal

Father, I have sinned against heaven, and in thy sight and am no more worthy to be called thy son.

LUKE 15:21 KJV

What this man was, is sufficiently declared in verse 13: [And not many days after the younger son gathered all together, and took his journey into a far country, and here wasted his substance with riotous living.]

1. A riotous spender of all—of time, talent, body, and soul.

2. He added to this his rebellion, great contempt of his father's house—he joined himself to a stranger, and became an associate with swine (vv. 15, 17). At last, indeed, he came to himself. But then observe—

1. He sought not justification by personal performances of his own.
2. Neither did he mitigate his wickedness;
3. Nor excuse himself before his father; but first resolved to confess his sin; and coming to his father, did confess it and that with aggravating circumstances. "I have sinned against heaven; I have sinned against thee; I am no more worthy to be called thy son" (v. 18). Now what he said was true or false. If true, then he had not righteousness. If false, he could not stand just in the sight of his father by virtue of his own performances. And, indeed, the sequel of the parable clears it. His "father said to his servant, bring forth the best robe," the justifying righteousness, "and put it on him; and put a ring on his hand, and shoes on his feet" (v. 22). This best robe, then, being in the father's house, was not in the prodigal's heart; neither stayed the father for further qualifications, but put it upon him as he was, surrounded with sin and oppressed with guilt. Therefore "men are justified from the curse, in the sight of God, while sinners in themselves."

JULY 4

A Wee Little Man Justified

For the Son of Man came to seek and to save the lost.

LUKE 19:10

The occasion of these words was, for that the Pharisees murmured because "Jesus was gone to be guest to one that was a sinner." Yea, a sinner of the publicans, and are most fitly applied to the case in hand. For though Zaccheus climbed the tree, yet Jesus Christ found him first and called him down by his name. Adding, "For to-day I must abide at thy house" (v. 5). Which being opened by verse nine, is as much as to say, I am come to be thy salvation. Now this being believed by Zaccheus, "he made haste and came down, and received him joyfully." And not only so, but to declare to all the simplicity of his faith and that he unfeignedly [genuinely] accepted this word of salvation. He said unto the Lord and that before all present, "Behold, Lord, the half of my goods I give to the poor; and if I have taken anything from any man by false accusation," a supposition intimating an affirmative, "I restore him fourfold." This being thus, Christ doubled his comfort, saying to him also, and that before the people, "This day is salvation come to this house." Then, by adding the next words, he expounds the whole of the matter, "For I am come to seek and save that which was lost." To seek it till I find it [and] to save it when I find it. He finds them that sought him not (Rom. 10:20); and Zaccheus said, "Behold me!" to a people that asked not after him. So, then, seeing Jesus finds this publican first, preaching salvation to him before he came down from the tree.

JULY 5

A Day In Paradise

And he said to him, "Truly, I say to you, today you will be with me in paradise."

LUKE 23:43

This was spoken to the thief upon the cross, who had lived in wickedness all his days. Neither had he so much as truly repented—no, not till he came to die. Nay, when he first was hanged, he then fell to railing on Christ; for though Luke leaves it out. Beginning but at his conversion; yet by Matthew's relating the whole tragedy, we find him at first as bad as the other (Matt. 27:44). This man then, had no moral righteousness, for he had lived in the breach of the law of God. Indeed, by faith he believed Christ to be King and that when dying with him. But what was this to a person performing the commandments? Or of restoring what he had oft taken away? Yea, he confessed his death to be just for his sin; and so, leaning upon the mediation of Christ he goes out of the world. Now he that truly confessed and acknowledged his sin, also acknowledged the curse to be due ... [him] from the righteous hand of God. So then, where the curse of God is due that man wanted righteousness. Besides, he that makes to another for help, has by that condemned his own, had he any, of utter insufficiency. But all these did this poor creature; wherefore he must stand "just from the law in the sight of God, while sinful in himself."

JULY 6

A Chosen Instrument

Lord, what wilt thou have me to do?

ACTS 9:6 KJV

What will thou have me to do? Ignorance is here set forth to the full. Paul hitherto knew not Jesus, neither what he would have him to do. Yet a mighty man for the law of works and for zeal towards God according to that. Thus, you see that he neither knew that Christ was Lord, nor what was his mind and will—"I did it ignorantly, in unbelief" (1 Timothy 1:13-15). I did not know him. I did not believe he was to save us. I thought I must be saved by living righteously—by keeping the law of God. This thought kept me ignorant of Jesus and of justification from the curse by him. Poor Saul! how many fellows . . . [like you are] yet alive! —every man zealous of the law of works. Yet none of them know the law of grace. Each of them seeking for life by doing the law, when life is to be had by nought [nothing] but believing in Jesus Christ.

[God answers Paul's question: "But the Lord said to him [Ananias], 'Go for he is a chosen instrument of mine to carry my name before the Gentiles and kings and the children of Israel. For I will show him how much he must suffer for the sake of my name.'" Acts 9:15-16.]

JULY 7

What Shall I Do To Be Saved?

And they said, "Believe in the Lord Jesus, and you will be saved, you and your household."

Acts 16:31

A little before [this], we find Paul and Silas in the stocks for preaching of Jesus Christ—in the stocks, in the inward prison, by the hands of a sturdy jailer. But at midnight; while Paul and his companion sang praises to God; the foundations of the prison shook, and every man's bands were loosed. Now the jailer being awakened by the noise of this shaking and supposing he had lost his prisoners, drew his sword, with intent to kill himself. "But Paul cried out, Do thyself no harm; for we are all here. Then he called for a light, and sprang in, and came trembling, and fell down before Paul and Silas, and brought them out, and said, 'Sirs, what must I do to be saved?'"

In all this relation here is not aught [anything] that can justify the jailer. For,

1. His whole life was idolatry, cruelty, and enmity to God. Yea,
2. Even now, while the earthquake shook the prison, he had murder in his heart—yea, and in his intentions too; murder, I say, and that of a high nature, even to have killed his own body and soul at once. Well,
3. When he began to shake under the fears of everlasting burnings, yet then his heart was wrapped up in ignorance as to the way of salvation by Jesus Christ: "What must I do to be saved?" He did not know what [to do]. His condition then was this: He neither had the righteousness to save him nor knew he how to get it. Now, what was Paul's answer? Why, "Believe in the Lord Jesus Christ," look for righteousness in Christ, "and then thou shalt be saved." This, then, still holds true, "men are justified from the curse, in the sight of God, while sinners in themselves."

JULY 8

All Are Unclean!

... [F]or all have sinned and fall short of the glory of God.

ROMANS 3:23

Men must be justified from the curse while sinners in themselves, because by nature all are under sin—"All have sinned and come short of the glory of God. He hath concluded all in unbelief; he hath concluded all under sin" (Rom. 3:23). Now having sinned, they are in body and soul defiled and become an unclean thing. Wherefore, whatever they touch, with an intent to work out righteousness thereby, they defile that also (Titus 1:15; Lev. 15:11; Isa. 64: 6). And hence, as I have said, all the righteousness they seek to accomplish is but as a menstruous cloth and filthy rags. Therefore, they are sinners still. Indeed, to some men's thinking, the Pharisee is holier than the publican. But in God's sight, in the eyes of divine justice, they stand alike condemned. "All have sinned;" there is the poison! Therefore, as to God, without Christ, all throats are an open sepulcher (Rom. 3:13).

The world in general is divided into two sorts of sinners—the open profane, and the man that seeks life by the works of the law. The profane is judged by all; but the other by a few. Oh! but God judges ... [both].

For a hypocrite, because notwithstanding he hath sinned, he would be thought to be good and righteous. And hence it is that Christ calls such kind of holy ones, "Pharisees, hypocrites! Pharisees hypocrites!" because by their gay outside they deceived those that beheld them. But said he, God sees your hearts; you are but like painted sepulchers, within you are full of dead men's bones (Matt. 23:27-30; Luke 11:26, 16:15). Such is the root from whence flows all their righteousness. But does the blind Pharisee think his state is such?

JULY 9

The Cross Is Foolishness

For the word of the cross is folly to those who are perishing, but to us who are being saved it is the power of God.
1 CORINTHIANS 1:18

God judges[,] "The preaching of the cross," that is, Christ crucified, "is to them that perish foolishness" (1 Cor. 1:18, 23). What says the merit-monger, will you look for life by the obedience of another man? Will you trust the blood that was shed upon the cross, that ran down to the ground, and perished in the dust? Thus, deridingly they scoff at, stumble upon, and are taken in the gin that attends the gospel, [but is] not to salvation, but to their condemnation. Because they have condemned the just, that they might justify their own filthy righteousness (Isa. 8:14).

But I say, if all have sinned, if all are defiled, if the best of a man's righteousness be but madness, blasphemy, injury; if for their righteousness they are judged hypocrites condemned as opposers of the gospel and as such have counted God foolish for sending his Son into the world; then must the best of "men be justified from the curse in the sight of God while sinners in themselves." Because they still stand guilty in the sight of God, their hearts are also still filthy infected—"Though thou wash thee with nitre [saline solution], and take thee much soap, yet thine iniquity is marked before ME, saith the Lord God" (Jer. 2:22). Wherefore, this vine is the vine of Sodom; these clusters are the clusters of Gomorrah; these grapes are grapes of gall; these clusters are bitter, they are the poison of dragons, and the cruel venom of asps (Matt. 3:7, 23). John [the Baptist] in his ministry gives the first rebuke and jostle to such still calling them serpents and vipers concluding it is impossible they should escape the damnation of hell. For of all sin, man's own righteousness, in special, bids defiance to Jesus Christ.

JULY 10

Righteous Before God

For all who rely on works of the law are under a curse; for it is written, "Cursed be everyone who does not abide by all things written in the Book of the Law, and do them."

GALATIANS 3:10

A[nother] ... reason why men must stand just in the sight of God from the curse, while sinners in themselves, is, because of the exactions of the law. For were it granted that men's good works arose from a holy root and were perfect in their kind, yet the demand of the law—for that is still beyond them would leave them sinners before the justice of God. And hence it is that holy men stand just in the sight of God from the curse. Yet [they] dare not offer their gifts by the law, but through Jesus Christ [alone]. [They] know ... that not only their persons but their spiritual service also would else be rejected of the heavenly Majesty (1 Pet. 2:5; Rev. 7:14-16).

For the law is itself so perfectly holy and good as not to admit of the least failure, either in the matter or manner of obedience—"Cursed is every one that continues not in all things that are written in the book of the law to do them" (Gal. 3:10). For they that shall keep the whole law, and yet offend in one point, are guilty of all, and convicted of the law as transgressors (James 2:9-10). And observe, the law leaves you not to your choice, when, or when not, to begin to keep it, but requires your obedience so soon as concerned. Now, if you sin before you begin to do, you are found by the law a transgressor. And so [you] stand by that convicted of sin. So, then, all your after-acts of righteousness are but the righteousness of a sinner, of one whom the law hath condemned already (John 3:18). "The law is spiritual, but thou art carnal, sold under sin" (Rom. 7:14).

JULY 11

A Deceitful Heart

The heart is deceitful above all things, and desperately sick; who can understand it?

JEREMIAH 17:9

[T]he law being absolutely perfect, does not only respect the matter and manner as to outward acts, but also the rise and root, the heart, from whence they flow. And an impediment there spoils all, were the executive part never so good—"Thou shalt love the Lord thy God with ALL thy heart, with ALL thy soul, with ALL thy mind, and with ALL thy strength" (Mark 12:30). Mark the repetition[:] with all, with all, with all; with all thy heart, with all thy soul, in all things, at all times, else you had as good to do nothing. But "every imagination of the thought of the heart of man is only evil continually" (Gen. 6:5). The ... [interpretation] "the whole imagination, the purposes, and desires." So that a good root is here wanting. "The heart is deceitful above all things, and desperately wicked: who can know it?" (Jer. 17:9). What thoughts, words, or actions can be clean, sufficiently to answer a perfect law that flows from this original? It is impossible. "Men must therefore be justified from the curse, in the sight of God, while sinners in themselves." But further yet to open the case. There are ... things that make it impossible that a man should stand just in the sight of God but while sinful in himself.

[One of these], Because the law under which he at present stands, holds him under the dominion of sin; for sin by the law hath dominion over all that are under the law (Rom. 6:14). Dominion, I say, both as to guilt and filth. Guilt hath dominion over him because he is under the curse. And filth, because the law giveth him no power, neither can he by it deliver his soul.

JULY 12

Sin Comes By The Law

But sin, seizing an opportunity through the commandment, produced in me all kinds of covetousness. For apart from the law, sin lies dead.

ROMANS 7:8

The law is so far from giving life or strength to do it, that it doth quite the contrary.

[First:] It weakens, it discourages, and disheartens the sinner, especially when it shows itself in its glory. [And] ... then it is the ministration of death and kills all the world. When Israel saw this, they fled from the face of God ... [for] they could not endure that which was commanded (Exod. 20:18-19). Yea, so terrible was the sight that Moses said, "I exceedingly fear and quake" (Heb. 12:20-21). Moses stood amazed to find himself and Israel yet alive, "Did ever [a] people," he said, "hear the voice of God speaking out of the midst of the fire, as thou hast heard, and live?" (Deut. 4:32-33). When that speaks, it shakes Mount Sinai, and writes death upon all faces, and makes the church itself cry out, A mediator! else we die (Exod. 20:19).

[Second:] It ... abundantly increases every sin. Sin takes the advantage of being by the law; [i.e.] the motions of sin are by the law. Where no law is there is no transgression (Rom. 4:15, 7:5): "When the commandment came, sin revived; for without the law, sin was dead" (Rom. 7:8-9). Sin takes an occasion to multiply by the law: "The law entered, that the offence might abound" (Rom. 5:20). "What shall we say then? Is the law sin? God forbid. Nay, I had not known sin, but by the law: for I had not known lust, except the law had said, 'Thou shalt not covet.' But sin, taking occasion by the commandment, wrought in me all manner of concupiscence. For without the law, sin was dead."

JULY 13

Is The Law Sin?

What then shall we say? That the law is sin? By no means!
ROMANS 7:7

These things then, are not infused or operated by the law from its own nature or doctrine but are occasioned by the meeting of and having to do with a thing directly opposite. "The law is spiritual, I am carnal." Therefore, every imposition is rejected and rebelled against. Strike a steel against a flint and the fire flies about you. Strike the law against a carnal heart and sin appears, sin multiplies, sin rages, sin is strengthened! And hence arises all these doubts, murmurings, and sinful complainings that are found in the hearts of the people of God. They have too much to do with the law. The law of works is now in the conscience, imposing duty upon the carnal part.

The law then, having to do with carnal men, by this they become worse sinners than before. For their heart now recoils desperately [and] opposes blasphemously. It gives way to despair. And then to conclude[:] There is no hope for the hereafter and so goes on in a sordid, ungodly course of life. I conclude, that "a man cannot stand just from the curse, in the sight of God but while sinful in himself."

As the law giveth neither strength nor life to keep it, so it neither giveth nor worketh repentance unto life if thou break it. Do this and live, break it and die—this is the voice of the law. All the repentance that such men have, it is but that of themselves—the sorrow of the world, that ends in death as Cain's and Judas' did, even such a repentance as must be repented of either here or in hell-fire (2 Cor. 7:10).

JULY 14

No Pity Under The Law

You are severed from Christ, you who would be justified by the law; you have fallen away from grace.

GALATIANS 5:4

As ... [the law] gives none so it accepts none of them that are under the law (Gal. 5:4). Sin and die is forever its language. There is no middle way in the law; they must bear their judgment, whosoever they be that stand and fall to the law. Cain was still a vagabond and Judas hanged himself. Their repentance could not save them—they fell headlong under the law. The law stays no man from the due reward of his deeds; it hath no ears to hear nor heart to pity its penitent ones (Gen. 4:9-11; Matt. 27:3).

All the promises annexed to the law are by the first sin, null and void. Our legalists then begin to talk too soon of having life by the law. Let them first begin without sin, and so throughout continue to death. And then if God will save them, not by Christ, but works, contrary to the covenant of grace, they may *hope* to go to heaven.

But, lastly ... [t]hou hast sinned; the law now calls for passive as well as active obedience. Yea, great contentedness in all you suffer for your transgressing against the law. So, then, will you live by the law? Fulfil it, then, perfectly till death, and afterwards go to hell and be damned. And abide there till the law and curse for your sin be satisfied for; and then, but not till then, you shalt have life by the law. "Can thine heart endure, or can thy hands be strong in the day that I shall deal with thee?" (Ezek. 22:14). O, it cannot be! "These must go away into everlasting punishment" (Matt. 25:46). So, then, men must stand just from the curse, in the sight of God, while sinners in themselves, or not at all.

JULY 15

No One Will Be Justified

... [S]o we also have believed in Christ Jesus, in order to be justified by faith in Christ and not by works of the law, because by works of the law no one will be justified.

GALATIANS 2:16

[Consider] ... these words, "The doers of the law shall be justified," there is no more proof of a possibility of saving yourself by the law than ... by this. The intent ... of the text ... is not to prove a possibility of man's salvation by the law, but to insinuate rather an impossibility—by asserting what [complete] perfections the law requires. And were I to argue against the pretended sufficiency of man's own righteousness, I would choose to frame my argument upon such a place as this—"The hearers of the law are not just before God." Therefore, the breakers of the law are not just before God. Not just ... by the law; but all have sinned and broken the law. Therefore, none by the law are just before God. For if all stand guilty of sin by the law, then that law that judges them sinners cannot justify them before God. And what if the apostle had said, "Blessed are they that continue in all things," instead of pronouncing a curse for the contrary. For where the blessing is pronounced, he is not the better that breaks the condition and where the curse is pronounced, he is not the worse that keeps it. But neither does the blessing nor curse in the law intend a supposition that men may be just by the law. But rather to show the perfection of the law, and that though a blessing be annexed, no man by it can obtain that blessing. For not the hearers of the law are justified before God but the doers; when they do it, they shall be justified. None but doers can by it be just before God: But none do[es] the law, no, not one (see Rom. 3:10-11)[!]

JULY 16

Christ: The End Of The Law

For Christ is the end of the law for righteousness to everyone who believes.

ROMANS 10:4

And whereas it is said Christ kept the law as our example, that we by keeping it might get to heaven as he; it is false, as before was showed—"He is the end of the law." Or [Christ] hath perfectly finished it, "for righteousness to everyone that believeth" (Rom. 10:4). No man can keep the moral law as Christ, unless he be first without sin, as Christ [was]. Unless he be God and man, as Christ [is]. And again; Christ cannot be our pattern in keeping the law for life because of the disproportion that is between him and us. For if we do it as he [did] when yet we are weaker than he; what is this but to out-vie [or] outdo and go beyond Christ? Wherefore we, not he, have our lives exemplary: Exemplary, I say, to him; for who do[es] the greatest work, they that take it in hand in full strength as Christ; or he that takes it in hand in weakness as we [do]? Doubtless the last if he fulfills it as Christ. So, then, by this doctrine, while we call ourselves his scholars, we make ourselves indeed the masters. But I challenge all the angels in heaven, let them but first sin as we have done, to fulfill the law, as Christ, if they can!

Again, if Christ be our pattern in keeping the law for life from the curse before God, then Christ fulfilled the law for himself. If so, he was imperfect before he fulfilled it. And how far short this is of blasphemy let sober Christians judge. For the righteousness he fulfilled was to justify from sin; but if it was not to justify us from ours, you know what remains (Dan. 9:26; Isa. 53:8-10).

JULY 17

Fallen From Grace?

You are severed from Christ, you who would be justified by the law; you have fallen away from grace.

GALATIANS 5:4

But when must we conclude we have kept the law? Not when we begin, because we have sinned first; nor when we are in the middle, for we may afterwards miscarry. But what if a man in this his progress has one sinful thought? I query, is it possible to come up to the pattern for justification with God? If yes, then Christ had such; if no, then who can fulfill the law as he? But should I grant that which is indeed impossible—namely, that you are justified by the law; what then? Are you now in the favor of God? No, you are fallen by this thy perfection, from the love and mercy of God: "Whosoever of you are justified by the law are fallen from grace" (Gal. 5:4). He speaks not this to them that are doing [it], but to such as think they have done it. And shows that the blessing that these have got thereby is to fall from the favor of God. Being fallen from grace, Christ profits them nothing, and so they still stand debtors to do the whole law. So then, they must not be saved by God's mercy, nor Christ's merits, but alone by ... [their] works of the law! But what should such men do in that kingdom that comes by gift, where grace and mercy reign? Yes, what should they do among that company that are saved alone by grace, through the redemption that is in Jesus Christ? Let them go to that kingdom that God hath prepared for them that are fallen from grace. "Cast out the bond-woman and her son; for he shall not be heir with the son of the free-woman" and of promise (Gal. 4:30).

JULY 18

How To Be Just Before God?

Now it is evident that no one is justified before God by the law, for "The righteous shall live by faith."

GALATIANS 3:11

[Consider] ... first ... Galatians 3:10: "As many as are of the works of the law are under the curse." Behold how boldly Paul asserts it! And observe it, he did not say here, so many as sin against the law—though that be true—but "As many as are of the works of the law." But what then are the works of the law? Not whoredom, murder, theft, and the like. But works that are holy and good, the works commanded in the ten commandments: As to love God, abhor idols, reverence the name of God, keeping the Sabbath, honoring your parents, abstaining from adultery, murder, theft, false-witness, and not to covet what is thy neighbour's—these are the works of the law. Now Paul said,... it [is] these who are under the curse of God. But what is it then to be [one] of these? Why, to be found in the practice of them and ... resting. This ... [one] is under the curse.

The second Scripture is the eleventh verse of the same chapter, "But that no man is justified by the law in the sight of God, it is evident; for, the just shall live by faith." These words, "the just shall live by faith," are taken out of the Old Testament, and are twice used by this apostle in the New [Testament:]

1. To show that nothing of the gospel can be apprehended but by faith: "For therein is the righteousness of God revealed from faith to faith. 'As it is written, The just shall live by faith'" (Rom. 1:17).
2. To show that the way to have relief and succor under temptation is then to live by faith: "Now the just shall live by faith" (Heb. 10:38).

JULY 19

No One Is Just Before The Law

Behold, his soul is puffed up; it is not upright within him, by the righteous shall live by his faith.

HABAKKUK 2:4

The word "just," therefore, in this place in special, respects a man that is just. Or that so esteems himself by the law and is here considered in a double capacity. First, what he is before men; secondly, what he is before God.

1. As he stands before men, he is just by the law; as Paul [was] before his conversion (Phil. 3:4).
2. As he stands in the sight of God; so, without the faith of Christ, he cannot be just, as is evident. For "the just shall live," not by his justice or righteousness by the law.

This is the true intent of this place. Because they carry with them a supposition that the just here intended may be excluded life, he is falling within the rejection asserted within the first part of the verse. No man is just by the law in the sight of God. For "the just shall live by faith": His justice cannot make him live, he must live by the faith of Christ. Again, the words are a reason dissuasive, urged to put a stop to those that are seeking life by the law. As if the apostle had said, Ye Galatians! What are you doing? Would you be saved by keeping the law? Would you stand just before God ... [by it]? Do you not hear the prophets, how they press faith in Jesus, and life by faith in him? Come, I will reason with you, by way of supposition. Were it granted that you all loved the law, yet that for life, will avail you nothing. For, "the just shall live by faith."

JULY 20

Jews: Justified By The Law?

... We know that a person is not justified by works of the law but through faith in Jesus Christ, so we also have believed in Jesus Christ, in order to be justified by faith in Christ and not by work of the law, because by works of the law no one will be justified.

GALATIANS 2:16

These words are the result of the experienced Christians in the primitive times. Yea, of those among them that had given up themselves before to the law, to get life and heaven thereby. The result, I say, of believing Jews—We who are Jews by nature. But how are they distinguished from the Gentiles?

Why, they are such that rest in the law, and make their boast of God. [They] ... know his will and approve the things that are excellent. [They] ... are guides to the blind, and a light to them that are in darkness. [They] ... are instructors of the foolish, teachers of babes, and which have the form of knowledge and of the truth of the law (Rom. 2:17-19). How far these attained we find by that of the Pharisee—I pray, I fast, I give tithes of all (Luke 18:11-12). The young man in the gospel [confessed]—"All these have I kept from my youth up." And Paul [also confessed]—"Touching the righteousness which is in the law, blameless" (Phil. 3:6). This was the Jew by nature, to do and trust in ... [the Law].

Now these attaining afterwards the sound knowledge of sin, the depravedness of nature, and the exactions of the law, fled from the command of the law to the Lord Jesus for life. We that are taught of God and that have found it by sad experience. We, even we, have believed in Jesus Christ—that we might be justified by the faith of Christ and not by the works of the law. These, even these now fly to Christ from the law, that they might be justified by the faith of Christ and not by the works of the law.

JULY 21

The Law Made Void

Now to the one who works, his wages are not counted as a gift but as his due.

ROMANS 4:4

Another reason why not one under heaven can be justified by the law, or by his own personal performances to it, is because since sin was in the world; God hath rejected the law and the works thereof for life (Rom. 7:10).

It is true, before man had sinned it was ordained to be unto life. But since, and because of sin, the God of love gave the word of grace. Take the law, then, as God hath established it; to wit, to condemn all flesh (Gal. 3:21). And then there is room for the promise and the law, the one to kill, the other to heal; and so, the law is not against the promises. But make the law a justifier and faith is made void, and the promise is made of none effect (Rom. 4:14). And the everlasting gospel, by so doing, you endeavor to root out of the world. Methinks—since it hath pleased God to reject the law and the righteousness thereof for life—such dust and ashes as we should strive to consent to his holy will. [It is] especially [true] when in the room of this [covenant] of works there is established a better covenant and that upon better promises. The Lord hath rejected the law, for the weakness and unprofitableness thereof; for, finding fault with them of the law, "The days come, saith the Lord, when I will make a new covenant with the house of Israel" (Heb. 8:8). Give God leave to find fault with us and to condemn our personal performances to death as to our justification before him thereby. And certainly, if ever he be pleased with us, it will be when he finds us in that righteousness that is of his own appointing.

JULY 22

Life In Christ By Faith

... And the life I now live in the flesh I live by faith in the Son of God, who love me and gave himself for me.

GALATIANS 2:20B

Notwithstanding all that hath or can be said, there are ... things that have great power with the heart to bend it to seek life before God by the law; of all which I would caution that soul to beware, that would have happiness in another world.

[One thing,] Take heed thou be not made to seek to the law for life, because of that name and majesty of God which thou find upon the doctrine of the law (Exod. 20:1). God indeed spoke all the words of the law and delivered them in that dread and majesty to men that shook the hearts of all that heard it. Now this is of great authority with some even to seek for life and bless[ing] by the law. "We know," said some, "that God spoke to Moses" (John 9:29). And Saul rejected Christ even of zeal towards God (Acts 22:3). What zeal? Zeal towards God according to the law, which afterwards he left and rejected because he had found out a better way. The life that he once lived, it was by the law; but afterwards, he saith, "The life which I now live," it is by faith, "by the faith of Jesus Christ" (Gal. 2:20). So that though the law was the appointment of God and had also his name and majesty upon it; yet now he will not live by the law. Indeed, God is in the law, but only as just and holy, not as gracious, and merciful; so, he is only in Jesus Christ. "The law," the word of justice, "was given by Moses, but grace and truth came by Jesus Christ" (John 1:17). Prevail with thee [not] to seek life by all the holy commandments of the law [but in Christ alone].

JULY 23

Beware the Conscience!

Speaking lies in hypocrisy; having their conscience seared with a hot iron.

1 TIMOTHY 4:2 KJV

[Another thing,] Take heed that the law, by taking hold on your conscience, does not make you seek life by the law (Rom. 2:13-15). The heart of man is the seat of the law. This being so, understanding and conscience must needs be in danger of being bound by the law. Man is a law unto himself and shows that the works of the law are written ... [on] his heart. Now, the law being thus nearly related to man, it easily takes hold of the understanding and conscience. By which hold, if it be not quickly broken off by the promise and grace of the gospel, it is captivated to the works of the law. For conscience is such a thing that if it once be possessed with a doctrine, yea, though but with the doctrine of an idol; it will cleave so fast ... [to it] that nothing but a hand from heaven can loosen it. And if it be not loosed no gospel can ... embraced [it] (1 Cor. 8:7). Conscience ... [brings] little-ease, if men resist it, whether it be rightly or wrongly informed. How fast then, will it hold when it knows it cleaves to the law of God! Upon this account, the condition of the unbeliever is most miserable. For not having faith in the gospel of grace, through which is tendered the forgiveness of sins, they [are] like men a-drowning. [They] hold fast that they have found, which being the law of God, they follow it. But because righteousness flies from them. They at last are found only accursed and condemned to hell by the law. Take heed, therefore, that your conscience be not entangled by the law (Rom. 9:31-32).

JULY 24

Beware Self Reasonings!

There is a way that seems right to a man, but its end is the way of death.

PROVERBS 14:12

[And again,] Take heed of fleshly wisdom. Reasoning suits much with the law. "I thought verily that I ought to do many things against the name of Jesus," and so to have sought for life by the law—my reason told me so. For thus will reason say: Here is a righteous law, the rule of life and death. Besides, what can be better than to love God and my neighbour as myself? Again, God has thus commanded, and his commands are just and good. Therefore, doubtless, life must come by the law. Further, to love God and keep the law are better than to sin and break it; and seeing men lost heaven by sin how should they get it again but by working righteousness? Besides, God is righteous and will therefore bless the righteous. O the holiness of the law! It [does] mightily sway with reason when a man [has] addicted himself to religion. The light of nature teaches that sin is not the way to heaven; and seeing no word does condemn sin more than the words of the ten commandments. It must needs be, therefore, the most perfect rule for holiness. Wherefore, says reason, the safest way to life and glory is to keep [your]self close to the law. But a little here to correct. Though the law indeed ... [is] holy, yet the mistake as to the matter in hand is as wide as the east from the west. For therefore the law can do you no good because it is holy and just. For what can he that has sinned expect from a law that is holy and just? Nought [nothing] but condemnation[!] Let them lean to it while they will, "there is one that accuseth you," said Christ, "even Moses, in whom you trust" (John 5:45).

JULY 25

The Law As A Veil

But their minds [Jews] were hardened. For to this day, when they read the old covenant, that same veil remains unlifted, because only through Christ is it taken away.

2 CORINTHIANS 3:14

[And again,] Man's ignorance of the gospel suits well with the doctrine of the law. They, through their being ignorant of God's righteousness, fall in love with that (Rom. 10:1-4). Yea, they do not only suit, but when joined in act, the one strengthens the other. That is, the law strengthens our blindness and binds the veil more fast about the face of our souls. The law suits much our blindness of mind. For until this day remains the veil untaken away in the reading of the Old Testament—especially in the reading of that which was written and engraved on stones. To wit, the ten commandments, that perfect rule for holiness which veil was done away in Christ (2 Cor. 3:15-16). But "even to this day, when Moses is read, the veil is over their hearts;" [and] they are blinded by the duties enjoined by the law from the sight and hopes of forgiveness of sins by grace. "Nevertheless, when IT," the heart, "shall turn to the Lord, the veil shall be taken away." The law, then, doth veil the heart from Christ, and holds the man so down to doing and working for the kingdom of heaven, that he quite forgets the forgiveness of sins by mercy through Christ. Now this veiling or blinding by the law is occasioned.

JULY 26

The Conscience Is Blind And Deaf

For I know my transgressions and my sin is ever before me.

PSALM 51:3

Good understanding giveth favour, but the way of the transgressor is hard.

PROVERBS 13:15 KJV

The law veils and blinds by that guilt and horror for sin that seizes the soul by the law. For guilt, when charged close upon the conscience is attended with such aggravations and that with such power and evidence. The conscience cannot hear, nor see, nor feel anything else but that. When David's guilt for murder and blood did roar by the law in his conscience, notwithstanding he knew much of the grace of the gospel—he could hear nothing else but terror, the sound of blood. The murder of Uriah was the only noise that he heard[!] Wherefore he cried to God that he would make him hear the gospel. "Make me to hear joy and gladness, that the bones which thou hast broken may rejoice" (Ps. 51:8). And as he could not hear, so neither could he see; the law had struck him deaf and blind: "I am," saith he, "not able to look up"—not up to Christ for mercy. [It is] as if David had said, O Lord, the guilt of sin, which is by the law, makes such a noise and horror in my conscience, that I can neither hear nor see the word of peace unless it is spoken with a voice from heaven! [Also,] The serpents that bit the people in the days of old were types of guilt and sin (Num. 21:6). Now, these were fiery serpents, and such as, I think, could fly (Isa. 14:29). Wherefore, in my judgment, they stung the people about their faces, and so swelled up their eyes, which made it the more difficult for them to look up to the brazen serpent, which was the type of Christ (see: John 3:14).

JULY 27

Sin Is A Deceiver

The very commandment that promised life proved to be death to me. For sin, seizing an opportunity through the commandment, deceived me and through it killed me.

ROMANS 7:10-11

Where the law comes with power, there it begets many doubts against the grace of God. For it is only a revealer of sin and ... [administers] death. That is, a doctrine that shews sin and condemns for the same. Therefore, as was hinted before, the law being the revealer of sin, where that is embraced, there sin must needs be discovered and condemned and the soul for the sake of that. Further, it is not only a revealer of sin but ... makes it abound. So that the closer any man sticks to the law for life the faster sin doth cleave to him. "That law," said Paul, "which was ordained to be unto life, I found to be unto death." For by the law, I became a notorious sinner; I thought to have obtained life by obeying the law, "but sin taking occasion by the commandment, deceived me, and by it slew me" (Rom. 7:10-14). A strange way of deceivableness is hidden from most men.

1. Man by nature is carnal and the law itself is spiritual: Now betwixt these two arises [a] great difference. The law is exceeding good, the heart exceeding bad; these two opposites. Therefore, the heart so abiding can by no means agree.
2. This being thus, the conscience perceiving this is a fault, begins to tremble at the sense of judgment. The law continues to command duty and to condemn for the neglect thereof. From this struggling from these two opposites arises doubts and fears that drive the heart into unbelief and make it blind to the word of the gospel, [so] it can neither see nor understand anything, but that it is a sinner and that the law must be fulfilled by it, if ever it be saved.

JULY 28

Is The Law Another Gospel?

But even if we or an angel from heaven should preach to you a gospel contrary to the one we preached to you, let him be accursed.... [S]o now I say again; if anyone is preaching to you a gospel contrary to the one you received, let him be accursed.

GALATIANS 1:8-9

[There is] ... another thing that hath great influence upon the heart to make it lean to the law for life. [That] ... is, the false names that Satan and his instruments have put upon it. Such as these—to call the law the gospel; conscience, the Spirit of Christ; works, faith; and the like. With these weak consciences have been mightily pestered; yea thousands deluded and destroyed. This was the way whereby the enemy attempted to overthrow the church of Christ of old; namely those in Galatia and at Corinth (2 Cor. 11:3-4, 13-14). By the feigned notion that the law was the gospel, the Galatians were removed from the gospel of Christ. And Satan, by appropriating to himself and his ministers the names and titles of the ministers of the Lord Jesus, prevailed with many at Corinth to forsake Paul and his doctrine. Where the Lord Jesus hath been preached in truth and something of his doctrine known it is not there so easy to turn people aside from the sound of the promise of grace—unless it be by the noise and sound of a gospel.

Therefore, the false apostles came thus among the churches: "[A]nother gospel, another gospel"; which in truth, said Paul, "is not another; but some would pervert the gospel of Christ." [They would] thrust it out of doors, by gilding [thinly covering] the law with that glorious name (Gal. 1:6-8). I say, [the Law] is of great force, especially being accompanied by so holy and just a doctrine as the word of the law is. For what better to the eye of reason than to love God above all, and our neighbour as ourselves.

JULY 29

Satan Encourages Circumcision

Look: I, Paul, say to you that if you accept circumcision, Christ will be of no advantage to you.

GALATIANS 5:2

Satan will yet go further; he will make use of something that may be at a distance from a moral precept and therewith bring souls under the law. Thus, he did with some of old; he did not make the Galatians fall from Christ by virtue of one of the ten words, but by something that was aloof [from them]. By circumcision, days, and months, that were Levitical ceremonies; for ... [Satan] knows it is no matter, nor in what Testament he found it,... he can ... hide Christ from the soul—"Behold, I Paul say unto you, that if ye be circumcised, Christ shall profit you nothing. For I testify again to every man that is circumcised, that he is a debtor to do the whole law" (Gal. 5:2-3). Why so, seeing circumcision is not one of the ten words [commandments]? Why, because they did it in [good] conscience to God, to stand just before him thereby.

Now here we may behold much cunning of the devil. He begins with some at a distance from that law which [is] cursed. So ... little ... [by] little [he] brings them under it; even as by circumcision the Galatians were ... brought under the law that condemned all men to the wrath and judgment of God. But I ... [understand] by Paul that by these things a man may reject and condemn the Lord Jesus. Which those do, that for life set up aught [anything else], whether moral or other institution, besides the faith of Jesus. Let men therefore warily distinguish betwixt names and things, betwixt statute and commandment, lest they by doing the one transgress against the other.

JULY 30

A Full And Final Atonement

For by a single offering he has perfected for all time those who are being sanctified.

Hebrews 10:14

[Christ] ... is said to have purged our sins by himself—"When he had by himself purged our sins, he sat down on the right hand of God" (Heb. 1:3). I have shown that in Christ, for the accomplishing of righteousness, there was both doing and suffering; doing, to fulfill all the commands of the law; suffering, to answer its penalty for sin. This ... is that which [is] in... the Hebrews ... especial[ly] intended by the apostle, where he said he has purged our sins. That is, by his precious blood; for it is that alone can purge our sins, either out of the sight of God or out of the sight of the soul (Heb. 9:14).

Now this was done by himself, said the apostle; that [it] is in or by his personal doings and sufferings. And hence it is when God had rejected the offerings of the law he said, "Lo, I come. A body hast thou prepared me,—to do thy will, O God" (Heb. 10:5-8). Now by this will of God, say the Scriptures, we are sanctified. By what will? Why, by the offering up of the body of Jesus Christ; for that was God's will, that ... [by it] we might be a habitation for him; as he said again—"Jesus also, that he might sanctify the people with his own blood, suffered without the gate" (Heb. 13:12).

As it is said, he hath purged our sins by himself, so it was by himself at once—"For by one offering he hath perfected forever them that are sanctified" ([Heb.] 10:14).

JULY 31

The Gift Of Righteousness

For if, because of one man's trespass, death reigned through that one man, much more will those who receive the abundance of grace and the free gift of righteousness reign in the life through the one man Jesus Christ.

ROMANS 5:17

It appears, in that by his resurrection from the dead the mercies of God are made sure to the soul. God declaring by that ... how well pleased he is by the undertaking of his Son for the salvation of the world: "And as concerning that he raised him up from the dead, now no more to return to corruption, he said on this wise, I will give you the sure mercies of David" (Acts 13:34). For Christ being clothed with man's flesh, and undertaking for man's sins, did then confirm all sure to us by his resurrection from the dead. So that by the rising of that man again, mercy and grace are made sure to him that have believed on Jesus. Wherefore, from these things, together with what has been discovered about his addressing himself to the work, I conclude: "that men can be justified from the curse, before God, while sinners in themselves, by no other righteousness than that long ago performed by the person of Christ." [So] "By the will of God we are sanctified, through the offering up of the body of Jesus Christ once for all."

[Since this] position is manifest—namely, that the righteousness by which we stand just from the curse before God, is only inherent in Jesus Christ. For if he hath undertaken to bring in a justifying righteousness, and that by works and merits of his own, then that righteousness must be inherent in him alone and ours only by imputation. And hence it is called, in that fifth to the Romans, the gift, the "gift of righteousness." Because neither wrought nor obtained by works of ours, but bestowed upon us, as a garment ... prepared, by the mercy of God in Christ.

AUGUST 1

The Wicked And The Righteous

The desire of the righteous ends only in good, the expectation of the wicked in wrath. One gives freely, yet grows all the richer; another withholds what he should give, and only suffers want.

PROVERBS 11:23-24

This book of Proverbs is so called because it is such as contains hard, dark, and pithy sentences of wisdom by which is taught unto young men knowledge and discretion ([Prov.]1-6). This book is not such as discloses truths by words antecedent or subsequent to the text, so as other Scriptures generally do. But has its texts or sentences more independent. For usually each verse stands upon its own bottom and presents by itself some singular thing to the consideration of the reader. So that I shall not need to bid my reader go back to what went before, nor yet to that which follows for the better opening of the text. And [I] shall therefore come immediately to the words and search into them for what hidden treasures are contained therein.

The words then, in the first place, present us with the general condition of the whole world. For all men are ranked under one of these conditions, the wicked or the righteous. For he that is not wicked is righteous and he that is not righteous is wicked. So again, "Lay not wait, O wicked man, against the dwelling of the righteous, spoil not his resting-place."

The world is also divided by other general terms, as by these—believers, unbelievers; saints, sinners; good, bad; children of God, and children of the wicked one. So that I say, the text, or these two terms in it, comprehend all men; the one all that shall be saved, the other all that shall be damned forever in hell-fire (Ps. 9:17, 11:6).

AUGUST 2

More Tolerable For Sodom

... For this is a people without discernment, therefore he who made them will not have compassion on them; he who formed them will show them no favor [grace].

ISAIAH 27:11

Of the wicked there are several sorts, some more ignorant, some more knowing. The more ignorant of them are such as go to be executed, as the ox goes to the slaughter, or as a fool to the correction of the stocks. That is as creatures whose ignorance makes them as unconcerned, while they are going down the stairs to hell. But alas! their ignorance will be no plea for them before the bar of God. For it is written, "It is a people of no understanding; therefore, he that made them will not have mercy on them, and he that formed them will show them no favour" (Isa. 27:11).

Though, I must confess, the more knowing the wicked is, or the more light and goodness such a one sins against, the greater will their judgment be. These shall have greater damnation: it shall be more tolerable at the judgment for Sodom than for them (Luke 10:12, 20:47). There is a wicked man that goes blinded, and a wicked man that goes with his eyes open to hell. There is a wicked man that cannot see, and a wicked man that will not see the danger he is in. But hell-fire will open both their eyes (Luke 16:23). There are that are wicked, and cover all with a cloak of religion, and there are that proclaim their profaneness. But they will meet both in the lake that burns with fire and brimstone; "The wicked shall be turned into hell, and all the nations that forget God" (Ps. 9:17).

There are also several sorts, if I may so express myself, of those that are truly righteous, as children, young men, fathers, or saints that fear God, both small and great (Rev. 11:18; 1 John 2).

AUGUST 3

Different Responses To Grace

[A]nd if he rescued righteous Lot, greatly distressed by the sensual conduct of the wicked....

2 PETER 2:7

Some have more grace than some and some do better [to] improve the grace they have than others of their brethren do. Some also are more valiant for the truth[1] upon the earth than others of their brethren are. Yea, some are so swallowed up with God, and love to his word and ways; they are fit to be a pattern or example in holiness to all that are about them. And some again have their light shining so dim, that they render themselves suspicious to their brethren; whether they are of the number of those that have grace or no. But being gracious they shall not be lost, although such will at the day of reward suffer loss. For this is the will of the Father that sent the Son to be the Saviour of the world, "That of all which he had given him he should lose nothing but should raise it up again at the last day" (John 6:37-39; 1 Cor. 3:15).

In the next place, we are here presented with some of the qualities of the wicked and the righteous. The righteous has his desires. The wicked has his fears. "The fear of the wicked, it shall come upon him; but the desire of the righteous shall be granted." Indeed, it seems to the godly that the wicked fear not, nor doth he after a godly sort. For he that fears God aright must not be reputed a wicked man. Yet for all that, the wicked at times are haunted: "Terrors," says Bildad, "shall make him afraid on every side." And again, "His confidence shall be rooted out of his tabernacle, and it shall bring him to the king of terrors" (Job 18:11-14).

1 "Valiant for Truth" is one of Buyan's characters in *Pilgrim's Progress*.

AUGUST 4

The Terror Of The Lord

Knowing therefore the terror of the Lord, we persuade men....
2 CORINTHIANS 5:11A KJV

A wicked man, though he may [bully someone] ... at times with his proud heart, as though he feared neither God nor hell; yet again, at times, his soul is even drowned with terrors. "The morning is to them even as the shadow of death; if one knew them, they are in the terrors of the shadow of death" (Job 24:14-17). At times, it is thus with them, especially when they are under warm convictions, that the day of judgment is at hand. Or when they feel in themselves as if death was coming as a tempest, to steal them away from their enjoyments, and lusts, and delights. Then the bed shakes on which they lie, then the proud tongue doth falter in their mouth and their knees knock one against another. Then their conscience stares, and roars, and tears, and arraigns them before God's judgment seat. Or [it] threatens to follow them down to hell, and there to wreck its fury on them, for all the abuses and affronts this wicked wretch offered to it in the day in which it controlled his unlawful deeds. O! none can imagine what fearful plights a wicked man is in sometimes. Though God in his just judgment towards them suffers them again and again to stifle and choke such awakenings, from a purpose to reserve them unto the day of judgment to be punished (2 Pet. 2:7-9).

[And also] ... as the wicked has his fears, so the righteous has his desires. "The desire of the righteous shall be granted." But this must not be taken exclusively, as if the wicked had nothing but fears, and the righteous nothing but desires. For both by Scripture and experience also, we find that the wicked has his desires, and the righteous man his fears.

AUGUST 5

The Boasts Of The Wicked

For the wicked boasts of the desires of his souls, and the one greedy for gain curses and renounces the LORD.

PSALM 10:3

For the wicked, they are not without their desires. "Let me die the death of the righteous, and let my last end be like his," was the desire of wicked Balaam (Num. 23:10) [I]n another place [it is] said, "the wicked boasts of his heart's desire." He is for heaven as well as the best of you all, but, even then, "he blesses the covetous, whom the Lord abhors" (Ps. 10:3). Wicked men have their desires and their hopes too, but the hope and desire of unjust men perishes (Prov. 11:7). Yea, and though they look and long, too, all day long, with desires of life and glory, yet their fears, and them only shall come upon them; for they are the desires of the righteous that shall be granted (Ps. 112:10).

The desires of the wicked want a good [stable] bottom. They flow not from a sanctified mind, nor of love to the God, or the heaven now desired. But only from such a sense as devils have of torments and so as they cry out, "I beseech thee torment me not" (Luke 8:28; 16:24).

Their fears, therefore, have a strong foundation; they also have matter to work upon, which is guilt and justice, the which they shall never be able to escape, without a miracle of grace and mercy (Heb. 2:3). Therefore, it saith and that with emphasis, "The fear of the wicked it shall come upon him." Wherefore his desires must die with him: for the promise of a grant of that which is desired is only entailed to righteousness. "The desire of the righteous shall be granted," but "grant not, O Lord, the desires of the wicked," said David (Ps. 140:8).

AUGUST 6

Whom Shall We Fear?

[Christ] ... himself likewise partook of the same things, that through death he might destroy the one who has the power of death, that is the devil, and deliver all those who through fear of death were subject to lifelong slavery.

HEBREWS 2:14B-15

The righteous [too are not] without their fears and that even all their life long. Through fear of death, some of them, are all their lifetime subject to bondage (Heb. 2:15). But as the desires of the wicked shall be frustrate[d], so shall also the fears of the godly. Hence you have them admonished, yea commanded, not to be afraid neither of devils, death, nor hell. For the fear of the righteous shall not come upon them to eternal damnation (Isa. 35:4, 41:10-14, 43:1, 44:28; Luke 8:50, 12:32; Rev. 1:17).

"The desire of the righteous shall be granted." No, they are not to fear what sin can do unto them, nor what all their sins can do unto them. I do not say they should not be afraid of sinning, nor of those temporal judgments that sin shall bring upon them. For of such things, they ought to be afraid as saith the Psalmist, "My flesh trembles for fear of thee, and I am afraid of thy judgments" (Ps. 119:120). But of eternal ruin, of that, they ought not to be afraid of slavish fear. "Wherefore should I fear," said the prophet, "in the days of evil, when the iniquity ... [on] my heels shall compass me about?" (Ps. 49:5). And again, "Ye have done all this wickedness, yet turn not aside from following the Lord;—for the Lord will not forsake his people, for his great name's sake" (1 Sam. 12:20-22).

AUGUST 7

Be Sober In Faith

Be sober-minded, be watchful. Your adversary the devil prowls around like a roaring lion, seeking someone to devour.

1 PETER 5:8

[The just are firm] ... because the righteous are secured by their faith in Christ Jesus. Also, their fears stand upon a mistake of the nature of the covenant in which they are wrapped up, which is ordered for them in all things and sure (2 Sam. 23:5; Isa. 55:3). Besides, God has purposed to magnify the riches of his grace in their salvation. Therefore, goodness and mercy shall, to that end, follow them all the days of their life that they may "dwell in the house of the Lord forever" (Ps. 23:6; Eph. 1:3-7).

They have also their intercessor and advocate ready with God; to take up matters for them in such a way as may maintain true peace betwixt their God and them. And as may encourage them to be sober, and hope to the end, for the grace that is to be brought unto them at the revelation of Jesus Christ (1 Pet. 1:13; 1 John 2:1-2). Wherefore, though the godly have their fears, yea, sometimes dreadful fears, and that of perishing for ever and ever; yet [their] day is coming. [The day] ... when their fears and tears shall be done away and when their desires only shall be granted: "The fear of the wicked, it shall come upon them; but the desire of the righteous shall be granted."

The words then, are a prediction or prophecy, and that both concerning the wicked and the righteous with reference to time and things to come and shall certainly be fulfilled in their season. Hence it is said concerning the wicked, that their triumphing is short and that the joy of the hypocrite is but for a moment (Job 20:5). O, their end will be bitter as wormwood, and will cut like a two-edged sword!

AUGUST 8

Their Damnation Does Not Sleep

... Their condemnation from long ago is not idle, and their destruction is not asleep.

2 PETER 2:3B

There ... [is a] desperate spirit that possesses the children of men, who, though they hear and read all this; yet cannot be reclaimed from courses that are wicked and that lead to such a condition (Prov. 5:7-14). I say they will not be reclaimed from such courses as lead to ways that go down to hell. Where their soul must mourn, even then when their flesh and their body are consumed. O! how dear bought are their pleasures and how will their laughter be turned into tears and anguish unutterable! And that presently for it is coming! Their "judgment now of a long time lingers not, and their damnation slumbers not" (2 Pet. 2:3).

But what good will their covenant of death then do them? And will their agreement of hell yield them comfort? Is not God as well mighty to punish as to save? (Isa. 28:18). Or can these sinners believe God out of the world or cause that he should not pay them home for their sins and recompense them for all the evil they have loved? (Job 21:29-31). Thou art bold now, I mean bold in a wicked way; you say now you will keep your sweet morsels of sin under thy tongue, you will keep them still within thy mouth. Poor wretch! Your sins shall lie down in the dust with thee (Job 20:11). You have sucked the poison of asps and the viper's tongue shall slay thee (Job 20:16). "Thou shalt not see the rivers, the streaming floods, the brooks of butter and honey [of heaven]" (Job 20:17). [And] "This is the portion of a wicked man from God and the heritage appointed to him by God" (Job 20:26-29).

AUGUST 9

The Desire Of The Righteous Granted

What the wicked dreads will come upon him, but the desire of the righteous will be granted.

PROVERBS 10:24

And as ... [the Scriptures] predict or prophesy what shall become of the wicked; so ... they plentifully foretell what shall happen to the righteous, when he said their desire shall be granted: of which more anon [soon]. Only here I will drop this short hint, That the righteous have great cause to rejoice; for what more pleasing, what more comfortable to a man, than to be assured and that from the Spirit of truth, that what he desires shall be granted? And this the righteous are assured of here; for ... [God] said it in words at length, "The desire of the righteous shall be granted." This then, should comfort them against their fears, and the sense of their unworthiness; it should also make them hold up their heads under all their temptations and the affronts that is usual for them to meet with in the world. The righteous! Who so vilified as the righteous? He, by the wise men of the world, is counted a very Abraham, [as] a fool; like to him who is the father of us all. But as he left all for the desire that he had of a better country and at last obtained his desire. For after he had patiently endured, he obtained the promise; so those that walk in the steps of that faith which our father Abraham had, even those also in the end shall find place in Abraham's bosom. Wherefore it is meet that we should cheer up and be glad, because what we desire shall be granted unto us (Heb. 6).

AUGUST 10

Who Are The Righteous?

Every way of a man is right in his own eyes, but the LORD *weighs the heart.*

PROVERBS 21:2

FIRST. There is one that is righteous in his own eyes and is yet far enough off from the blessing of the text: "There is a generation that are pure or righteous in their own eyes, and yet is not washed from their filthiness" (Prov. 30:12). The evangelist Luke said some trusted "in themselves that they were righteous, and despised others" (Luke 18:9). These are set so low by this their foolish confidence in the eyes of Jesus Christ, that he even preferred a praying publican before them (Luke 18:13-14).

SECOND. There are those that by others are counted righteous; I mean they are so accounted for by their neighbours. Thus, Korah and his company are called the people of the Lord and all the congregation by them also called holy, every one of them (Num. 16:3, 41). But as he who commends himself is not approved, so it is no great matter if all the world shall count us righteous.

THIRD. There are those that indeed are righteous when compared with others: "I came not to call the righteous" [and] "for scarcely for a righteous man will one die," and the like are texts ... to be understood. For such as these are as to life moral better than others. If they are none otherwise righteous than by acts and works of righteousness of their own, are not the people contained in the text that are to have their desires granted.

FOURTH. The righteous man therefore ... is and ought to be thus described:

1. He is one whom God makes righteous by reckoning him so.
2. He is one that God makes righteous by possessing of him with a principle of righteousness.
3. He is one that is practically righteous.

AUGUST 11

Description Of The Righteous

[The LORD] ... has clothed me with garments of salvation; he has covered me with the robe of righteousness, as a bridegroom decks himself like a priest with a beautiful headdress, and as a bride adorns herself with her jewels.

ISAIAH 61:10

He is one that God makes righteous. Now, if God makes him righteous, his righteousness is not his own. I mean this sort of righteousness: "Their righteousness is of me saith the Lord" (Isa. 54:17). God then makes a man righteous by putting righteousness upon him—by putting the righteousness of God upon him (Phil. 3:6-9). Hence, we are said to be made the righteousness of God in Christ: "For God hath made him to be sin for us, who knew no sin, that we might be made the righteousness of God in him" (2 Cor. 5:21). Thus God, reckons one righteous, even by imputing that unto us which can make us so: "Christ of God is made unto us—righteousness" (1 Cor. 1:30). Wherefore he saith again, "In the Lord shall all the seed of Israel be justified and shall glory" (Isa. 45:25).

The righteousness then by which a man is made righteous with righteousness to justification of life before God, for that is it we are speaking of now: [It] is the righteousness of another than he who is justified thereby. Hence it is said again, by the soul thus justified and made righteous, "The Lord hath clothed me with the garments of salvation, he hath covered me with the robe of righteousness" (Isa. 61:10). As he also saith in another place, "I spread my skirts over thee, and covered thy nakedness"[1] (Ezek. 16:8).

1 "Nakedness" sometimes in Scripture is a metaphor for sinfulness.

AUGUST 12

Sanctified In Christ

To the church of God that is in Corinth, to those sanctified in Christ Jesus, called to be saints together with all those who in every place call upon the name of our Lord Jesus Christ, both their Lord and ours.

1 CORINTHIANS 1:2

[Now] ... this righteousness by being bestowed upon us, is [not] severed from Jesus Christ; for it is still his and in him. How then, may some say, doth it become ours? I answer by our being put into him. For of God are we in Christ Jesus, who is made unto us, of him, "righteousness." And again, we are made "the righteousness of God in him." So then, the righteousness of Christ covers his, as a man's garments cover the members of his body, for we are "the body of Christ, and members in particular" (1 Cor. 12:27). The righteousness therefore is Christ's; resides still in him, and covers us, as the child is lapped up in its father's skirt, or as the chicken is covered with the feathers of the hen. I make use of all these similitudes thereby to inform you of my meaning. For by all these things are set forth the way of our being made righteous to justification of life (Matt. 23:37; Ezek. 16:8; Ps. 36:7).

Now thus a man is made righteous, without any regard to what he has or to what is of him. For as to him, it is utterly another's. Just as if I should, with the skirts of my garments, take up and clothe some poor and naked infant that I find cast out into the open field. Now if I cover the person, I cover scabs and sores, and ulcers, and all blemishes. Hence God, by putting this righteousness upon us, is said to hide and cover our sins. "Blessed are they whose iniquities are forgiven, and whose sins are covered. Blessed is the man to whom the Lord will not impute sin" (Rom. 4:7-8).

AUGUST 13

A Tree Is Known By Its Fruit

Either make the tree good and its fruit good, or make the tree bad and its fruit bad, for the tree is known by its fruit.

MATTHEW 12:33

Thus ... a man [is] made righteous even of God by Christ or through his righteousness. Now if ... a man is thus made righteous, then in this sense he is good before God. Before he has done anything of that which the law calls good before men. For God maketh not men righteous with this righteousness, because they have been, or have done good, but before they can do good at all. Hence, we are said to be justified while ungodly, even as an infant is clothed with the skirt of another, while naked, as touching itself (Rom. 4:4-5). Works therefore do not precede but follow after this righteousness. And even thus it is in nature, the tree must be good before it bears good fruit, and so also must a man. It is as impossible to make a man bring forth good fruit to God, before he is of God made good, as it is for a thorn or bramble bush to bring forth figs or grapes (Matt. 7:15-16).

But again, a man must be righteous before he can be good; righteous by imputation; before his person, his intellectuals, can be qualified with good, as to the principle of good. For neither faith, the Spirit, nor any grace is given unto the sinner before God has made him righteous with this righteousness of Christ. Wherefore it is said, that after he had spread his skirt over us, he washed us with water, that is, with the washing of sanctification (Ezek. 16:8-9). And to conclude otherwise, is as much as to say that an unjustified man has faith, the Spirit, and the graces thereof; which to say is to overthrow the gospel.

AUGUST 14

The Righteous Do Righteousness

And to the one who does not work but believes in him who justifies the ungodly, his faith is counted as righteousness.
ROMANS 4:5

God makes a man righteous by possessing ... him with a principle of righteousness even with the spirit of righteousness (Rom. 4:4-5). For though, as to justification before God from the curse of the law, we are made righteous while we are ungodly. And yet sinners; yet being made free from sin, thus we become through a change which the Holy Ghost works in our minds, the servants of God (Rom. 5:7-9). Hence it is said, "There is therefore now no condemnation to them which are in Christ Jesus, who walk not after the flesh, but after the Spirit" (Rom. 8:1). For though, as the apostle also insinuates here, that being in Christ Jesus is antecedent to our walking after the Spirit. Yet a man can make no demonstration of his being in Christ Jesus, but by his walking in the Spirit, because the Spirit is an inseparable companion of imputed righteousness, and immediately follows it, to dwell with whosoever it is bestowed upon. Now it is dwelling in us, principles us in all the powers of our souls with that which is righteousness in the habit and nature of it. Hence the fruits of the Spirit are called "the fruits of goodness and righteousness," as the fruits of a tree are called the fruit of that tree (Eph. 5:9).

And again, "He that doth righteousness is righteous," not only in our first sense, but even in this also. For who can do righteousness without he be principled so to do? Who can act reason that hath not reason? So, none can bring forth righteousness that hath not in him the root of righteousness, which is the Spirit of God. Which comes to us by virtue of our being made sons of God (1 John 2:19, 3:7; Gal. 4:5-7).

AUGUST 15

Root And Fruit Both Agree

You will recognize them by their fruits. Are grapes gathered from thornbushes, or figs from thistles?

MATTHEW 7:16

[Justification before God] ... comes to us before we do any act [that is] spiritually good. How can a man act righteous but from a principle of righteousness? And seeing this principle is not of or by nature but of and by grace through Christ it follows that as no man is just before God that is not covered with the righteousness of Christ. So, no man can do righteousness but by the power of the Spirit of God which must dwell in him. Hence, we are said through the Spirit to mortify the deeds of the body, which works are preparatory to fruitful actions. The husbandman ... must first be partaker of the fruit; he that worketh righteousness, must first be blessed with a principle of righteousness (2 Tim. 2:1-6). Men must have eyes before they see, tongues before they speak, and legs before they go; so, must a man be made habitually good and righteous before he can work righteousness.... God makes a man righteous by possessing him with a principle of righteousness; which principle is not of nature but of grace; not of man but of God.

The man in the text is practically righteous or one that declares himself by works that are good; a virtuous, a righteous man, even as the tree declares by the apple or plum it bears what manner of tree it is: "Ye shall know them by their fruits" (Matt. 7:16). Fruits show outwardly what the heart is principled with: show me then thy faith, which abides in the heart by thy works in a well spent life. Mark how the apostle words it, we being, said he, "made free from sin, and become servants to God, have our fruit unto holiness, and the end everlasting life" (Rom. 6:23).

AUGUST 16

According To His Mercy

[H]e saved us, not because of works done by us in righteousness, but according to his own mercy, by the washing of regeneration and renewal of the Holy Spirit.

TITUS 3:5

[F]irst we are made free from sin; now that is by being justified freely by the grace of God through the redemption which is in Jesus Christ. Whom God has set forth ... [as] a propitiation through faith in his blood. Now this is God's act, without any regard at all to any good that the sinner has or can accomplish; "not by works of righteousness which we have done, but according to his mercy" has he saved us (Titus 3:5; Rom. 3:24; 2 Tim. 1:9). Now, being made free from sin, what follows? We become the servants of God, by that turn which the Holy Ghost makes upon our heart when it reconciles it to the Word of God's grace. For that ... is the effect of the indwelling and operation of the Holy Ghost. Now having our hearts ... changed by God and his Word, the fruits of righteousness put forth themselves by us. For as when we were in the flesh, the motions of sin which is in our members did bring forth fruit unto death, so now, if we are in the Spirit and we are not in the flesh; the Spirit of Christ dwells in us, by the motions and workings of that we have our fruit unto holiness and the end everlasting life[; we are justified] (Rom. 8:6, 9).

But now by these fruits we are neither made righteous nor good; for the apple maketh not the tree good, it only declares it so to be. Here therefore all those are mistaken that think to be righteous by doing of righteous actions or good by doing good. A man must first be righteous, or he cannot do righteousness; to wit, that which is evangelically such.

AUGUST 17

By Faith Abel Offered

By faith Abel offered to God a more acceptable sacrifice than Cain, through which he was commended as righteous, God commending him by accepting his gifts. And through his faith though he died, he still speaks.

HEBREWS 11:4

How can a man without grace and the spirit of grace, do good; nature is defiled even to the mind and conscience; how then can good fruit come from such a stock (Titus 1:15)? Besides, God accepts not any work of a person which is not first accepted of him; "The Lord hath respect unto Abel and to his offering" (Gen. 4:4). To Abel first ... before ... [what] Abel offered. But how could God have respect to Abel—if Abel was not pleasing in his sight? And how could Abel be yet pleasing in his sight for the sake of his own righteousness, when it is plain that Abel had not yet done good works?

He was therefore first made acceptable in the sight of God, by and for the sake of that righteousness which God of his grace had put upon him to justification of life. Through and by which also the Holy Ghost in the graces of it dwelt in Abel's soul. Now Abel being justified and also possessed with this holy principle, he offers his sacrifice to God. Hence it is said that he offered "by faith," by the faith which he had precedent to his offering. For if through faith he offered, he had that faith before he offered; that is plain. Now his faith looked not for acceptance for the sake of what he offered, but for the sake of that righteousness which it did apprehend God had already put upon him and by which he was made righteous. Wherefore his offering was the offering of a righteous man, of a man made righteous first and so the text saith: "By faith Abel offered unto God a more excellent sacrifice than Cain, by which he obtained witness that he was righteous" (Heb. 11:4).

AUGUST 18

Submission to God's Righteousness

For, being ignorant of the righteousness of God, and seeking to establish their own, they did not submit to God's righteousness.
ROMANS 10:3

The want of understanding of ... [justification by faith] is that which keeps so many in a mist of darkness about the way of salvation. When they hear of the need they have of a righteousness to commend them to God that is, of that which God imputes to a man and that by which he counts him righteous; [they] have it not in their thoughts to accept ...[it] unto justification of life. But presently betake [journey] themselves to the law of works and fall to work there for the performing of a righteousness that they may be accepted of God for the same. So, submit not themselves to the righteousness of God by which ... the soul stands just before God (Rom. 10:1-3). It is necessary that this be distinctly laid down. That a man must be righteous first even before he doth righteousness. The argument is plain from the order of nature: "For a corrupt tree cannot bring forth good fruit," wherefore make the tree good, and so his fruit good; or the tree corrupt, and his fruit corrupt (Luke 6:43)....

It is manifest, that the person must be accepted before the duty performed can be pleasing unto God. And if the person must first be accepted, it is evident that the person must first be righteous. But if the person be righteous before he does good, then it follows that he is made righteous by righteousness that is none of his own. [So] ... he hath no hand in [it], further than to receive it as the gracious gift of God. Deny this, and it follows that God accepts men without respect to righteousness; and then what follows ... but that Christ is dead in vain?

AUGUST 19

The Righteous Do Righteousness

Herein is our love made perfect, that we may have boldness in the day of judgment: because as he is, so are we in this world.
1 JOHN 4:17 KJV

We must not ... be deceived, "He that doeth righteousness is righteous, even as he," the Lord, "is righteous" (1 John 3:7). He does not say he that doth righteousness shall be righteous as if his doing works would make him so before God. But he that does righteousness IS righteous, antecedent to his doing righteousness. And it must be thus understood, else that which follows signifies nothing. For he said, "He that doth righteousness is righteous, even as he," the Lord his God, "is righteous." But how is the Lord righteous? Even antecedent to his works. The Lord was righteous before he wrought righteousness in the world; and even so are we, to wit, every child of God. "As he is, so are we, in this world" (1 John 4:17).

But we must in this admit this difference; the Lord was eternally and essentially righteous before he did any work. But we are imputatively righteous, and made so by a second work of creation, before we do good works. It holds therefore only as to order; God was righteous before he made the world and we are righteous before we do good works. Therefore, we have described the righteous man:

First, he is one whom God makes righteous by reckoning or imputation.

Second, he is one that God makes righteous by possessing of him with a principle of righteousness. Third. He is one that is practically righteous. Nor dare I give a narrower description of a righteous man than this; nor otherwise than thus.

I dare not give a narrower description of a righteous man than this, because whoever pretends to justification, if he be not sanctified, pretends to what he is not.

AUGUST 20

The Desires Of The Righteous

... As a deer pants for flowing streams, so pants my soul for you, O God. My soul thirsts for God, for the living God. When shall I come and appear before God?

PSALM 42:1-2

For the first; desire in general may be thus described—They are the workings of the heart or mind after that of which the soul is persuaded that it is good to be enjoyed. This, I say, is so without respect to regulation. For we speak not now of good desires but of desires themselves even as they flow from the heart of a human creature. I say, desires are or may be called, the working of the heart after this or that; the strong motions of the mind unto it. Hence the love of women to their husbands is called "their desires" (Gen. 3:16). And the wife also is called "the desire of thine" [in] the husband's "eyes" (Ezek. 24:16). Also love to woman to make her one's wife is called by the name of "desire" (Deut. 21:10-11). Now, how strong the motions or passions of love are, who is there that is an utter stranger thereto? (Song 8:6-7).

Hunger is also a most vehement thing; and that which is called "hunger" in one place is called "desire" in another. And he desired "to be fed with the crumbs which fell from the rich man's table" (Luke 16:21; Ps. 145:16). Exceeding lusts are called "desires" to show the vehemency of desires (Ps. 106:14; 78:27-30). Longings, pantings, thirstings, prayers; if there be any life in them are all fruits of a desirous soul. Desires therefore flow from the consideration of the goodness, or profitableness, or pleasurableness of a thing. Yea, all desires flow from there. For a man desires not that about which he has had no consideration nor neither on which he has thought—if he does not judge it will yield him something worth desiring.

AUGUST 21

Lusts Of The Flesh

For all that is in the world—the desires of the flesh and the desires of the eyes and pride of life—is not from the Father but is from the world.

1 JOHN 2:16

When Eve saw that the forbidden fruit was a beautiful tree—though her sight deceived her—then she desired it. And [then] took ... herself and gave to her husband and he did eat. Yea, says the text, "when she saw that it was a tree to be desired, to make one wise, she took" (Gen. 3:6). Hence that which is called "coveting" in one place is called "desiring" in another. For desires are craving; and by desires a man seeks to enjoy what is not his (Exod. 20:17). From all these things, therefore we see what desire is. It is the working of the heart. After that which the soul is persuaded that it is good to be enjoyed; and of them there are these two effects.

One is—on a supposition that the soul is not satisfied with what it has—to cause the soul to range and hunt through the world for something that may fill up that vacancy. Yet the soul finds and would have supplied [it]. Hence desires are said to be wandering and the soul said to walk by them; "Better is the sight of the eyes than the wandering of the desire" or than the walking of the soul (Eccles. 6:8-9). Desires are hunting things and how many things some empty souls seek after ... as to the world and as to religion, who have desirous minds!

The second effect is: If desires are strong, they carry all away with them. They are all like Samson, they will pull down the gates of a city. But they will go out abroad; nothing can stop the current of desires but the enjoyment of the thing desired or a change of opinion as to the worth or want of worth of the thing that is desired.

AUGUST 22

The Desires Of The Righteous

The desires of the righteous ends only in good, the expectation of the wicked in wrath.

PROVERBS 11:23

We ... now come to ... [a] more particular thing: ... To show what are the desires of the righteous; that is that which the text calls us to the consideration of, because it saith, "The desire of the righteous shall be granted."

We have ... spoken of desires, as to the nature of them, without respect for them as good or bad. But now we shall speak to them as they are the effects of a sanctified mind, as they are the breathings, pantings, lustings, hungerings, and thirstings of a righteous man. The text says, "the desire of the righteous shall be granted," What then are the desires of the righteous? Now I will ... speak to their desires in general or with reference to them as to their bulk. Next, I will speak to them more particularly as they work this way and that.

For their desires in general, the same Solomon said, "The desire of the righteous shall be granted," said also, "The desire of the righteous is only good" (Prov. 11:23). This text gives us, in a general description of the desires of a righteous man and a sharp and smart description it is. For where, may some say, is then the righteous man or the man that hath none but good desires? And if it be answered they are good in the main or good in the general, yet that will seem to come short of an answer. For in that he said, "the desires of the righteous are only good," it is as much as to say, that a righteous man has none but good desires, or desires nothing but things that are good. I must labour to reconcile the experience of good men with this text [in the following readings].

AUGUST 23

The Flesh Lusts Against The Spirit

For the desires of the flesh are against the Spirit, and the desires of the Spirit are against the flesh, for these are opposed to each other, to keep you from doing the things you want to do.

GALATIANS 5:17

A righteous man is to be considered more generally ... [and] more strictly.

[First,] more generally, as he consists of the whole man, of flesh and spirit, of body and soul, of grace and nature; now consider him thus. And you can by no means reconcile the text with his experience, nor his experience with the text. For as he is body, flesh, and nature—for all these are with him, though he is a righteous man—so he has desires vastly different from those described by this text. Vastly differing from what is good. Yea, what is it not, that is naught, that the flesh and nature, even of a righteous man, will not desire? "Do ye think that the Scripture saith in vain, The spirit that dwelleth in us lusts to envy?" (James 4:5). And again, "In me, that is, in my flesh, dwelleth no good thing" (Rom. 7:18). And again, "The flesh lusts against the spirit" (Gal. 5:17). And again, the lusts thereof do "war against the soul" (1 Pet. 2:11).

From all these texts we find that a righteous man has other workings, lusts, and desires than such only that are good. Here then, if we consider of a righteous man thus generally, is no place of agreement betwixt him and this text. We must consider him, then, in the next place, more strictly, as he may and is to be distinguished from his flesh, his carnal lusts, and sinful nature.

AUGUST 24

Consent To The Law's Goodness

Now if I do what I do not want, I agree with the law, that it is good.

ROMANS 7:16

[Secondly and] more strictly ... a righteous man is [considered by his] SECOND CREATION. And so ... his desires are regarded as only good.

He is taken sometimes as to or for his best part, or as he is a second creation, as these Scriptures declare: "If any man be in Christ, he is a new creature—all things are become new" (2 Cor. 5:17). "Created in Christ Jesus" (Eph. 2:10). "Born of God" (John 3; 1 John 3:9). Become heavenly things, renewed after the image of him that created them. (See Col. 3:10; Heb. 9:23; etc.). By all which places, the sinful flesh, the old man, the law of sin, the outward man, all which are corrupt according to the deceitful lusts, are excluded. And so pared off from the man, as he is righteous; for his "delight in the law of God" is "after the inward man." And Paul himself was forced ... to distinguish of himself, before he could come to make a right judgment in this matter said, "That which I do, I allow not; what I would, do I not; but what I hate, that do I." See you not here how he cleaves [divides] himself in two, severing himself as he is spiritual, from himself as he is carnal. And [he] ascribes his motions to what is good to himself only as he is spiritual or the new man: "If then I do that which I would not, I consent to the law that it is good" (Rom. 7:16).

AUGUST 25

The Flesh Serves The Law Of Sin

I was once alive apart from the law, but when the commandment came, sin came alive and I died.

ROMANS 7:9

But I [believe] ... your consenting to what is good is not by that part which does what you would not. No, no, he says, that which does do what I would not. I disown and count it no part of sanctified Paul: "Now then it is no more I that do it, but sin that dwelleth in me; for—in me, that is, in my flesh, dwelleth no good thing: for to will is present with me; but how to perform that which is good, I find not: for the good that I would, I do not; but the evil which I would not, that I do: Now, if I do that I would not, it is no more I that do it, but sin that dwells in me" (Rom. 7:18-20). Thus, you see Paul is forced to make two men of himself saying; I and I; I do; I do not; I do[!] I would not do; what I hate, that I do. Now it cannot be the same I unto whom these contraries are applied. But his sinful flesh is one I, and his godly mind the other: And indeed, so he concludes it in this chapter, saying, "So then with the mind I myself serve the law of God, but with the flesh the law of sin."

Therefore, the Christian man must distinguish concerning himself; and doing so, he shall find, though he has flesh, and as he is such, he hath lusts contrary to God: Yet as he is a new creature, he allows not, but hates the motions and desires of the flesh, and consents to, and wills and delights in the law of God (Rom. 15:17-22). Yea, as a new creature, he can do nothing else.

AUGUST 26

Evil Is Always Present

So I find it to be a law that when I want to do right, evil lies close at hand.

Romans 7:21

As the righteous man must here be taken for the best part for the I[1] that would do good, for the I ... hates the evil. So again, we must consider of the desires of this righteous man as they flow from that fountain of grace which is the Holy Ghost within him. And as they are immediately mixed with [other] ... channels, in and through [which] they must pass before they can be put forth into acts. For though the desire, as to its birth and first being, is only good. Yet before it comes into much motion it gathers that from the defilements of the passages through which it comes as makes it to bear a tang of flesh and weakness in the skirts of it. And the evil that dwells in us is so universal and always so ready; that as sure as there is any motion to what is good, so sure evil is present with it: "[F]or when" or whenever "I would do good," Paul says, "evil is present with me" (Rom. 7:21). Hence it follows, that all our graces, and so our desires, receive disadvantage by our flesh; mixing itself with what is good and so abates the excellency of the good.

There is a spring that yields water good and clear but the channels through which this water comes to us are muddy, foul, or dirty. Now, of the channels the waters receive a disadvantage and so come to us as savouring of what came not with them from the fountain but from the channels. This is the cause of the coolness and of the weakness of flatness and of the many extravagancies that attend some of our desires.

---

1 See August 25 Devotional as segue to this reading. The "I" is the apostle Paul.

AUGUST 27

How To Perform Righteousness?

For I delight in the law of God, in my inner being.

ROMANS 7:22

You read in Solomon's Ecclesiastes of a time when desires fail for that "man goes to his long home" (Eccles. 12:5). And as to good desires, there is not one of them, when we are in our prime, but they fail also as to the perfecting of that which a man desires to do. "To will is present with me," Paul says, "but how to perform that which is good I find not" (Rom. 7:18). To will or to desire, that is present with me but when I have willed or desired to do, to perform is what I cannot attain to. But why not attain to a performance? Why, he asks, I find a law "in my members warring against the law of my mind." This law takes me prisoner and brings "me into captivity to the law of sin, which is in my members" (Rom. 7:23). Now, where things willed and desired meet with such obstructions, no marvel if our willing and desiring, though they set out lustily at the beginning, come yet lame home in conclusion.

There is a man, when he first prostrates himself before God, does it with desires as warm as fire coals. But erewhile [some time ago] he finds that the metal of those desires, were it not revived with fresh supplies would be quickly spent and grow cold. But the desire is good, and only good, as it comes from the breathing of the Spirit of God within us. We must therefore ... distinguish betwixt what is good and that which doth annoy it as gold is to be distinguished from the earth and dross that doth attend it. The man that believed desired to believe better, and so cries out, "Lord, help mine unbelief" (Mark 9:24).

AUGUST 28

Outward Desires: The Pulse Of The Inner Man

So, we do not lose heart. Though our outer self is wasting away, our inner self is being renewed day by day.

2 CORINTHIANS 4:16

There is another thing to be considered [about the inner struggle.] That is, the different frames that our inward man is in while we live as pilgrims in the world. A man, as he is not always well without so neither is he always well within. Our inward man is subject to transient though not to utter decays (Isa. 1:5). And ... when the outward man is sick, strength and stomach, and lust, or desire fails. So, it is when our inward man has caught a cold likewise (Ezek. 34:4).

The inward man I call the new creature, of which the Spirit of God is the support as my soul supports my body. But I say, this new man is not always well. He knows nothing ... [who] knows not this. Now being sick, things fail. As when a man is not in health of body, his pulse beats to declare that he is sick. So, when a man is not well within, his inward pulse, which are his desires—for I count the desires for the pulse of the inward man—they also declare that the man is not well within. They beat too little after God, weak and faintly after grace. They also have their halts, they beat not evenly, as when the soul is well, but to manifest all is not well there.

Yet "life is life," we say if there is a pulse, or breath, though breath scarce able to shake a feather, we cast not away all hope of life. Desires then, though they be weak are, notwithstanding, true desires. If they be the desires of the righteous thus described, and therefore are truly good, according to our text.

AUGUST 29

The Flesh Lusts Against The Spirit

For the desires of the flesh are against the Spirit, and the desires of the Spirit are against the flesh, for these are opposed to each other, to keep you from doing the things that you want to do.

GALATIANS 5:17

We read that the church of Sardis was under sore sickness, insomuch that some of her things were quite dead and they that were not so yet ready to die (Rev. 3:2). Yet "life is life," we say and if there is a pulse or breath though breath scarce able to shake a feather, we cast not away all hope of life. Desires then, though they be weak, are, notwithstanding true desires, if they are the desires of the righteous thus described. Therefore, are truly good, according to our text. David says he "opened his mouth and panted" for he longed for God's commandments (Ps. 119:131). This was a sickness, but not such a one as we have been speaking of. The spouse also cried out that she was "sick of love." Such sickness would do us good, for in it the pulse beats strongly well (Song 5:8).

There is not a Christian under heaven but has desires that run both ways, as is manifest from what hath been said already. Flesh will be flesh; grace shall not make it otherwise. By flesh I mean that body of sin and death that dwelleth in the godly (Rom. 6:6). As grace will act according to its nature, so sin will act according to the nature of sin (Eph. 2:3). Now, the flesh has desires, and the desires of the flesh and of the mind are both one in the ungodly; thank God it is not so in thee! (Rom. 7:24). The flesh I say, hath its desires in the godly. Hence it is said to lust enviously; it lusts against the Spirit; "The flesh lusts against the Spirit" (Gal. 5:17; Rom. 7:25).

AUGUST 30

Grace Trumps The Deeds Of The Flesh

Now the works of the flesh are evident: sexual immorality, impurity, sensuality, idolatry, sorcery, enmity, strife, jealousy, fits of anger, rivalries, dissentions, divisions, envy, drunkenness, orgies, and things like these.

GALATIAN 5:19-21

The works of the flesh are manifest; that is, more plainly discovered even in the godly than are the works of the Holy Ghost (Gal. 5:19). And this their manifestation arises from these following particulars:

1. We know the least appearance of a sin better by its native hue than we know a grace of the Spirit.

2. Sin is sooner felt in its bitterness to and upon a sanctified soul than is the grace of God. A little aloe will be tasted sooner than will much sweet though mixed with it.

3. Sin is dreadful and murderous in the sight of a sanctified soul: Wherefore the apprehending of that makes us often forget and often question whether we have any grace or no[t].

4. Grace lies deep in the hidden part but sin lies high, and floats above in the flesh; Wherefore it is easier, oftener seen than is the grace of God (Ps. 51:6). The little fishes swim on the top of the water, but the biggest and best keep down below and so are seldom seen.

5. Grace, as to quantity, seems less than sin. What is leaven or a grain of mustard seed to the bulky lump of a body of death (Matt. 13:31-33).

6. Sin is seen by its own darkness and in the light of the Spirit. But the Spirit itself neither discovers itself nor yet its graces by every glance of its own light.

7. A man may have the Spirit busily at work in him, he may also have many of his graces in their vigorous acts, and yet may be greatly ignorant of either. Wherefore we are not competent judges in this case. There may be a thousand acts of grace pass through your soul, and you are sensible of few, if any of them.

AUGUST 31

God's Love Is Shed Abroad In Our Hearts

... [H]ope does not put us to shame, because God's love has been poured into our hearts through the Holy Spirit who has been given to us.

ROMANS 5:5

Question: But since I have lusts and desires how shall I know to which my soul adheres?

Answer: These are how it may be known:

1. Which would you have prevail? The desires of the flesh or the lusts of the spirit; whose side are you on? Does not your soul now inwardly say and that with a strong indignation, "O let God, let grace, let my desires that are good, prevail against my flesh for Jesus Christ's sake?"

2. What kind of secret wishes do you have in your soul when you feel the lusts of your flesh rage? Do you not inwardly and with indignation against sin say, "O that I might never, never feel one such motion more? O that my soul was so full of grace, that there might be longer no room for ever for the least lust to come into my thoughts!"

3. What kind of thoughts do you have in yourself, now that you see these desires of yours that are good so briskly opposed by those that are bad? Do you not say, "O! I am the basest of creatures, I could even spew at myself[!] There is no man in all the world in my eyes so loathsome as myself. I abhor myself; a toad is not so vile as I am. O Lord, let me be anything but a sinner, anything, so thou subdue mine iniquities for me!"

4. How do you like the discovery of that which you think is grace in other men? Do you not cry out, "O, I bless them in my heart! O, methinks [I think] grace is the greatest beauty in the world! Yea, I could be content to live and die with those people that have the grace of God in their souls."

SEPTEMBER 1

Desire For God

My soul yearns for you in the night, my spirit within me earnestly seeks you. For when your judgments are in the earth the inhabitants of the world learn righteousness.

ISAIAH 26:9

And is it thus with your soul indeed? Happy man! It is grace that has your soul, though sin at present works in thy flesh. Yea, all these breathings are the very actings of grace; even of the grace of desire, of love, of humility, and of the fear of God within you. Be of good courage, you are on the right side. Your desires are only good; for that you have desired against your sin, your sinful self; which indeed is not yourself but sin that dwells in thee.

[Consider] The distinct or particular desires of the righteous.

I come ... to speak of desires more distinctly or particularly, as they work this way and that. First ... the desires of the righteous are either such as they would have accomplished here [while alive]; or, Second, such as they know they cannot come at the enjoyment of till after death.

[There are some] Desires that may be accomplished or enjoyed in this life.

For the first of these, the desires of the righteous are for such good things as they could have accomplished here. That is, in this world, while they are on this side glory. And they, in general, are comprised under these two general heads:

1. Communion with their God in spirit or spiritual communion with him.
2. The liberty of the enjoyment of his holy ordinances. And indeed, this second is, that they may both attain to and have the first maintained with them.

SEPTEMBER 2

Contrasting Desires

They say to God, "Depart from us! We do not desire the knowledge of your ways."

JOB 21:14

Now, to desire declares one already made righteous. For herein there appears a mind reconciled to God. Wherefore the wicked are set on the other side, even in that opposition to these; "[T]hey say unto God, depart from us, for we desire not the knowledge of thy ways" (Job 21:14). They neither love his presence nor to be frequenters of his ordinances. "What is the Almighty that we should serve him? and what profit should we have if we pray unto him?" (Job 21:15). So, again, speaking of the wicked, he said, "Ye have said it is vain to serve God, and what profit is it that we have kept his ordinance?" (Mal. 3:14). This, then, to desire truly to have communion with God, is the property of a righteous man, of a righteous man only. For this desire arises from a suitableness which is in the righteous unto God "Whom," said the Prophet, "have I in heaven but thee? and there is none upon earth that I desire beside thee" (Ps. 73:25). This could never be the desire of a man, were he not a righteous man, a man with a truly sanctified mind. "The carnal mind is enmity against God, for it is not subject to the law of God, neither indeed can be" (Rom. 8:7).

When Moses, the man of God, was with the children of Israel in the wilderness, he prays that God would give them his presence unto Canaan or else to let them die in that place. It was death to him to think of being in the wilderness without God! And he said unto God, "If thy presence go not with me, carry us not up hence [there]" (Exod. 33:14-15). Here then, are the desires of a righteous man—namely, after communion with God.

SEPTEMBER 3

Reasons For Righteous Desires

You make known to me the path of life; in your presence there is fullness of joy, at your right hand are pleasures forevermore.
PSALM 16:11

The reasons of these desires are many. In communion with God is life and favour. Yea, the very presence of God with a man is a token of it (Ps. 30:3-5). For by his presence he helps, succors [assists], relieves, and supports the hearts of his people and therefore is communion with him desired: "I will, David said, "behave myself wisely in a perfect way; O when wilt thou come unto me?" (Ps. 101:2). The pleasures that such a soul finds in God that has communion with him are surpassing all pleasures and delights; yea, infinitely surpassing them. "In thy presence is fullness of joy, at thy right hand there are pleasures for evermore" (Ps. 16:11). Upon this account ... [God] is called the desire of all nations—of all ...[the] nations that know him. Job desired God's presence, that he might reason with God. "Surely," he said, "I would speak to the Almighty, and I desire to reason with God" (Job 13:3). And again, "O that one would hear me! Behold my desire is that the Almighty would answer me" (Job 31:35). But why does Job thus desire to be in the presence of God! O! he knew that God was good, and that he would speak to him that which would do him good. "Will he plead against me with his great power? No: but he would put strength into me. There the righteous might dispute with him; so should I be delivered forever from my judge" (Job 23:6-7).

SEPTEMBER 4

In God's Presence Is Safety

What then shall we say to these things? If God is for us, who can be against us?

ROMANS 8:31

God's presence is the safety of a man. If God be with one, who can hurt one? As HE said, "If God be for us, who can be against us?" Now, if so much safety flows from God's being for one, how safe are we when God is with us? "The beloved of the Lord," Moses said, "shall dwell in safety by him, and the Lord shall cover him all the day long and he shall dwell between his shoulders" (Deut. 33:12). God's presence keeps the heart awake to joy and will make a man sing in the night (Job 35:10). "Can the children of the bridechamber mourn as long as the bridegroom is with them?" (Matt. 9:15). God's presence is feasting, and feasting is made for mirth (Rev. 3:20; Eccles. 10:19). God's presence keeps the heart tender and makes it ready to fall in with what is made known as duty or privilege (Isa. 64:1). "I will run the ways of thy commandments," the Psalmist said, "when thou shalt enlarge my heart" (Ps. 119:32). The presence of God makes a man affectionately and sincerely good. Yea, [and] makes him willing to be searched and stripped from all the remains of iniquity (Ps. 26:1-3).

SEPTEMBER 5

All Marvel In God's Presence

He said to them, "Where is your faith?" And they were afraid, and they marveled, saying to one another, "Who then is this, that he commands even winds and water, and they obey him?"
LUKE 8:25

What, what shall I say? God's presence is renewing, transforming, seasoning, sanctifying, commanding, sweetening, and enlightening to the soul! [There is] Nothing like it in all the world[!] His presence supplies all wants, heals all maladies, saves from all dangers; is life in death, heaven in hell; all in all. No marvel, then, if the presence of and communion with, God, is become the desire of a righteous man (Ps. 26:9). To conclude this, by the presence of God being with us, it is known to ourselves, and to others, what we are. "If thy presence," said Moses, "go not with me, carry us not up hence [from now on]. For wherein shall it be known here that I and thy people have found grace in thy sight, is it not in that thou goest with us? So shall we be separated, I and thy people, from all the people that are upon the face of the earth" (Exod. 33:15-16).

They are then best known to themselves. They know they are his people because God's presence is with them. Therefore, he saith, "My presence shall go with thee, and I will give thee rest" (Exod. 33:14). That is, [to] let you know that you have found grace in my sight and are accepted of me. For if God withdraws himself or hides his presence from his people, it is hard for them to bear up in the steadfast belief that they belong to him. "Be not silent to me," O Lord, David said, "lest I become like them that go down into the pit" (Ps. 28:1). "Be not silent unto me," that is, as he has it in another place, "Hide not thy face from me. Hear me speedily, O Lord," (Ps. 143:7).

SEPTEMBER 6

The Glory Of The Lord

Now the appearance of the glory of the LORD was like a devouring fire on the top of the mountain in the sight of the people of Israel.

EXODUS 24:17

[Because] ... the presence of God being with us we know ourselves to be the people of God. So, by this presence of God the world themselves are sometimes convinced who we are also.

Abimelech saw that God was with Abraham (Gen. 21:22). Thus, Pharaoh knew that God was with Joseph (Gen. 41:38). Saul "saw and knew that the Lord was with David" (1 Sam. 18:28). Saul's servant knew that the Lord was with Samuel (1 Sam. 9:6). Darius knew, also, that God was with Daniel. And when the enemy saw the boldness of Peter and John, "they took knowledge of them that they had been with Jesus" (Acts 4:13). There is a glory upon them that have God with them, a glory that sometimes glances and flashes out into the faces of those that behold the people of God (Acts 6:15).

The reason[s] are:

1. Such have with them the wisdom of God (2 Sam. 14:17-20).
2. Such, also, have special bowels [inner being, heart] and compassions of God for others.
3. Such have more of his majesty upon them than others (1 Sam. 16:4).
4. Such, their words, and ways, their ... [manner of life], are attended with that of God that others are destitute of (1 Sam. 3:19-20).
5. Such are holier and of more convincing lives in general than other people are (2 Kings 4:9). Now there is both comfort and honor in this. For what comfort like that of being a holy man of God? And what honor like that of being a holy man of God?

SEPTEMBER 7

The Place Of Blessing

... [I]n every place where I cause my name to be remembered I will come to you and bless you.

EXODUS 20:24

And "The Glory of the Lord"[1] ... leads me to the second thing, namely: The liberty of the enjoyment of his holy ordinances. For next to God himself, nothing is so dear to a righteous man as the enjoyment of his holy ordinances.

"One thing," said David, "have I desired of the Lord, that will I seek after." Namely, "that I may dwell in the house of the Lord all the days of my life, to behold the beauty of the Lord, and to inquire in his temple" (Ps. 27:4). The temple of the Lord was the dwelling-house of God. There he recorded his name and there he made known himself unto his people (Ps. 11:4). Wherefore this was the cause why David so earnestly desired to dwell there too: "To behold," saith he, "the beauty of the Lord, and to inquire in his temple." There ... [God] had promised his presence to his people. Yea, and to bring thither [there] a blessing for them; "In all places where I record my name, I will come unto thee, and I will bless thee" (Exod. 20:24). For this cause, therefore, as I said, it is why the righteous do so desire that they may enjoy the liberty of the ordinances and appointments of their God; To wit, that they may attain to and have communion maintained with him. Alas! the righteous are as it were undone, if God's ordinances be taken from them: "How amiable are thy tabernacles, O Lord of hosts. My soul longs, yea, even faints for the courts of the Lord, my heart, and my flesh cries out for the living God" (Ps. 84:1-2). Yea, and his heart and his flesh cried out for the God that dwelt in the temple at Jerusalem.

1 See yesterday's reading.

SEPTEMBER 8

A Doorkeeper In God's House

For a day in your courts is better than a thousand elsewhere. I would rather be a doorkeeper in the house of my God than to dwell in the tents of wickedness.

Psalm 84:10

Yea ... [the Psalmist's] words [seem] to envy the very birds that could more commonly frequent the temple than he: "The sparrow," saith he, "hath found a house and the swallow a nest for herself, where she may lay her young, even thine altars, O Lord of hosts, my King, and my God" (Ps. 84:3). And then blessed [are] all them that had the liberty of temple worship saying, "Blessed are they that dwell in thy house, they will be still praising thee" (Ps. 84:4). Then he cries up the happiness of those that in Zion do appear before God (Ps. 84:7). After this he cries out unto God, that he would grant him to be partaker of this high favour saying, "O Lord God of hosts, hear my prayer"[!] "For a day in thy courts is better than a thousand: I had rather be a doorkeeper in the house of my God than to dwell in the tents of wickedness" (Ps. 84:8-10).

But why is all this? What ails the man to express himself this way? Why, as I said, the temple was the great ordinance of God. This was, I say, the reason why the Psalmist chose out and desired this one thing. There were to be seen the shadows of things in the heavens; the candlestick, the table of shewbread, the holiest of all, where was the golden censer, the ark of the covenant overlaid roundabout with gold, the golden pot that had manna, Aaron's rod that budded, the tables of the covenant, and the cherubim of glory overshadowing the mercy-seat, which were all of them then things by which God showed himself merciful to them (Heb. 9:1-5; cf. Heb. 9:23, 8:5).

SEPTEMBER 9

Church Ordinances As Love Letters

... Do this in remembrance of me.

1 CORINTHIANS 11:24

Are [love letters] not desired between lovers? ... God's ordinances, they are his love-letters and his love-tokens. [Do not] marvel then if the righteous do so desire them: "More to be desired are they than gold, yea, than much fine gold; sweeter also than honey and the honeycomb" (Ps. 19:10, 119:72-127). Yea, this judgment wisdom itself passes upon these things. "Receive," he said, "my instruction, and not silver, and knowledge rather than choice gold. For wisdom is better than rubies: and all the things that may be desired, are not to be compared to it" (Prov. 8:10-11). For this cause therefore are the ordinances of God so much desired by the righteous. In them they meet with God; and by them they are built and nourished up to eternal life. "As newborn babes," says Peter, "desire the sincere milk of the word, that ye may grow thereby (1 Pet. 2:2). As milk is nourishing to children, so is the word heard, read, and meditated on, to the righteous. Therefore, it is their desire.

Christ made himself known to them in breaking of bread. Church fellowship/communion of saints is the place where the Son of God loves to walk. His first walking was in Eden, there he converted our first parents: "And come, my beloved," says he, "let us get up to the vineyards; let us see if the vines flourish, whether the tender grapes appear, and the pomegranates bud forth; there will I give thee my loves" (Song 7:12). Church fellowship is the glory of all the world. No place, no community, no fellowship, is adorned and bespangled with those beauties as is a church rightly knit together to their head and lovingly serving one another. "In his temple doth everyone speak of his glory" (Ps. 29:9).

SEPTEMBER 10

David's One Desire

One thing have I desired of the Lord, that will I seek after; That I may dwell in the house of the Lord all the days of my life, To behold the beauty of the Lord, and to inquire in his temple.

Psalm 27:4 KJV

No marvel then if this be the one thing that David desired, and that which he would seek after, namely, "to dwell in the house of the Lord all the days of his life." And this also shows you the reason why God's people of old used to venture so hardly for ordinances, and to get to them with the peril of their lives, "because of the sword of the wilderness" (Lam. 5:9).

They were their bread, they were their water, they were their milk, they were their honey. Hence the sanctuary was called "the desire of their eyes, and that which their soul pitieth, or the pity of their soul." They had rather have died than lost it, or than that it should have been burned down as it was (Ezek. 24:21, 25).

When the children of Israel had lost the ark, they count that the glory was departed from Israel. But when they had lost all, what a complaint made they then! "He hath violently taken away his tabernacles, as if it were of a garden, he hath destroyed his places of the assembly. The Lord hath caused the solemn feasts and sabbaths to be forgotten in Sion, and hath despised, in the indignation of his anger, the king and the priest" (Lam. 2:6). Wherefore, upon this account, it was that the church in those days counted the punishment of her iniquity greater than the punishment of Sodom (Lam. 4:6; 1 Sam. 4:22).

By these few hints you may perceive what is the "desire of the righteous." But this is spoken of with reference to things present, to things that the righteous desire to enjoy while they are here; communion with God while here; and his ordinances in their purity while here. I come, therefore, in the second place, to show you that the righteous have desires that reach further, desires that have so long a neck as to look into the world to come.

SEPTEMBER 11

Is Your Desire To See Christ?

I am hard pressed between the two. My desire is to depart and be with Christ, for that is far better.

PHILIPPIANS 1:23

[Let us consider one of the] desires that can only be accomplished or enjoyed [by God's people] in eternity.

Then the desires of the righteous are after that which yet they know cannot be enjoyed till after death. And those are comprehended under these two heads—

1. They desire that presence of their Lord which is personal.
2. They desire to be in that country where their Lord personally is, that heavenly country.

They desire that presence of their Lord which is personal. For the first of these, says Paul, "I have a desire to depart, and to be with Christ." Thus, you have it in Philippians 1:23, "I have a desire to be with Christ."

In ... [this] sort of desire, I told you that the righteous desired spiritual communion with God; and now I tell you they desire to be with Christ's person—"I have a desire to be with Christ." That is, with his person that I may enjoy his personal presence, such a presence of his as we are not capable to enjoy while here. Hence, he says, "I have a desire to depart, that I might be with him,." Knowing as he says in another place, "that whilst [while] we are at home in the body, we are" and cannot be, "absent from the Lord" (2 Cor. 5:6). Now this desire, as I said, is a desire that hath a long neck. For it can look over the brazen wall of this [world], quite into another world. And as it hath a long neck so it is very forcible and mighty in its operation.

SEPTEMBER 12

Take The Whole World But Give Me Jesus!

... But one thing I do: forgetting what lies behind and straining forward to what lies ahead.

PHILIPPIANS 3:13B

The desire [to see Christ] breeds a divorce, a complete divorce betwixt [between] the soul and all inordinate love and affections to relations. This desire makes a married man live as if he had no wife; a rich man lives as if he possessed not what he has (1 Cor. 7:29-30). This is a soul-sequestering desire. This desire makes a man willing rather to be absent from all enjoyments that he may be present with the Lord. This is a famous desire; none hath this desire but a righteous man. There ... [are those who] profess much love to Christ, yet never had such a desire in them all their life long. No, the relation they ... [had with] the world, together with those many flesh-pleasing accommodations with which they are surrounded; would never yet suffer such a desire to enter their hearts.

The strength of this desire is such that it is ready so far ... as it can, to dissolve that sweet knot of union that is betwixt body and soul. A knot more dear to a reasonable creature than can be which is betwixt wife and husband, parent and child, or a man and his estate. For even "all that a man hath will he give for his life" and to keep body and soul firmly knit together. But now, when this desire comes, this "silver cord is loosed"—is loosed by consent. This desire grants him that comes to dissolve this union leave to do it delightfully. "We are confident and willing rather to be absent from the body, and to be present with the Lord" (2 Cor. 5:8). Yea, this desire makes this flesh [even] this mortal life a burden. The man that has this desire exercises self-denial, while he waits till his desired change comes.

SEPTEMBER 13

The Desire To Depart

I am hard pressed between the two. My desire is to depart and be with Christ, for that is far better.

PHILIPPIANS 1:23

The strength of this desire shows itself in this. Namely, in that it is willing to grapple with the king of terrors [Satan] rather than to be detained from that sweet communion that the soul looks for when it comes into the place where its Lord is. Death is not to be desired for itself; the apostle chose rather to be clothed upon with his house which is from heaven, "that mortality might be swallowed up of life" (2 Cor. 5:1-4). Rather than he would be absent from the Lord, he was willing to be absent from the body. Death, in the very thoughts of it, is grievous to flesh and blood. And nothing can so master it in our apprehensions as that by which we attain to these desires. These desires do deal with death as Jacob's love to Rachel did deal with the seven long years he was to serve for her. It made them seem few, or but a little time. Now so, I say, do these desires deal with death itself. They make it seem little ... [not a servant but a privilege]. For ... [by it] a man may come to enjoy the presence of his beloved Lord. "I have a desire to depart," to go from the world and relations, to go from my body, that great piece of myself; I have a desire to venture the tugs and pains, and the harsh handling of the king of terrors, so I may be with Jesus Christ! These are desires of the righteous.

SEPTEMBER 14

Why Do The Righteous Desire To See Christ?

Beloved, we are God's children now, and what we will be has not yet appeared; but we know that when he appears we shall be like him, because we shall see him as he is.

1 JOHN 3:2

[I might also ask.] Why does the wife—that is, as the loving hind [doe]—love to be in the presence of her husband?

Christ in glory is worth ... [seeing]. If the man out of whom the Lord Jesus cast a legion [of demons] prayed that he might be with him; [with] all the trials that attended him in this life, how can it be but a righteous man must desire to be with him now he is in glory? What we have heard concerning the excellency of his person, the unspeakableness of his love, the greatness of his sufferings, and the things that he still is doing for us; [does he] need command our souls into a desire to be with him[?]

When we have heard of a man among us that has done for us some excellent thing, the ... thing that our hearts [long to have], I would set mine eyes upon him. But was ever heard the like to what Jesus Christ has done for sinners? Who then that has faith ... [in] him can do otherwise but desire to be with him? It was that which some time comforted John, that the time was coming that he should see him (1 John 3:2). But that consideration made him bray like a hart [stag], to hasten the time that he might set his eyes upon him quickly (Rev. 22:20). To see Jesus Christ, then, to see him as he is, to see him as he is in glory, is a sight that is worth going from relations, and out of the body, and through the jaws of death to see. For this is to see him head overall, to see him possessed of heaven for his church.

SEPTEMBER 15

A Personal Meditation

... I saw the LORD sitting upon a throne, high and lifted up; and the train of his robe filled the temple.

ISAIAH 6:1

Your eyes will behold the king in his beauty; they will see a land that stretches afar ...

ISAIAH 33:17

I have a desire to be with him, to see myself with him; this is more blessed still. For a man to see himself in glory, this is a sight worth seeing. Sometimes I look upon myself and say, "Where am I now?" and do quickly return answer to myself again, "Why, I am in an evil world, a great way from heaven; in a sinful body, among devils and wicked men; sometimes benighted, sometimes beguiled, sometimes fearing, sometimes hoping, sometimes breathing, sometimes dying, and the like." But then I turn the tables, and say, "But where shall I be shortly? Where shall I see myself anon [soon], after a few times more have passed over me? And when I can but answer this question thus—I shall see myself with Jesus Christ." This yields glory, even glory to one's spirit now: No marvel, then, if the righteous desire to be with Christ.

I have a desire to be with Christ. There, the spirits of the just are perfected; there the spirits of the righteous are as full as they can hold (Heb. 12:23). A sight of Jesus in the Word, some know how it will change them from glory to glory (2 Cor. 3:18). But how then shall we be changed and filled when we shall see him as he is? "When he shall appear, we shall be like him, for we shall see him as he is" (1 John 3:2). Moses and Elias appeared to Peter, and James, and John at the transfiguration of Christ, in glory. How so? Why, they had been in the heavens and came thence with some of the glories of heaven upon them[!]

SEPTEMBER 16

True Desires Come Forth

The earth produces by itself, first the blade, then the ear, then the full grain in the ear.

MARK 4:28

[Consider an objection.] But if this be the character of a righteous man, to desire to depart and to be with Christ, [one might say] I am none of them. For I never had such a desire in my heart. No, my fears of perishing will not suffer me either to desire to die to be with Christ nor that Christ should come to judge the world.

Though yours is a case that must be excepted for ... your desires may not yet be grown so great. Yet if you are a righteous man your heart has in it the very seeds required. There are therefore desires and desires to desire. As one child can reach so high and the other can but desire to do so. You, if you are a righteous man, you have desires. These desires [are] ready to put forth into act when they are grown a little stronger or when their impediment is removed. Many times it is with our desires as it is with saffron [flower], it will bloom and blossom, and be ripe and all in a night. Tell me, do you not desire to desire? Yea, do you not vehemently desire to desire to depart and to be with Christ? I know, if you are a righteous man, you do desire this. There is a man [who] sows his field with wheat, but as he sows soon it is covered with great clods. Now that grows as well as the rest, though it runs not upright yet. It grows and yet is kept down. So do your desires and when one shall remove the clod the blade will soon point upwards.

SEPTEMBER 17

A Godly Desire To Be With Christ

I am hard pressed between the two. My desire is to depart and be with Christ, for that is far better.

PHILIPPIANS 1:23

I know your mind; that which keeps you that you cannot yet arrive to this—to desire to depart and to be with Christ. [It] is because some strong doubt or clod of unbelief as to your eternal welfare lies hard upon your desiring spirit. Now let Jesus Christ remove this clod and your desires will quickly start up to be gone. I say, let Jesus Christ give you one kiss and with his lips as he kisses you whisper to you the forgiveness of your sins and you will quickly break out and say, "Nay Lord, let me die in peace since my soul is persuaded of thy salvation!"

There is a man upon the bed of languishing; but O! he dares not die. For all is not as he would have it betwixt God and his poor soul. And many a night he lies there in great horror of mind. But do you think that he does not desire to depart? Yes, he also waits and cries to God to set his desires at liberty. At last, the visitor comes and sets his soul at ease by persuading him that he belongs to God: and what then? "O! now let me die, welcome death!" Now he is like the man in Essex, who, when his neighbour at his bedside prayed for him, that God would restore him to health, started up in his bed, and pulled him by the arm, and cried out, "No, no, pray that God will take me away for to me it is best to go to Christ." He can and will cut the cord some time or other: And then you shalt be able to say, "I have a desire to depart, and to be with Jesus Christ."

SEPTEMBER 18

Heaven: A Person And A Place

For here we have no lasting city, but we seek the city that is to come.

Hebrews 13:14

Meantime, be earnest to desire to know your interest in the grace of God. For there is nothing short of the knowledge of that can make you desire to depart that you may be with Christ. This is what Paul laid as the ground of his desires to be gone: "We know," he said, "that if our earthly house of this tabernacle were dissolved, we have a building of God, a house not made with hands, eternal in the heavens. For in this we groan, earnestly desiring to be clothed upon with our house, which is from heaven" (2 Cor. 5:1-2). And know, that if your desires be right they will grow as other graces do, from strength to strength. Only in this they can grow no faster than faith grows as to justification and then hope grows as to glory. But ... [consider another] thing.

[Many] ... desire to be in that country where their Lord personally is. As the righteous men desire to be present with Jesus Christ, so they desire to be with him in that country where he is: "But now they desire a better country, that is, a heavenly; wherefore God is not ashamed to be called their God, for he hath prepared for them a city" (Heb. 11:14-16). "But now they desire a better country." Here is a comparison. There was another country, to wit, their native country, the country from where they came out, that in which they left their friends and their pleasures for the sake of another world, which, indeed, is a better country, as is manifest from its character. "It is heavenly." As high as heaven is above the earth, so much better is that country, which is heavenly, than is this in which now we are.

SEPTEMBER 19

God Prepares Them A City

For he [Abraham] was looking forward to the city that has foundations, whose designer and builder is God.

HEBREWS 11:10

[They desire a] heavenly country, where there is a heavenly Father (Matt. 6:14-16), a heavenly host (Luke 2:13), heavenly things (John 3:12), heavenly visions (Acts 26:19), heavenly places (Eph. 1:3, 20), a heavenly kingdom (2 Tim. 4:18), and the heavenly Jerusalem (Heb. 12:22), for them that are partakers of the heavenly calling (Heb. 3:1), and that are the heavenly things themselves (Heb. 9:23). This is a country to be desired and therefore no marvel if any, except those that have lost their wits and senses, refuse to choose themselves a habitation here.

Here is the "Mount Zion, the city of the living God, the heavenly Jerusalem, and an innumerable company of angels: here is the general assembly and church of the firstborn, and God the Judge of all, and Jesus, and the spirits of just men made perfect" (Heb. 12:22-24). Who would not be here? This is the country that the righteous desire for a habitation: "[B]ut now they desire a better country, that is, an heavenly; wherefore God is not ashamed to be called their God, for he hath prepared for them a city" (Heb. 11:16).

Mark [this], they desire a country and God [has] prepared for them a city. He goes beyond their desires, beyond their apprehensions, beyond all their hearts conceive to ask. There is none that is weary of this world from a gracious disposition that they have to a heavenly. But God will take notice of them, will own them, and not be ashamed to own them. Yea, such shall not lose their longing. They desire a handful; God gives them a seaful. They desire a country, God prepares for them a city—a city that is a heavenly; a city that has foundation, a city whose builder and maker is God.

SEPTEMBER 20

The Desire Of The Righteous Granted

What the wicked dreads will come upon him, but the desire of the righteous will be granted.

PROVERBS 10:24

We then ... come to inquire into *what is meant*, or to be understood, *by the granting of the righteous their desires*; "The desire of the righteous shall be granted."

First, to grant is to yield to what is desired, to consent that it shall be even so as is requested: "The Lord hear thee in the day of trouble, the name of the God of Jacob defend thee; send thee help from the sanctuary, and strengthen thee out of Zion, remember all thy—sacrifices: grant thee according to thine own heart and fulfil all thy counsel" (Ps. 20:1-4).

Scond, to grant is to accomplish what is promised: Thus, God granted to the Gentiles repentance unto life, namely, for that he had promised it by the prophets from the days of old (Acts 11:18; Rom. 15:9-12).

Third, to grant ... is an act of grace and condescending favour. For if God is said to humble himself when he beholds things in heaven, what condescension is it for him to hearken to a sinful wretch on earth and to tell him. Have the thing which you desire. A wretch, I call him, if compared to him that hears him though he is a righteous man, when considered as the new creation of God.

Fourth, to grant, then, is not to part with the thing desired, as if a desire merited, purchased, earned, or deserved it. But of bounty and goodwill, to bestow the thing desired upon the humble. Hence God's grants are said to be gracious ones (Ps. 119:29).

Fifth, I will add, that to grant is sometimes taken for giving one authority or power to do, or possess, or enjoy such and such privileges [as He deems].

SEPTEMBER 21

David's Desires Granted

Delight yourself in the LORD *and he will give you the desires of your heart.*

PSALM 37:4

[The Desire of the Righteous Granted] ... is acknowledged by David, where he said to God, "Thou hast given him his heart's desire, and hast not withholden the request of his lips" (Ps. 21:2). And this is promised unto all that delight themselves in God, "Delight thyself also in the Lord, and he shall give thee the desires of thy heart" (Ps. 37:4). And again, "He will fulfil the desire of them that fear him, he also will hear their cry, and will save them" (Ps. 145:19). By all these places it is plain, that the promise of granting desires is entailed to the righteous and that the grant to them is an act of grace and mercy. But it also follows, that though the desires of the righteous are not meritorious; yet they are pleasing in his sight; and this is manifest several ways, besides the promise of a grant of them.

SEPTEMBER 22

God Desires Men's Heart

Of David. To you, O Lord, I lift up my soul.

Psalm 25:1

God's desire is to the work of his hands and the righteous are for surrendering that up to him.

1. In giving up the heart unto him; "My son," says God, "give me thy heart" (Prov. 23:26). "I lift my soul to thee," says the righteous man (Ps. 25:1). There is an agreement between God and the righteous. God desires it, the righteous man desires it. Yea, he desires it with a groan saying, "Incline my heart unto thy testimony" (Ps. 119:36).

2. They are also agreed about the disposing of the whole man: God is for body, and soul, and spirit; and the righteous desires that God should have it all. Hence, they are said to give themselves to the Lord (2 Cor. 8:5) and to addict themselves to his service (1 Cor. 15:16).

3. God desires truth in the inward parts, that is, that truth may be at the bottom of all (Ps. 51:6, 16) and this is the desire of the righteous man likewise: "Thy word have I hid in my heart," said David, "that I might not sin against thee" (Ps. 119:11).

4. They agree in the way of justification, in the way of sanctification, in the way of preservation, and in the way of glorification. Wherefore, who should hinder the righteous man or keep him back from enjoying the desire of his heart?

5. They also agree about the sanctifying of God's name in the world, "Thy will be done on earth as it is in heaven." There is a great agreement between God and the righteous; "[H]e that is joined to the Lord is one spirit" (1 Cor. 6:17). No marvel, then, if their desires in the general, so far as the righteous man doth know the mind of his God.

SEPTEMBER 23

God Knows Our Hidden Desires

O Lord, all my longing is before you; my sighing is not hidden from you.

Psalm 38:9

The desires of the righteous are the life of all their prayers; and it is said, "The prayer of the upright is God's delight."

Jesus Christ put a difference betwixt the form and spirit that is in prayer and intimates the soul of prayer is in the desires of a man; "Therefore," saith he, "I say unto you, What things soever ye desire when ye pray, believe that ye receive them, and ye shall have them" (Mark 11:24). If a man prays never so long and has never so many brave expressions in prayer: Yet God counts it prayer no further than there are warm and fervent desires in it, after those things the mouth maketh mention of. David saith: "Lord, all my desire is before thee, and my groaning is not hid from thee" (Ps. 38:9). Can you say what you desire, when you pray? Or that your prayers come from the braying, panting, and longing of your hearts? If not, they shall not be granted: For God looks, when men are at prayer to see if their heart and spirit is in their prayers. For he counts all other but vain speaking. "You shall seek me and find me," says he, "when you shall search for me with all your heart" (Rom. 8:26-27; Matt. 6:7; Jer. 29:12). The people that you read of in 2 Chronicles 15 are there said to do what they did "with all their heart, and with all their soul." "For they sought God with their whole desire" (2 Chron. 15:11-15). When a man's desires put him upon prayer, run along with him in his prayer, break out of his heart and ascend up to heaven with his prayers, it is a good sign that he is a righteous man and that his desire shall be granted.

SEPTEMBER 24

O! What Does A Righteous Man Desire?

Whom have I in heaven but you? And there is nothing on earth that I desire besides you.

PSALM 73:25

By [his] desire a righteous man shows more of his mind for God than he can by any manner of way besides. Hence it is said, "The desire of man is his kindness, and a poor man," that is sincere in his desires, "is better than" he that with his mouth shows much love if he be "a liar" (Prov. 19:22).

Desires, desires, are copious things; you read that a man may "enlarge his desire as hell" (Hab. 2:5), that is, if they be wicked. Yea, and a righteous man may enlarge his desires as heaven (Ps. 73:25). No grace is so extensive as desires. Desires out-go [outdo] all. Who believes as he desires to believe and loves as he desires to love and fears as he desires to fear God's name? (Neh. 1:11). Might it be as a righteous man doth sometimes desire it should be, both with God's church, and with his own soul. Stranger things would be than there are; faith, and love, and holiness, would flourish more than it does! O! what does a righteous man desire? What do you think the prophet desired, when he said, "O that thou wouldest rend the heavens and—come down?" (Isa. 64:1). And Paul, when he said, he could wish that himself were accursed from Christ, for the vehement desire that he had that the Jews might be saved? (Rom. 9:1-3, 10:1). Yea, what do you think John desired, when he cried out to Christ to come quickly?

SEPTEMBER 25

Love To God Is Kindness To Him

Go and proclaim in the hearing of Jerusalem, Thus says the LORD, *"I remember the devotion of your youth, your love as a bride, how you followed me in the wilderness in a land not sown."*

JEREMIAH 2:2

Love to God ... is more seen in desires than in any Christian act. Do you think that the woman with her two mites cast in all that she desired to cast into the treasury of God? Or do you think when David said that he had prepared for the house of God with all his might, that his desires stinted [restricted] when his ability was at its utmost (1 Chron. 29)? No, no; desires go beyond all actions. Therefore, I said it is the desires of a man that are reckoned for his kindness. Kindness is that which God will not forget. I mean the kindness which his people show to him, especially in their desires to serve him in the world. When Israel was come out of Egypt, you know how many stumbles they had before they got to Canaan.

But forasmuch as they were willing or desirous to follow God, he passes by all their failures, saying, "I remember thee," and that almost a thousand years after, "the kindness of thy youth, the love of thine espousals, when thou wentest after me in the wilderness, in a land that was not sown" (Jer. 2:2). Israel was holiness to the Lord and the first fruits of his increase. There is nothing that God likes of ours better than he likes our true desires. For indeed true desires they are the smoke of our incense, the flower of our graces, and the very vital part of our new man. They are our desires that ascend, and they that are the sweet of all the sacrifices that we offer to God. The man of desires is the man of kindness.

SEPTEMBER 26

Our Desires Carry Us Along

For he grew up before him like a young plant, and like a root out of dry ground; he had no form or majesty that we should look at him, no beauty that we should desire him.

ISAIAH 53:2

All convictions, conversions, illuminations, favours, tastes, revelations, knowledge, and mercies will do nothing if the soul abides without desires. All is but like rain upon stones or favours bestowed upon a dead dog. O! but a poor man with desires, a man that sees but little, that knows but little, that finds in himself but little; if he has but strong desires they will supply all. His desires take him up from his sins, from his companions, from his pleasures and carry him away to God. Suppose you were a minister and were sent from God with a whip, whose cords were made of the flames of hell. You might lash long enough before you could so much as drive one man that abides without desires to God. Or [drive him] to his kingdom by that you could with a whip. Suppose again that you were a minister and were sent from God to sinners with a crown of glory in your hand, to offer to him that first comes to you for it. Yet none can come without desire. What is the reason that men will with mouth commend God, and commend Christ, and commend and praise both heaven and glory[?] And yet all the while fly from him and from his mercy, as from the worst of enemies? Why, they . . . [require] good desires; their desires being mischievous, carry them another way. You entreat your wife, your husband, and the son of your womb, to fall in with your Lord and your Christ, but they will not. Ask them the reason why they will not, and they know none, only they have no desires. "When we shall see him, there is no beauty in him that we should desire him" (Isa. 53:1-3).

SEPTEMBER 27

Faith Begets Desires

But as it is, they desire a better country, that is, a heavenly one. Therefore, God is not ashamed to be called their God, for he has prepared for them a city.

HEBREWS 11:16

But now, desires, desires that are right, will carry a man quite away to God and to do his will, let the work be never so hard. Take an instance or two for this:

You may see it in Abraham, Isaac, and Jacob. The text says plainly, they were not mindful of that country from whence they came out, through their desires of a better (Heb. 11:8-16). God gave them intimation of a better country and their minds did cleave to it with desires of it; and what then? Why, they went forth and desired to go, though they did not know whither [where] they went. Yea, they all sojourned in the land of promise because it was but a shadow of what was designed for them by God. Wherefore they also cast that behind their back, looking for that city that had foundations, of which mention was made before. Had not now these men desires that were mighty? It was their desires that thus separated them from their dearest and choice relations and enjoyments.

You may see it in Moses, who had a kingdom at his foot and was the alone visible heir thereof. But desire of a better inheritance made him refuse it and choose rather to take part with the people of God in their afflicted condition than to enjoy the pleasures of sin for a season. You may say the Scripture attributes this to his faith. I answer, so it is attributed to Abraham's faith his leaving of his country. But his faith begat in him these desires after the country that is above. So indeed, Moses saw these things by faith; and therefore, his faith begat in him these desires. For it was because of his desires that he did refuse and did choose as you read.

SEPTEMBER 28

Desire To Partake Of A Better Resurrection

And he said to them, "I have earnestly desired to eat this Passover with you before I suffer."

LUKE 22:15

The women also ... [that we read] and others that would not, upon unworthy terms, accept ... deliverance from torments and sundry trials, that they might or because they had a desire to be made partakers of a better resurrection. "And others," saith he, "had trial of cruel mockings and scourgings; yea, moreover, of bonds and imprisonments. They were stoned, they were sawn asunder, were tempted, were slain with the sword; they wandered about in sheep skins, and goat skins, being destitute, afflicted, tormented; of whom the world was not worthy. They wandered in deserts, and in mountains, and caves of the earth" (Heb. 11:35-38).

But we will come to the Lord Jesus himself. Whither did his desires bring him? Whither did they carry him? And to what did they make him stoop? For they were his desires after us and after our good, that made him humble himself to do as he did (Song 7:10). What was it, do you think, that made him cry out: "I have a baptism to be baptized with, and how am I straitened till it be accomplished"! (Luke 12:50). What was that baptism but his death? And why did he so long for it but of desire to do us good? Yea, his desires to suffer for his people made him go with more strength to lay down his life for them than they, for want of them, had to go to see him suffer. And they were in their way going up to Jerusalem, he to suffer, and they to look on, "And Jesus went before them, and they were amazed, and as they followed, they were afraid" (Mark 10:32; Matt. 20:17).

SEPTEMBER 29

The Desire Of The Wicked Will Perish

The wicked man sees it and is angry; he gnashes his teeth and melts away; the desire of the wicked will perish!

PSALM 112:10

You have heard what hath been said of desires [to this point] and what pleasing things right desires are unto God. But you must know that they are the desires of his people of the righteous, that are so. No wicked man's desires are regarded (Ps. 112:10). These men must be informed of [them] lest their desires become a snare to their souls. You read of a man whose "desire killeth him" (Prov. 21:25).

The natural man desires to be saved and to go to heaven when he dies. Ask any natural man and he will tell you so. Besides, we see it is so with them, especially in certain seasons. As when some guilt or conviction for sin takes hold upon them or when some sudden fear terrifies them. [Or] when they are afraid that the plague or pestilence will come upon them and break up house-keeping for them. Or when death has taken them by the throat and is hauling them downstairs to the grave. Then, O then, "Lord, save me, Lord, have mercy upon me; good people, pray for me! O! whither [where] shall I go when I die, if sweet Christ has not pity for my soul?" And now the bed shakes and the poor soul is loath [hate] to go out of the body for fear the devil should catch it. As the poor bird is to go out of the bush, while it sees the hawk waits there to receive her. But the fears of the wicked must come upon the wicked. They are the desires of the righteous that must be granted. Pray, take good notice of this. And to back this with the authority of God, consider that Scripture, "The wicked man travaileth with pain all his days, and the number of years is hidden to the oppressor."

SEPTEMBER 30

One's Wicked Desires Take Him Away

Then they will call upon me, but I will not answer; they will seek me diligently but will not find me.

PROVERBS 1:28

Can it be imagined that when the wicked [or hypocrite is] ... in this distress but that they will desire to be saved? There is the hypocrite's desire. Now his desire seems to have life and spirit in it. Also, he desires, in his youth, his health, and the like; yet it comes to naught. You shall see him drawn to life in Mark 10:17. He comes running and kneeling and asking and that, as I said, in youth and health and that is more than men merely natural do. But all to no purpose. He went as he came, without the thing desired. The conditions propounded were too hard for this hypocrite to comply withal (Mark 10:21-22). Some indeed make a great noise with their desires over some again do. But in conclusion all comes to one, they meet there where they go whose desires are not granted.

"For what is the hope of the hypocrite, though he has gained" to a higher strain of desires, "when God taketh away his soul?" [For,] "Will God hear his cry when trouble cometh upon him?" (Job 27:8-9). Did he not, even when he desired life, yet break with God in the day when conditions of life were propounded to him? Did he not, even when he asked what good things were to be done that, he might have eternal life, refuse to hear or to comply with what was propounded to him? How then can his desires be granted, who himself refused to have them answered? No marvel then if he perishes like his own dung, if they that have seen him shall say they miss him among those that are to have their desires granted.

OCTOBER 1

A Great High Priest

For every high priest chosen from among men is appointed to act on behalf of men in relation to God, to offer gifts and sacrifices for sins.

HEBREWS 5:1

First, I begin, then, with the first; that is, to show you what intercession is. Intercession is prayer; but all prayer is not intercession. Intercession then, is that prayer that is made by a third person about the concerns that are between two. And it may be made either to set them at further difference or to make them friends. For intercession may be made against as well as for a person or people. "Wot ye not [do you not know] what the Scripture saith of Elias? how he maketh intercession to God against Israel." (Rom. 11:2) But the intercession that we are now to speak of is not an intercession of this kind, not an intercession against but an intercession for a people. "He ever lives to make intercession for them." The high priest is ordained for, but not to be against the people. "Every high priest taken from among men is ordained for men in things pertaining to God," to make reconciliation for the sins of the people; or "that he may offer both gifts and sacrifices for sins" (Heb. 5:1). This, then, is intercession; and the intercession of Christ is to be between two, between God and man for man's good. And it extends itself unto these:

1. To pray that the elect may be brought all home to him; that is, to God.
2. To pray that their sins committed after conversion may be forgiven them.
3. To pray that their graces which they receive at conversion may be maintained and supplied.
4. To pray that their persons may be preserved unto his heavenly kingdom.

OCTOBER 2

Christ Our Ransom

For even the Son of Man came not to be served but to serve, and to give his life as a ransom for many.

MARK 10:45

[Christ] ... prays for all the elect, that they may be brought home to God and so into the unity of the faith [for] ... he said, "Neither pray I for these alone." That is, for those only that are converted: "But for them also which shall believe on me through their word." For all them that shall, that are appointed to believe; or as you have it a little above, "for them which thou hast given me." (John 17:9, 20; Isa. 53:12) And the reason is, for ... he hath paid a ransom for them. Christ, therefore, when he maketh intercession for the ungodly and all the unconverted elect are such; doth [as a] petitionary ask for his own, his purchased ones, those for whom he died. That they might be saved by his blood.

When any of them are brought home to God, he yet prays for them. Namely, that the sins which through infirmity they, after conversion, may commit, may also be forgiven them.

This is showed us by the intercession of the high priest under the law; that was to bear away the iniquities of the holy things of the children of Israel. Yea, and by his atonement for them that sinned. For it said, "And the priest shall make an atonement for him, for his sin which he hath sinned, and it shall be forgiven him" (Lev. 5:10). This also is intimated even where our Lord doth make intercession, saying, "I pray not that thou shouldest take them out of the world, but that thou shouldest keep them from the evil" (John 17:15).

OCTOBER 3

Grace For Grace

For the law was given through Moses; grace and truth came through Jesus Christ.

JOHN 1:17

In ... [Christ's] intercession he prays also that those graces which we receive at conversion may be maintained and supplied. This is clear where he saith, "Simon, Simon, behold, Satan hath desired to have you, that he may sift you as wheat; but I have prayed for thee, that thy faith fail not." (Luke 22:31-32) Aye, may some say, he is said to pray here for the support and supply of faith. But does it therefore follow that he prayed for the maintaining and supply of all our graces? Yes, in that he prayed for the preservation of our faith, he prayed for the preservation of all our graces. For faith is the mother grace, the root grace, the grace that hath all others in the bowels [heart] of it. And that from which all others flow. Yea, it is that which gives being to all our other graces and that by which all the rest do live. Let, then, faith be preserved, and all graces continue and live—that is, according to the present state, health, and degree of faith. So, Christ prayed for the preservation of every grace when he prayed for the preservation of faith. That text ... [continues], "Keep through thine own name those whom thou hast given me" (John 17:11). Keep them in thy fear, in the faith, in the true religion, in the way of life by thy grace, by thy power, by thy wisdom.

He also in his intercession prays that our persons be preserved and brought safe unto his heavenly kingdom. And this he does,

1. By pleading interest in them.
2. By pleading that he had given, by promise, glory to them.
3. By pleading his own resolution to have it so.
4. By pleading the reason why it must be so.

OCTOBER 4

Christ's Pleas

I have manifested your name to the people whom you gave me out of the world. Yours they were, and you gave them to me, and they have kept your word.

JOHN 17:6

[Christ] ... prays that their persons may come to glory, for that they are his and that by the best of titles: "Thine they were, and thou gavest them me" (John 17:6). Father, I will have them; Father, I will have them, for they are mine: "Thine they were, and thou gavest them me." What is mine, my wife or my child or my jewel or my joy; sure, I may have it with me. Thus, therefore, he pleads or cries in his intercession, that our persons might be preserved to glory: They are mine, and thou gave them [to] me.

He also pleads that he had given—given already, that is, in the promise—glory to them. Therefore, they must not go without it. "And the glory which thou gavest me I have given them" (John 17:22). Righteous men, when they give a good thing by promise, they design the performance of that promise. [No] ... they more than design it, they purpose, they determine it. As the mad prophet also said of God, "Hath he said and shall he not do it? Or hath he spoken, and shall he not make it good?" (Num. 23:19). Hath Christ given us glory and shall we not have it? Yea, hath the truth [Christ himself] ... bestowed it upon us. And shall those to whom it is given, even given by Scripture of truth, be yet deprived thereof?

He pleads in his interceding that they might have glory, his own resolution to have it so. "Father, I will that they also, whom thou hast given me, be with me where I am" (John 17:24). Behold you here, he is resolved to have it so. It must be so. It shall be so. I will have it so!

OCTOBER 5

Jesus Prays For His Disciples Joy To Be Full

Father, I desire that they also, whom you have given me, may be with me where I am, to see my glory that you have given me because you loved me before the foundation of the world.

JOHN 17:24

[Jesus] ... also ... in this his intercession, urges a reason why he will have it so, namely, "That they may behold my glory, which thou hast given me; for thou lovedst me before the foundation of the world" (v. 24). And this is a reason to the purpose; it is as if he had said, Father: These have continued with me in my temptations; these have seen me under all my disadvantages; these have seen me in my poor, low, contemptible condition; these have seen what scorn, reproach, slanders, and disgrace I have borne for thy sake in the world. And now I will have them also be where they shall see me in my glory. I have told them that I am thy Son and they have believed that. I have told them that you love me and they have believed that. I have also told them that you would take me again to glory and they have believed that. But they have not seen my glory nor can they but be like the Queen of Sheba. They will but believe by the halves unless their own eyes do behold it. Besides, Father, these are they that love me and it will be an increase of their joy if they may but see me in glory. It will be as a heaven to their hearts to see their Saviour in glory. I will, therefore, that those which "thou hast given me be with me where I am, that they may behold my glory." This, therefore, is a reason why Christ Jesus our Lord intercedes to have his people with him in glory.

OCTOBER 6

Christ Prays As High Priest

Consequently, he is able to save to the uttermost those who draw near to God through him, since he always lives to make intercession for them.

HEBREWS 7:25

I come now to ... [another] thing, namely, to show you what is to be inferred from Christ's making intercession for us.

This is to be inferred from hence, that saints—for I will here say nothing of those of the elect uncalled—do ofttimes give occasion of offense to God, even [after] they that have received grace. For intercession is made to continue one in the favor of another and to make up those breaches that at any time shall happen. [They occur] to be made by one to the alienating of the affections of the other. And thus, he makes reconciliation for iniquity; for reconciliation may be made for iniquity two ways. First, by paying of a price, secondly, by insisting upon the price paid for the offender by way of intercession. Therefore you read that as the goat was to be killed, so his blood was, by the priest, to be brought within the veil, and in a way of intercession, to be sprinkled before and upon the mercy-seat: "Then shall he kill the goat of the sin-offering, that is, for the people, and bring his blood within the veil, and do with that blood as he did with the blood of the bullock, and sprinkle it upon the mercy-seat, and before the mercy-seat; and he shall make an atonement for the holy place, because of the uncleanness of the children of Israel, and because of their transgressions in all their sins: and so shall he do for the tabernacle of the congregation that remaineth among them, in the midst of their uncleanness" (Lev. 16:15-16). This was to be done, as you see, that the tabernacle, which was the place of God's presence and graces, might yet remain among the children of Israel, notwithstanding their uncleannesses and transgressions.

OCTOBER 7

Christ: Our Mediator And Intercessor

... Jesus, the mediator of a new covenant, and to the sprinkled blood that speaks a better word than the blood of Abel.
HEBREWS 12:24

By Christ's intercession I gather, that awakened men and women such as the godly are, dare not, after offense given, come in their own names to make unto God an application for mercy. God, in himself, is a consuming fire and sin has made the best of us as stubble is to fire. Wherefore, they may not, they cannot, they dare not approach God's presence for help but by and through a mediator and intercessor.

When Israel saw the fire, the blackness and darkness, and heard the thunder, and lightning, and the terrible sound of the trumpet, "they said unto Moses, Speak thou with us, and we will hear: but let not God speak with us, lest we die" (Exod. 20:19; Deut. 18:16). Guilt and sense of the disparity that is betwixt [between] God and us will make us look out for a man that may lay his hand upon us both and that may set us right in the eyes of our Father again. This ... I infer from the intercession of Christ. For, if there had been a possibility of our ability to have approached God with advantage without, what need had there been of the intercession of Christ?

Absalom did not approach—no, not the presence of his father—by himself, without a mediator and intercessor. Wherefore, he sends to Joab to go to the king and make intercession for him. Also, Joab did not go upon that errand himself but by the mediation of another. Sin is a fearful thing; it will quash and quail the courage of a man and make him afraid to approach the presence of him whom he has offended though the offended is but a man.

OCTOBER 8

Job: An Intercessor Like Christ

And the L*ORD restored the fortunes of Job when he had prayed for his friends. And the* L*ORD gave Job twice as much as he had before.*

JOB 42:10

It [can be inferred] ... that should we, out of an ignorant boldness and presumption, attempt, when we have offended, by ourselves to approach the presence of God, God would not accept us. He told Eliphaz so. What Eliphaz thought, or was about to do, I know not. But God said unto him, "My wrath is kindled against thee, and against thy two friends; for ye have not spoken of me the thing that is right, as my servant Job hath. Therefore take unto you now seven bullocks, and seven rams, and go to my servant Job, and offer up for yourselves [that is, by him] a burnt-offering, and my servant Job shall pray for you; for him will I accept; lest I deal with you after your folly, in that ye have not spoken of me the thing which is right, like my servant Job." See here, an offense is a bar and an obstruction to acceptance with God, but by a mediator, but by an intercessor. He that comes to God by himself, God will answer him by himself—that is, without an intercessor: I will tell you; such are not like to get any pleasant [response]. I will answer him that so cometh according to the multitude of his idols. "And I will set my face against that man, and will make him a sign and a proverb, and I will cut him off from the midst of my people; and ye shall know that I am the Lord" (Ezek. 14:7-8).

He that intercedes ... with a holy and just God had need be clean himself, lest he with whom he so busies himself say to him: First clear thyself, and then come and speak for thy friend. Wherefore, this is the very description and qualification of this our High Priest and blessed intercessor.

OCTOBER 9

Christ As Our Intercessor

For every high priest is appointed to offer gifts and sacrifices; thus it is necessary for this priest also to have something to offer.
HEBREWS 8:3

Since Christ is an intercessor, he has ... [means] in readiness to answer to any demands that may be propounded by him that hath been by us offended. To a renewing of peace and letting out of that grace to us that we have sinned away and yet have need of. Well, you come to me about this man. What interest he has in you is one thing, what offense he has committed against me is another. I speak now after the manner of men. Now, what can an intercessor do if he is not able to answer this question? But now, if he can answer this question—that is, according to law and justice, no question but he may prevail with the offended for him for whom he makes intercession.

Why this is our case; we have offended a just and a holy God and Jesus Christ is become intercessor. He also knows full well, that for our parts, if it would save us from hell, we cannot produce towards a peace with God so much as poor two farthings; that is, not anything that can by law and justice be esteemed worth a halfpenny; yet he makes intercession. "Every high priest is ordained to offer gifts and sacrifices: wherefore it is of necessity that this man have somewhat also to offer." (Heb. 8:3); "For if he were on earth, he should not be a priest." (v. 4) These gifts, therefore, and this sacrifice, he now offereth in heaven by way of intercession, urging and pleading as an intercessor, the valuableness of his gifts for the pacifying of that wrath that our Father hath conceived against us for the disobediences that we are guilty of. "A gift in secret pacifieth anger; and a reward in the bosom strong wrath" (Prov. 21:14).

OCTOBER 10

Our Ransom Is Our Intercessor

Who gave himself a ransom for all, which is the testimony given at the proper time.

1 TIMOTHY 2:6

Since Christ is an intercessor ... believers should not rest at the cross for comfort [or] justification they should look for there. But, being justified by his blood, they should ascend up after him to the throne. At the cross you will see him in his sorrows and humiliations, in his tears and blood. But follow him to where he is now and then you shall see him in his robes, in his priestly robes, and with his golden girdle about his paps [chest]. Then you shall see him wearing the breastplate of judgment and with all your names written upon his heart. Then you shall perceive that the whole family in heaven and earth is named by him and how he prevailed with God the Father of mercies—for you.

What gifts these are the Scripture everywhere testifies. He gave himself; he gave his life, he gave his all for us. (John 6, Gal. 1:4, 1 Tim. 2:6, Matt. 20:28) These gifts, as he offered them up at the demand of justice on Mount Calvary for us, so now he is in heaven he presents them continually before God as gifts and sacrifice valuable for the sins. For all the sins that we, through infirmity, do commit, from the day of our conversion to the day of our death. And these gifts are so satisfactory, so prevalent with God, that they always prevail for a continual remission of our sins with him. Yea, they prevail with him for more than for the remission of sins. We have, through their procurement, our graces often renewed, the devil often rebuked, the snare often broken, guilt often taken away from the conscience and many a blessed smile from God and love-look from his life-creating countenance (Eph. 3:12).

OCTOBER 11

The Justified Freed To Serve God

But now that you have been set free from sin and have become slaves of God, the fruit you get leads to sanctification and its end, eternal life.

ROMANS 6:22

What it is to be saved, namely, in a way ... [it is] justification. ... To be saved is to be delivered from guilt of sin that is by the law as it is the ministration of death and condemnation. Or to be set free therefrom before God. This is to be saved; for he that is not set free therefrom, whatever he may think of himself, or whatever others may think concerning him, he is a condemned man. It said not, he shall be but he is condemned already. (John 3:18) The reason is, for that he has deserved the sentence of the ministration of condemnation, which is the law. Yea, that law has already arraigned, accused, and condemned him before God for that it hath found him guilty of sin. Now he that is set free from this, or, as the phrase is, "being made free from sin" (Rom. 6:22); that is, from the imputation of guilt, there can, to him, be no condemnation, no condemnation to hell fire. But the person thus made free may properly be said to be saved. Wherefore, as sometimes it [is] said, we shall be saved, respecting saving in the second sense or the utmost completing of salvation. So ... [the Scripture] says, we are saved, as respecting our being already secured from guilt and so from condemnation to hell for sin. And so set safe and quit from the second death before God (1 Cor. 1:18; Eph. 2:5).

Now, saving thus comes to us by what Christ did for us in this world, by what Christ did for us as suffering for us. I say, it comes to us; thus, that is, it comes to us by grace through the redemption that is in Christ (1 Cor. 15:1-4, Rom. 5:8-10).

OCTOBER 12

Saved By His Life

For if while we were enemies we were reconciled to God by the death of his Son, much more, now that we are reconciled, shall we be saved by his life.

ROMANS 5:10

To be saved is called justification, justification to life. Because one thus saved [is] acquitted from guilt and that everlasting damnation to which for sin he had made himself obnoxious by the law (1 Cor. 15:1-4; Rom. 5:8-10).

Hence, we are said to be saved by his death, justified by his blood, and reconciled to God by the death of his Son. All which must respect his offering of himself on the day he died and not his improving of his so dying in a way of intercession. Because in the same place the apostle reserves a second or an additional salvation and applies that to his intercession: "Much more then, being now," or already, "justified by his blood, we shall be saved from wrath through him." That is, through what he will further do for us. "For if, when we were enemies, we were reconciled to God by the death of his Son, much more, being reconciled." That is, by his death, "we shall be saved by his life," his intercession which he ever lives so to complete (v. 9-10).

See here, we are said to be justified, reconciled already, and therefore we shall be saved, justified by his blood and death. And [we are] saved through him by his life. Now the saving intended in the text is saving in this second sense. That is, saving us by preserving us, by delivering of us from all those hazards that we run between our state of justification and our state of glorification.

OCTOBER 13

Christ: Ever Alive To Intercede

Consequently, he is able to save to the uttermost those who draw near to God through him, since he always lives to make intercession for them.

HEBREWS 7:25

Now the saving intended in the text is saving in ... [another] sense. That is, a saving of us by preserving us, by delivering of us from all those hazards that we run betwixt our state of justification and our state of glorification. Yea, such a saving of us as we that are justified need to bring us into glory.

When he saith he is able to save, seeing he ever lives to make intercession, he added saving to saving. Saving by his life to saving by his death; saving by his improving of his blood to saving by his spilling of his blood. He gave himself a ransom for us and now improves that gift in the presence of God by way of intercession. The high priests under the law took the blood of the sacrifices that were offered for sin and brought it within the veil. And there sprinkled it before and upon the mercy-seat and by it made intercession for the people to an additional way of saving them, the sum of which Paul thus applies to Christ when he saith, "He can save, seeing he ever liveth to make intercession."

That also in the Romans is clear to this purpose, "Who is he that condemneth? It is Christ that died" (Rom. 8:31-39). That is, who is he that shall lay anything to the charge of God's elect to condemnation to hell, since Christ has taken away the curse by his death from before God? Then he adds that there is nothing that shall yet happen to us, shall destroy us, since Christ also lives to make intercession for us. "Who shall condemn? It is Christ that died; yea, rather, that is risen again, who is even at the right hand of God, who also maketh intercession for us."

OCTOBER 14

Saved By Christ's Life

For if while we were enemies we were reconciled to God by the death of his Son, much more, now that we are reconciled, shall we be saved by his life.

ROMANS 5:10

Christ, then, by his death saves us as we are sinners, enemies, and in a state of condemnation by sin. And Christ by his life saves us as considered justified and reconciled to God by his blood. So, then, we have salvation from that condemnation that sin had brought us unto and salvation from those ruins that all the enemies of our souls would yet bring us unto but cannot; for the intercession of Christ prevents [it] (Rom. 6:7-10).

Christ hath redeemed us from the curse of the law. Whatever the law can take hold of to curse us for, that Christ has redeemed us from, by being made a curse for us. But this curse that Christ was made for us, must be confined to his sufferings, not to his exaltation, and, consequently, not to his intercession. For Christ is made no curse but when he suffered, not in his intercession. So then, as he died, he took away the curse and sin that was the cause thereof by the sacrifice of himself (Gal. 3:13). And through his life, his intercession, he saves us from all those things that attempt to bring us into that condemnation again.

The salvation, then, that we have by the intercession of Christ, as was said—I speak now of them that can receive comfort and relief by this doctrine—is salvation that follows upon or that comes after, justification. We that are saved as to justification of life need yet to be saved with that that preserves to glory. For though by the death of Christ we are saved from the curse of the law, yet attempts are made by many that we may be kept from the glory that justified persons are designed for and from these we are saved by his intercession.

OCTOBER 15

Heir Of Wrath Or Heir Of Grace?

And if children, then heirs—heirs of God and fellow heirs with Christ, provided we suffer with him in order that we may also be glorified with him.

ROMANS 8:17

A man, then, that must be eternally saved is to be considered,

1. As an heir of wrath.
2. As an heir of God.

An heir of wrath he is in himself by sin. An heir of God he is by grace through Christ (Eph. 2:3; Gal. 4:7) Now, as an heir of wrath he is redeemed and as an heir of God he is preserved. As an heir of wrath, he is redeemed by blood and as an heir of God he is preserved by this intercession. Christ by his death, then, puts me, I being reconciled to God thereby, into a justified state. And God accepts me to grace and favour through him. But this does not hinder but that, notwithstanding, there are [those], that would frustrate me of the end to which I am designed. By this reconciliation to God, by redemption through grace; and from the accomplishing of this design—I am saved by the blessed intercession of our Lord Jesus Christ. [And I am not an heir of wrath.]

OCTOBER 16

Delivered From The Wrath To Come

And ... [we] wait for his Son from heaven, whom he raised from the dead, Jesus who delivers us from the wrath to come.

1 THESSALONIANS 1:10

We are saved from all punishment in hell fire by the death of Christ. Jesus has "delivered us from the wrath to come" (1 Thess. 1:10). So that as to this great punishment, God for his sake has forgiven us all trespasses (Col. 2:13). But we are being translated from being slaves of Satan to be sons of God. God reserves yet this liberty in his hand, to chastise us if we offend as a father chastises his son (Deut. 8:5). But this chastisement is not in legal wrath but in fatherly affection. Not to destroy us but that still we might be made to get advantage thereby, even be made partakers of his holiness. This is, that we might "not be condemned with the world" (Heb. 12:5-11, 1 Cor. 11:32). [Further,] There do ... many things happen betwixt or between the cup and the lip [when we drink]. Many things attempt to overthrow the work of God and to cause that we should perish through our weakness. Notwithstanding the price that hath by Christ been paid for us. But what says the Scripture? "Who shall separate us from the love of Christ? shall tribulation, or distress, or persecution, or famine, or nakedness, or peril, or sword? As it is written, for thy sake we are killed all the day long; we are accounted as sheep for the slaughter. Nay, in all these things we are more than conquerors through him that loved us. For I am persuaded, that neither death, nor life, nor angels, nor principalities, nor powers, nor things present, nor things to come, nor height, nor depth, nor any other creature, shall be able to separate us from the love of God, which is in Christ Jesus our Lord" (Rom. 8:35-39).

OCTOBER 17

A Persuaded Apostle

... But I am not ashamed, for I know whom I have believed, and I am convinced [persuaded] that he is able to guard until that day what has been entrusted to me.

2 TIMOTHY 1:12

Thus, the apostle reckons up all the disadvantages that a justified person is incident to in this life and by way of challenge declares: That not any one of them, nor all together, shall be able to separate us from the love of God; that is towards us by Christ, his death, and his intercession.

[There] ... may be [a] further objection, that the apostle does here leave out sin, unto which we know the saints are subject, after justification. And sin of itself, we need no other enemies, is of that nature as to destroy the whole world.

[The answer comes:] Sin is sin, in the nature of sin, wherever it is found. But sin as to the damning effects thereof is taken away from them unto whom righteousness is imputed for justification. Nor shall any or all the things, though there is a tendency in every one of them to drive us unto sin, drown us, through it, in perdition and destruction. I am persuaded, says Paul, they shall never be able to do that. The apostle, therefore, does implicitly, though to expressly, challenge sin. Yea, sin by all its advantages and then glories in the love of God in Christ Jesus. From which he concludes, it shall never separate the justified. Besides, it would now have been needless to have expressly here put in sin by itself, seeing before, he had argued that those he speaks of were freely justified therefrom.

OCTOBER 18

The Chastisement Of Sons And Daughters

If you are left without discipline, in which all have participated, then you are illegitimate children and not sons.

HEBREWS 12:8

One word more before I go ... ahead. The Father, as I told you, has reserved to himself a liberty to chastise his sons, to wit, with temporal chastisements if they offend. This still abides to us, notwithstanding God's grace[; that is] Christ's death or blessed intercession. And this punishment is so surely entailed to the transgressions that we who believe shall commit, that it is impossible that we should be utterly freed therefrom. Insomuch that the apostle positively concludes them to be bastards, what pretenses to sonship soever they have that are not, for sin, partakers of fatherly chastisements.

For the reversing of this punishment, it is that we should pray, if perhaps God will remit it, when we are taught to say, "Our Father, forgive us our trespasses." And he that admits of any other sense as to this petition, derogates from the death of Christ, or faith, or both. For either he concludes that for some of his sins Christ did not die, or that he is bound to believe that God, though he did has not yet, nor will forgive them, till from the petitioner some legal work be done. Forgive us as we forgive them that trespass against us (Matt. 6:14-15). But now, apply this to temporal punishments and then it is true that God has reserved a liberty in his hand to punish even the sins of his people upon them. Yea and will not pardon their sin, as to the remitting of such punishment, unless some good work by them be done; "If ye forgive not men their trespasses, neither will your Father forgive your trespasses" (Matt. 6:15, 18:28-35).

OCTOBER 19

Sons: Not Condemned With The World

But when we are judged by the Lord, we are disciplined so that we may not be condemned along with the world.

1 CORINTHIANS 11:32

And this [chastisement] is the cause why some that belong to God are yet so under the afflicting hand of God. They have sinned and God, who is their Father, punishes. Yea and this is the reason why some who are dear to God have this kind of punishment never forgiven. But it abides with them to their lives' end, goes with them to the day of their death. Yea, is the very cause of their death. By this punishment they are cut off out of the land of the living. But all this is that they might "not be condemned with the world" (1 Cor. 11:32).

Christ died not to save from this punishment. Christ intercedes not to save from this punishment. Nothing but a good life will save from this punishment; nor always that either.

The hidings of God's face, the harshness of his providences, the severe and sharp chastisements that ofttimes overtake the very spirits of his people, plainly show that Christ died not to save from temporal punishments. [He] ... prays not to save from temporal punishments—that is absolutely [true]. God has reserved a power to punish, with temporal punishments, the best and dearest of his people, if need[s] be. And sometimes he remits them, sometimes not, even as it pleases him. [But in either case] Christ saves to the uttermost.

OCTOBER 20

Christ Saves To The Uttermost

... He is able to save to the uttermost those who draw near to God through him.

HEBREWS 7:25

I shall now show you something of what it is for Christ, by his intercession, to save to the "uttermost." [For the Scripture says:] "He is able to save them to the uttermost."

This is a great expression and carries with it much. "Uttermost" signifies to the outside, to the end, to the last, to the furthest part. And it hath respect both to persons and things. (Gen. 49:26; Deut. 30:4; Matt. 5:26; Mark 13:27; Luke 15).

Some persons are in their own apprehensions even further from Christ than anybody else. [They are] afar off, a great way off, yet a-coming, as the prodigal was. Now, these many times are exceedingly afraid; the sight of that distance that they think is betwixt Christ and them makes them afraid. As it is said in another case, "They that dwell in the uttermost parts are afraid at thy tokens" (Ps. 65:8). So these are afraid they shall not speed, not obtain that for which they come to God. But the text says: He is able to save to the uttermost, to the very hindermost, them that come to God by him.

Two sorts of men seem to be far, very far from God:

1. The town sinner.

2. The great backslider (Neh. 1:9). But both these, if they come, he is able to save to the uttermost. He is able to save them from all those dangers that they fear will prevent their obtaining that grace and mercy they would have to help them in time of need. The publicans and harlots enter into the kingdom of heaven [the Pharisees].

OCTOBER 21

O Lord! Have Mercy!

And he cried out, "Jesus, Son of David, have mercy on me!"
LUKE 18:38

[Consider the town sinner and the great backslider.[1]] There is a more than ordinary breaking up of the corruptions of their nature. It seems as if all their lusts and vile passions of the flesh were become masters and might now do what they will with the soul. Yea, they take this man and toss and tumble him like a ball in a large place. This man is not master of himself, of his thoughts, nor of his passions—"His iniquities, like the wind, do carry him away" (Isa. 64:6). He thinks to go forward but this wind blows him backward. He labours against this wind but cannot find that he gets ground. He takes what advantage opportunity does minister to him but all he gets is to be beat out of heart, out of breath, out of courage. He stands still, and pants, and gapes as if for life. "I opened my mouth, and panted," said David, "for I longed for thy commandments" (Ps. 119:131). He sets forward again but has nothing but labour and sorrow.

Nay, to help forward his calamity, Satan [and his] angels will not be wanting. Both to trouble his head with the fumes of their stinking breath nor to throw up his heels in their dirty places—"And as he was yet a-coming, the devil threw him down and tare him" (Luke 9:42). How many strange, hideous, and amazing blasphemies have those, some of those, that are coming to Christ, had injected, and fixed upon their spirits against him. Now help, Lord; now, Lord Jesus, what shall I do? Now, Son of David, have mercy upon me! I say, to say these words is hard work for such a one. But he can save to the uttermost this comer to God by him.

1 See previous devotional reading.

OCTOBER 22

The Backslider's Lot

The backslider in heart shall be filled with his own ways; and a good man shall be satisfied from himself.

PROVERBS 14:14 KJV

There are also the oppositions of sense and reason hard at work for the devil [in the town sinner and the great backslider], against ... [his] soul. The men of his own house are revolted against him. One's sense and reason, one would think, should not fall in with the devil against us. And yet nothing more common, nothing more natural, than for our own sense and reason to turn the unnatural and are both against our God and us. And now it is hard coming to God. Better can a man hear and deal with any objections against himself than with those that himself does [he] make against himself. They lie close, stick fast, speak aloud, and will be heard. Yea will haunt and hunt him as the devil does some, in every hole and corner. But come, man, come; for ... [Christ] can save to the uttermost!

Now guilt is the consequence and fruit of all this. And what so intolerable a burden as guilt! They talk of the stones and of the sands of the sea. But it is guilt that breaks the heart with its burden. And Satan has the art of making the uttermost of every sin. He can blow it up, make it swell, make every hair of its head as big as a cedar. He can tell how to make it a heinous offense and unpardonable offense, an offense of that continuance and committed against so much light, he says it is impossible, it should ever be forgiven. But, soul, Christ is able to save to the uttermost, he can "do exceeding abundantly above all that we ask or think" (Eph. 3:20).

OCTOBER 23

He Works His Will In Us

For it is God who works in you, both to will and to work for his good pleasure.

PHILIPPIANS 2:13

Join to all this the rage and terror of men, which thing of itself is sufficient to quash and break to pieces all desires to come to God by Christ. Yea and it doth do so to thousands that are not willing to go to hell. Yet thou art kept and made to go panting on. A whole world of men and devils and sin are not able to keep thee from coming. But how does it to pass that you are so hearty, that you set your face against so much wind and weather? I dare say it arises not from yourself nor from any of thine enemies. This comes from God, though you are not aware thereof. And is obtained for you by the intercession of the blessed Son of God, who is also able to save ... to the uttermost [those] that come to God by him.

I will add that there is much of the honor of the Lord Jesus engaged as to the saving of the coming man to the uttermost: "I am glorified in them," he said (John 17:10). He is exalted to be a Saviour (Acts 5:31). And if the blessed One does count it an exaltation to be a Saviour, surely it is an exaltation to be a Saviour, and a great one. "They shall cry unto the Lord because of the oppressors, and he shall send them a Saviour, and a great one, and he shall deliver them" (Isa. 19:20). If it is a glory to be a Saviour, a great Saviour, then it is a glory for a Saviour, a great one, to save, and save, and save to the uttermost—to the uttermost man, to the uttermost [from] sin, to the uttermost [from] temptation.

OCTOBER 24

The LORD—The Merciful

The LORD passed before him and proclaimed, "The LORD, the LORD, a God merciful and gracious, slow to anger, and abounding in steadfast love and faithfulness."

EXODUS 34:6

When Moses said, "I beseech thee, show me thy glory," the answer was, "I will make all my goodness pass before thee, and I will proclaim the name of the Lord before thee" (Exod. 33:18-19). And when he came indeed to make proclamation, then he proclaimed: "The Lord, The Lord God, merciful and gracious, long-suffering, and abundant in goodness and truth, keeping mercy for thousands, forgiving iniquity and transgression and sin, and that will by no means clear the guilty" (Exod. 34:6-7). That will by no means clear them that will not come to me that they may be saved.

See here, if it is not by himself accounted his glory to make his goodness, all his goodness, pass before us. And how can that be, if he saves not to the uttermost them that come unto God by him? For goodness is by us no ways seen but by those acts by which it expressed itself to be so. And, I am sure, to save, to save to the uttermost, is one of the most eminent expressions by which we understand it is great goodness. I know goodness has many ways to express itself to be what it is to the world; but then it expresses its greatness when it pardons and saves, when it pardons and saves to the uttermost. My goodness, Christ says, extends not itself to my Father, but to my saints (Ps. 16:2-3). My Father has no need of my goodness, but my saints have. Therefore, it shall reach forth itself for their help, in whom is all my delight.

OCTOBER 25

A Full And Final Atonement

For by a single offering he has perfected for all time those who are being saved.

HEBREWS 10:14

In Christ's ability to save lies our safety.

But ... [one might ask:], What is the meaning of this word able? "Wherefore he is able to save." He is able to save the uttermost. How does it come to pass that his power to save is rather put in ... his willingness. I will speak ... [a few] words to this question:

By this word "able" is suggested to us the sufficiency of his merit, the great worthiness of his merit. For, as intercessor, he sticks fast by his merit. All his petitions, prayers, or supplications are grounded upon the worthiness of his person as mediator and on the validity of his offering as priest. This is the more clear, if you consider the reason why those priests and sacrifices under the law could not make the worshippers perfect. It was, I say, because they wanted in them worthiness and merit in their sacrifices. But this man, when he came and offered his sacrifice, he did by that one act "perfect for ever them that are sanctified," or set apart for glory. "But this man, after he had offered one sacrifice for sins, for ever sat down on the right hand of God" (Heb. 10:1-12).

When Moses prayed for the people of Israel, thus he said, "And now, I beseech thee, let the power of my Lord be great, according as thou hast spoken." But what had he spoken? "The Lord is long-suffering, and of great mercy, forgiving iniquity and transgression, and by no means clearing the guilty—Pardon, I beseech thee, the iniquity of this people according unto the greatness of thy mercy, and as thou hast forgiven this people, from Egypt even until now" (Num. 14:17-19).

OCTOBER 26

Safe In Christ's Ability

All that the Father gives me will come to me, and whoever comes to me I will never cast out.

JOHN 6:37

Has ... [Christ] power, we know he is willing, else he would not have promised. It is also his glory to pardon and save. So, then, in his ability lies our safety. What if he were never so willing, if he were not of ability sufficient, what would his willingness do? But he has showed ... his willingness by promising: "Him that cometh to me I will in no wise cast ot: (John 6:37). So now our comfort lies in his power, in that he is able to make good his word (Rom. 4:20-21).

And this also will then be seen when he hath saved them that come to God by him, when he hath saved them to the uttermost. Not to the uttermost of his ability but to the uttermost of our necessity. For to the uttermost of his ability I believe he will never be put to it to save his church. Not for that he is loath to save but because there is no need to save. He shall not need to put out all his power and to press the utmost of his merit for the saving of his church. Alas! there is sufficiency of merit in him to save a thousand times as many more as are like to be saved by him: "he is able to do exceeding abundantly above all that we ask or think."

Measure not, therefore, what he can do by what he has, does, or will do. Neither ... [should you] interpret this word to the uttermost, as if it related to the uttermost of his ability. But rather as it relates, for so it does indeed, to the greatness of your necessity.

OCTOBER 27

Questions Concerning Christ's Ability

... he is able to save to the uttermost ...

HEBREWS 7:25A

What! shall not the worthiness of the Son of God be sufficient to save from the sin of man? Or shall the sin of the world be of that weight to destroy [his ability?] That it shall put Christ Jesus to the uttermost of the worth of his person and merit to save therefrom? I believe it is blasphemy to think so. We can easily imagine that he can save all the world—that is, that he is of ability to do it. But we cannot imagine that he can do no more than we can think he can. But our imagination and thoughts set no bound to his ability. "He is able to do exceeding abundantly above all that we ask or think." But what is ... [it], I say, no man can think [or] no man can imagine. So, then, Jesus Christ can do more than ever any man thought he could do as to saving. He can do we know not what. This, therefore, should encourage comers to come to him and them that come to hope. This, I say, should encourage them to let out, to lengthen, and heighten their thoughts by the word, to the uttermost, seeing he can "save to the uttermost them that come to God by him."

OCTOBER 28

Complete In Christ

And ye are complete in him, which is the head of all principality and power.

COLOSSIANS 2:10 KJV

And now I come to ... [a] thing ... I should speak to and that is, to ... [an] inference that may be gathered from the ... [former readings].

Are they that are justified by Christ's blood such as have need yet to be saved by his intercession? Then from hence it follows that justification will stand with imperfection. It does not therefore follow that a justified man is without infirmity. For he that is without infirmity—that is, perfect with absolute perfection, has no need to be yet saved by an act yet to be performed by a mediator and his mediation.

When I say justification will stand with imperfection; I do not mean that it will allow, countenance, or approve ... [of imperfection]. But I mean there is no necessity of our perfection, of our personal perfection as to our justification and that we are justified without it. Yea, in justified persons, [it] remains. Again, when I say that justification will stand with imperfection, I do not mean that in our justification we are imperfect. For in that we are complete; "we are complete in him" who is our justice (Col. 2:10). If otherwise, the imperfection is in the matter that justifies us which is the righteousness of Christ. Yea, and to say so would conclude that wrong judgment proceeds from him that imputes that righteousness to us to justification, since an imperfect thing is imputed to us for justification. But far be it from any that believe that God is true to imagine such a thing: All his works are perfect, there is nothing wanting in them as to the present design.

OCTOBER 29

Christ—Our Rest

Come to me, all who labour and are heavy laden, and I will give you rest.

MATTHEW 11:28

And this is ... one reason why they that are justified have need of an intercessor. To wit, to save us from the evil of the sin that remains in our flesh after we are justified by grace through Christ and set free from the law as to condemnation. Therefore, as it is said, "He is able also to save them to the uttermost that come unto God by him, seeing he ever liveth to make intercession for them." The godly ... feel in themselves many things even after justification by which they are convinced they are still attended with personal, sinful imperfections:—

1. They feel unbelief, fear, mistrust, doubting, despondings, murmurings, blasphemies, pride, lightness, foolishness, avarice, fleshly lusts, heartlessness to good, wicked desires, [and] low thoughts of Christ.
2. They feel in themselves an aptness to incline to errors, as to lean to the works of the law for justification; to question the truth of the resurrection and judgment to come; to dissemble and play the hypocrite in profession and in performance of duties.
3. They feel an inclination in them, in times of trial, to faint under the cross, to seek too much to save themselves, to dissemble the known truth for the obtaining a little favour with men and to speak things . . . they ought not [to speak].
4. They feel wearisomeness in religious duties but a natural propensity to things of the flesh. They feel a desire to go beyond bounds both at board, and bed, and bodily exercise, and in all lawful recreation.

OCTOBER 30

Incomplete Work If Grace

Simon, Simon, behold, Satan demanded to have you, that he might sift you like wheat, but I have prayed for you, that your faith may not fail ...

LUKE 22:31-32A

Again; [let it be said] the justified man is imperfect in his graces and therefore needs to be saved by the [perpetual] intercession of Christ from the bad fruit that ... [his] imperfection yields.

Justifying righteousness is accompanied with graces—the graces of the Spirit. Though these graces are not ... [a] matter by and through which we are justified nor any part ... [of it]. [For it is] ... only the obedience of Christ imputed to us of [his] mere pleasure and good will. But, I say, they come when justification comes (Rom. 9). And though they are not so easily discerned at the first, they show forth themselves afterwards. But I say, no matter how many soever they are and how fast soever they grow, their utmost arrivement here is but a state short of perfection. None of the graces of God's Spirit in our hearts can do their work in us without shortness and that because of their own imperfections, and also because of the oppositions that they meet with from our flesh.

Faith, which is the root-grace, the grand grace, its shortness is sufficiently manifest by its shortness of apprehension of things pertaining to the person, offices, relations, and works of Christ—now in the heavenly place for us. It is also very defective in its fetching of comfort from the Word to us. And in continuing of it with us when at any time we attain unto it. In its receiving of strength to subdue sin, and in its purifyings of the heart, though indeed it does what it does in reality. Yet how short is it of doing of it thoroughly? Oftentimes, were it not for supplies by virtue of the intercession of Christ, faith would fail of performing its office in any measure (Luke 22:31-32).

OCTOBER 31

A Litany Of Graces

... Clothe yourselves, all of you, with humility toward one another, for "God opposes the proud but gives grace to the humble."

1 PETER 5:5B

There is hope, another grace of the Spirit bestowed upon us and how often is that also as to the excellency of working, made to flag? "I shall perish," saith David; "I am cut off from before thine eyes," said he (Ps. 31:22). And now where was his hope[found], in the right discovery of the gospel?

There is love that should be in us as hot as fire. It is compared to fire, to fire of the hottest sort. Yea, it is said to be hotter than the coals of juniper (Song 8:6-7). But who finds this heat in love so much as for one poor quarter of an hour together?

The grace of humility, whe[re] is it? Who has a thimbleful ... [of it]? Where is he that is "clothed with humility," and that does what he is commanded "with all humility of mind"?

For zeal, where is that also? Zeal for God against sin, profaneness, superstition, and idolatry. I speak now to the godly. [Those] who have this zeal in the root and habit. But oh, how little of it puts forth itself into actions in such a day as this is!

There is reverence, fear, and standing in awe of God's Word and judgments, where are the excellent workings thereof to be found? And where it is most, how far short of perfect acts is it?

Simplicity and godly sincerity also, with how much dirt is it mixed in the best; especially among those of the saints that are rich, who have got the poor and beggarly art of complimenting? For the more compliment, the less sincerity. Many words will not fill a bushel. But "in the multitude of words there wanteth not sin" (Prov. 10:19).

NOVEMBER 1

Holy Fear Of The Almighty's Splendor

Out of the north comes golden splendor; God is clothed with awesome majesty.

JOB 37:22

By this word fear ... we are to understand God himself, who is the object of our fear: For the divine majesty goes often under this very name himself. This name Jacob called him by, when he and Laban [did] chide together on Mount Gilead, after that Jacob had made his escape to his father's house: "Except," said he, "the God of my father, the God of Abraham, and the fear of Isaac had been with me, surely thou hadst sent me away now empty." So again, a little after, when Jacob and Laban agree to make a covenant of peace each with [the] other, though Laban, after the jumbling way of the heathen by his oath, puts the true God and the false together. Yet "Jacob sware by the fear of his father Isaac" (Gen. 31:42, 53).

By the fear, that is, by the God of his father Isaac [made he the covenant]. And indeed, God may well be called the fear of his people. Not only because they have by his grace made him the object of their fear, but because of the dread and terrible majesty that is in him. "He is a mighty God, a great and terrible, and with God is terrible majesty" (Dan. 7:28, 10:17; Neh. 1:5, 4:14, 9:32; Job 37:22). Who knows the power of his anger? "The mountains quake at him, the hills melt, and the earth is burned at his presence. Yea, the world, and all that dwell there. Who can stand before his indignation? who can abide in the fierceness of his anger? His fury is poured out like fire, and the rocks are thrown down by him" (Nahum 1:5-6).

NOVEMBER 2

There Remains No Strength In Me!

And behold, one in the likeness of the children of man touched my lips. Then I opened my mouth and spoke. I said to him who stood before me, "O my lord, by reason of the vision pains have come upon me, and I retain no strength. How can my lord's servant talk with my lord? For now no strength remains in me, and no breath is left in me."

DANIEL 10:16-17

[There was a] ... time ... when Jacob had that memorable visit from God. In which he gave him power as a prince to prevail with him. Yea and gave him a name, that by his remembering it he might call God's favour the better to his mind. Yet even then and there such dread of the majesty of God was upon him, that he went away wondering that his life was preserved (Gen. 32:30). Man crumbles to dust at the presence of God. Yea, though he shows himself to us in his robes of salvation. We have read how dreadful and how terrible even the presence of angels have been unto men and that when they have brought them good tidings from heaven (Judg. 13:22; Matt. 28:4; Mark 16:5-6).

Now, if angels, which are but creatures, are through the glory that God has put upon them, so fearful and terrible in their appearance to men; how much more dreadful and terrible must God himself be to us, who are but dust and ashes! When Daniel had the vision of his salvation sent him from heaven, for so it was: "O Daniel," said the messenger, "a man greatly beloved." Yet behold the dread and terror of the person speaking fell with that weight upon this good man's soul, that he could not stand nor bear up under it. He stood trembling and cries out, "O my lord, by the vision my sorrows are turned upon me, and I have retained no strength. For how the servant of this my lord can talk with this my lord? For as for me, straightway there remained no strength in me" (Dan. 10:16-17).

NOVEMBER 3

His Presence Is Dreadful To Us

When I saw him, I fell at his feet as though dead. But he laid his right hand on me, saying, "Fear not, I am the first and the last."

REVELATION 1:17

[One reason] ... is God's own greatness and majesty. The discovery of this or of himself thus, even as no poor mortals can conceive of him is altogether unsupportable. The man dies to whom he thus discovers himself. "And when I saw him," John says, "I fell at his feet as dead" (Rev. 1:17). It was this ... that Job would have avoided in the day that he would have approached unto him. "Let not thy dread," he says, "make me afraid. Then call thou and I will answer; or let me speak, and answer thou me" (Job 13:21-22). But why does Job after this manner ... speak to God? Why! it was from a sense that he had of the dreadful majesty of God, even the great and dreadful God that kept covenant with his people. The presence of a king is dreadful to the subject. Yea, [even] though he carries it never so condescendingly. If then there be so much glory and dread in the presence of the king, what fear and dread must there be, think you, in the presence of the eternal God?

When God gives his presence to his people: That his presence causes them to appear to themselves more what they are than at other times, by all other light, they can see. "O my lord," said Daniel, "by the vision my sorrows are turned upon me." And why was that but because by the glory of that vision, he saw his own vileness more than at other times. So again: "I was left alone," says he, "and saw this great vision," and what follows? Why, "and there remained no strength in me; for my comeliness was turned into corruption, and I retained no strength" (Dan. 10:7-8, 16).

NOVEMBER 4

God's Presence Begets Reverence

Comfort, comfort my people, says your God.

ISAIAH 40:1

By the presence of God, when we have it indeed, even our best things, our comeliness, our sanctity, and righteousness; all do immediately turn to corruption and polluted rags. The brightness of his glory dims them as the clear light of the shining sun puts out the glory of the fire or candle and [it] covers them with the shadow of death. See also the truth of this in that vision of the prophet Isaiah. "Wo[e] is me," said he, "for I am undone, because I am a man of unclean lips, and I dwell in the midst of a people of unclean lips." Why, what is the matter? how came the prophet by this sight? [For] ... "mine eyes have seen the King, the Lord of hosts" (Isa. 6:5).

But do you think that this outcry was caused by unbelief? No; nor ... begotten by slavish fear. This was to him the vision of his Saviour with whom also he had communion before (vv. 2-5). It was the glory of that God with whom he had now to do. [This] turned ... Daniel, his comeliness in him into corruption and that gave him yet greater sense of the disproportion that was betwixt his God and him; and so, a greater sight of his defiled and polluted nature.

The revelation of God's goodness and it must needs make his presence dreadful. Notwithstanding his greatness, goodness in his heart, and mercy to bestow upon him: this makes his presence yet the more dreadful. They "shall fear the Lord and his goodness" (Hosea 3:5). The goodness as well as the greatness of God doth beget in the heart of his elect an awful reverence of his majesty. "Fear ye not me? saith the Lord; will ye not tremble at my presence?"

NOVEMBER 5

Why Some Tremble Before God

I will restore the fortunes of Judah and the fortunes of Israel, and rebuild them as they were at first. I will cleanse them from all the guilt of their sin against me, and I will forgive all the guilt of their sin and rebellion against me.

JEREMIAH 33:7-8

And what mean the tremblings, the tears, those breakings and shakings of heart that attend the people of God, when in an eminent manner they receive the pronunciation of the forgiveness of sins at his mouth? But that the dread of the majesty of God is in their sight mixed therewith? God must appear like himself, speak to the soul like himself. Nor can the sinner, when under these glorious discoveries of his Lord and Saviour keep out the beams of his majesty from the eyes of his understanding. "I will cleanse them," says he, "from all their iniquity, whereby they have sinned against me, and I will pardon all their iniquities whereby they have sinned, and whereby they have transgressed against me."

And what then? "And they shall fear and tremble for all the goodness, and for all the prosperity that I procure unto it" (Jer. 33:8-9). Alas! there is a company of poor, light, frothy professors in the world, that carry it under that which they call the presence of God—more like to antics than sober sensible Christians. Yea, more like to a fool of a play than those that have the presence of God. They would not carry it so in the presence of a king nor yet of the lord of their land, were they but receivers of mercy at his hand. They carry it even in their most eminent seasons, as if the sense and sight of God and his blessed grace to their souls in Christ, had a tendency in them to make men wanton: But indeed, it is the most humbling and heart-breaking sight in the world; it is fearful.

NOVEMBER 6

Rejoice And Tremble

Serve the LORD *with fear, and rejoice with trembling.*

PSALM 2:11

I would have you ... [know], when God shall tell you that your sins are pardoned indeed, "rejoice with trembling" (Ps. 2:11). For then you have solid and godly joy; a joyful heart, and wet eyes, in this will stand very well together and it will be so more or less. For if God shall come to you indeed and visit you with the forgiveness of sins, that visit removes the guilt, but increases the sense of thy filth and the sense of this that God hath forgiven a filthy sinner. [These] ... will make you both rejoice and tremble. O, the blessed confusion that will then cover your face while you, even you, so vile a wretch, shalt stand before God to receive at his hand your pardon and so the first fruits of thy eternal salvation—"That thou mayest remember, and be confounded, and never open thy mouth anymore because of thy shame (thy filth), when I am pacified toward thee for all that thou hast done, saith the Lord God" (Ezek. 16:63).

But, as the presence, so the name of God, is dreadful and fearful: Wherefore his name doth rightly go under the same title, "That thou mayest fear this glorious and fearful name, *the* LORD *thy God*" (Deut. 28:58). The name of God, what is that but that by which he is distinguished and known from all others? Names are to distinguish by; so, man is distinguished from beasts, and angels from men; so heaven from earth, and darkness from light. Especially when by the name, the nature of the thing is signified and expressed; and so, it was in their original name, for then names expressed the nature of the thing so named.

NOVEMBER 7

Where Is Our Fear Of God?

A son honors the father, and a servant his master. If then I am a father, where is my honor? And if I am a master, where is my fear?

MALACHI 1:6A

[We tremble and fear] his name: I am, Jah, Jehovah. What is by them intended but his nature, as his power, wisdom, eternity, goodness, and omnipotency—might be expressed and declared. The name of God is therefore the object of a Christian's fear. David prayed to God that he would unite his heart to fear his name (Ps. 86:11). Indeed, the name of God is a fearful name, and should always be reverenced by his people: Yea his "name is to be feared for ever and ever," and that not only in his church, and among his saints but even in the world and among the heathen—"So the heathen shall fear the name of the Lord, and all kings thy glory" (Ps. 102:15). God tells us that his name is dreadful and that he is pleased to see men be afraid before his name. Yea, one reason why he executes so many judgments upon men as he does, is that others might see and fear his name. "So shall they fear the name of the Lord from the west, and his glory from the rising of the sun" (Isa. 59:19; Mal. 2:5).

The name of a king is a name of fear—"And I am a great king, saith the Lord of hosts" (Mal. 1:14). The name of master is a name of fear—"And if I be a master, where is my fear? saith the Lord" (v 6). Yea, rightly to fear the Lord is a sign of a gracious heart. And again, "To you that fear my name," saith he, "shall the sun of righteousness arise with healing in his wings" (Mal. 4:2). Yea, when Christ comes to judge the world, he will give reward to his servants the prophets, and to his saints, "and to them that fear his name, small and great" (Rev. 11:18).

NOVEMBER 8

Worship His Majesty

You shall not take the name of the LORD your God in vain, for the LORD will not hold him guiltless who takes his name in vain.

EXODUS 20:7

Always make mention then of the name of the Lord with great dread of his majesty upon our hearts and in great soberness and truth. To do otherwise is to profane the name of the Lord and to take his name in vain; "the Lord will not hold him guiltless that taketh his name in vain." God said that he will cut off the man that does it. So jealous is he of the honor due unto his name (Exod. 20:7; Lev. 20:3). This ... shows you the dreadful state of those that lightly, vainly, lyingly, and profanely make use of the name. This fearful [use] of God['s name], either by their blasphemous cursing and oaths or by their fraudulent dealing with their neighbour [is godless]. For some men have no way to prevail with their neighbour to bow under a cheat. But [only] by calling falsely upon the name of the Lord to be witness that their wickedness is good and honest. But how these men will escape, when they shall be judged, devouring fire and everlasting burnings, for their profaning and blaspheming of the name of the Lord, [it] becomes them ... [early] to consider of (Jer. 14:14-15; Ezek. 20:39; Exod. 20:7).

The presence and name of God are dreadful and fearful in the church—so is his worship and service. I say his worship or the works of service to which we are by him enjoined while we are in this world, are dreadful and fearful things. This David con[fessed] when he said, "But as for me, I will come into thy house in the multitude of thy mercy, and in thy fear will I worship toward thy holy temple" (Ps. 5:7).

NOVEMBER 9

Reverential Fear In Worship

But I, through the abundance of your steadfast love, will enter your house, I will bow down toward your holy temple in the fear of you.

PSALM 5:7

As the presence and name of God are dreadful and fearful in the church, so is his worship and service. I say his worship or the works of service to which we are by him enjoined while we are in this world, [they] are dreadful and fearful things. David conceives when he saith, "But as for me, I will come into thy house in the multitude of thy mercy, and in thy fear will I worship toward thy holy temple" (Ps. 5:7). And again, "Serve the Lord with fear." To praise God is a part of his worship. But, Moses says, "Who is a God like unto thee, glorious in holiness, fearful in praises, doing wonders?" (Exod. 15:11). To rejoice before him is a part of his worship but David bids us "rejoice with trembling" (Ps. 2:11). Yea, the whole of our service to God and every part thereof, ought to be done by us with reverence and godly fear. And therefore, let us, as Paul said, "Cleanse ourselves from all filthiness of the flesh and spirit, perfecting holiness in the fear of God" (2 Corinthians 7:1; Hebrews 12).

That which makes the worship of God so fearful a thing, is, for that it is the worship of GOD: All manner of service carries dread and fear along with it, according as the quality or condition of the person is to whom the worship and service is done. This is seen in the service of subjects to their princes, the service of servants to their lords and the service of children to their parents. Divine worship, then, being due to God, for it is now of divine worship we speak—his worship must therefore be a fearful thing.

NOVEMBER 10

We Worship A Jealous God

For the LORD your God in your midst is a jealous God—lest the anger of the LORD your God be kindled against you, and he destroy you from off the face of the earth.

DEUTERONOMY 6:15

Besides, this glorious Majesty is himself present to behold his worshippers in their worshipping him. "When two or three of you are gathered together in my name, I am there." That is, gathered together to worship him, "I am there," [Jesus] says. And so, again, he is said to walk "in the midst of the seven golden candlesticks" (Rev. 1:13). That is, in the churches and that with a countenance like the sun, with a head and hair as white as snow, and with eyes like a flame of fire. This puts dread and fear into his service; and therefore, his servants should serve him with fear.

Above all things, God is jealous of his worship and service. In all the ten [commandments], he tells us not anything of his being a jealous God, but in the second, which respects his worship (Exod. 20). Look to yourselves therefore, both as to the matter and manner of your worship; "for I the Lord thy God," says he, "am a jealous God, visiting the iniquity of the fathers upon the children." This therefore does also put dread and fear into the worship and service of God.

NOVEMBER 11

Holiness Unto The Lord

You shall be holy to me, for I the LORD am holy and have separated you from the peoples, that you should be mine.

LEVITICUS 20:26

The judgments that sometimes God has executed upon men for their want of godly fear, while they have been in his worship and service, [to] put fear and dread upon his holy appointments.

1. Nadab and Abihu were burned to death with fire from heaven because they attempted to offer false fire upon God's altar. And the reason rendered why they were so served, was, because God will be sanctified in them that come nigh him (Lev. 10:1-3). To sanctify his name is to let him be your dread and your fear and to do nothing in his worship but what is well-pleasing to him. But because these men had not grace to do this, therefore they died before the Lord.
2. Eli's sons, for want of this fear, when they ministered in the holy worship of God, were both slain in one day by the sword of the uncircumcised Philistines (see 1 Sam. 2).
3. Uzzah was smitten, and died before the Lord for but an unadvised touching of the ark when the men forsook it (1 Chron. 13:9-10).
4. Ananias and Sapphira his wife, for telling a lie in the church when they were before God, were both stricken dead upon the place before them all. Because they ... [lacked] the fear and dread of God's majesty, name, and service, when they came before him (Acts 5).

This ... should teach us ... that next to God's nature and name, his service, his instituted worship, is the most dreadful thing under heaven. His name is upon his ordinances, his eye is upon the worshippers, and his wrath and judgment upon those that worship not in his fear.

NOVEMBER 12

Rebukes To Those Whose Heart Is Far From God

And the LORD said: "Because this people draw near with their mouth and honor me with their lips, while their hearts are far from me, and their fear of me is a commandment taught of men ..."

ISAIAH 29:13

[First:] Such as regard not to worship God at all. Be sure they have no reverence of his service, nor fear of his majesty before their eyes. Sinner, you do not come before the Lord to worship him; you do not bow before the high God. You neither worship him in your closet nor in the congregation of saints. The fury of the Lord and his indignation must in [a] short time be poured out upon you and upon the families that call not upon his name (Ps. 79:6; Jer. 10:25).

[Second:] This rebukes such as count it enough to present their body in the place where God is worshipped. [They don't] mind with what heart or with what spirit they come thither [there]. Some come into the worship of God to sleep there. Some come thither to meet with their chapmen [peddler] and to get into the wicked fellowship of their vain companions. Some come thither to feed their lustful and adulterous eyes with the flattering beauty of their fellow-sinners. O what a sad account will these worshippers give when they shall [give ac]count for all this and be damned for it. Because they come not to worship the Lord with that fear of his name; became [for] them to come in when they presented themselves before him!

[Third:] This also rebukes those that care not, so they worship, how they worship. How, where, or after what manner they worship God. Those, I mean, whose fear towards God "is taught by the precept of men." They are hypocrites; their worship also is vain and [are] a stink in the nostrils of God. Thus, I conclude this first thing, namely, that God is called our dread and fear.

NOVEMBER 13

The Word Of The Lord Brings Godly Fear

The law of the Lord is perfect, reviving the soul; the testimony of the Lord is sure, making wise the simple.

Psalm 19:7

But again, this word *fear* is sometimes to be taken for *the Word*, the written Word of God. For that also is and ought to be, the rule and director of our fear. So, David calls it in the nineteenth Psalm: "the fear of the Lord," he said, "is clean, enduring forever." The fear of the Lord, that is, the Word of the Lord, the written Word. For that which he calleth in this place the fear of the Lord, even in the same place he calls the law, statutes, commandments, and judgments of God. "The law of the Lord is perfect, converting the soul: the testimony of the Lord is sure, making wise the simple: the statutes of the Lord are right, rejoicing the heart: the commandment of the Lord is pure, enlightening the eyes: the fear of the Lord is clean, enduring forever: the judgments of the Lord are true and righteous altogether." All these words have respect to the same thing, to wit, to the Word of God, jointly designing the glory of it. Among which phrases, as you see, this is one, "The fear of the Lord is clean, enduring forever." This written Word is therefore the object of a Christian's fear. This is also which David intended when he said, "Come, ye children, hearken unto me, I will teach you the fear of the Lord" (Ps. 34:11). I will teach you the fear, that is, I will teach you the commandments, statutes, and judgments of the Lord, even as Moses commanded the children of Israel—"Thou shalt teach them diligently unto thy children, and shalt talk of them when thou sittest in thine house, and when thou walkest by the way, and when thou liest down, and when thou risest up" (Deut. 6:4-7).

NOVEMBER 14

Learn To Fear The LORD

Hear, O Israel: The LORD *our God, the* LORD *is one ... You shall teach them diligently to your children, and shall talk of them when you sit in your house, and when you walk by the way, and when you lie down, and when you rise.*

DEUTERONOMY 6:4, 7

The eleventh of Isaiah intends the same [idea to fear the *LORD*], where the Father said of the Son, he shall be of quick understanding in the fear of the Lord. [H]e may judge and smite the earth with the rod of his mouth. This rod in the text is nothing other than the fear [and] the Word of the Lord. For he was to be of a quick understanding, that he might smite, that is, execute it according to the will of his Father, upon and among the children of men.

Now this ... is called the fear of the Lord because it is called the rule and director of our fear. For we know not how to fear the Lord in a saving way without its guidance and direction. As it is said of the priest that was sent back from the captivity to Samaria to teach the people to fear the Lord, so it is said concerning the written Word. It is given to us and left among us that we may read therein all the days of our life and learn to fear the Lord (Deut. 6:1-3, 24; 10:12; 17:19). And here it is, trembling at the Word of God, is even by God himself not only taken notice of, but counted as laudable and praiseworthy as is evident in the case of Josiah (2 Chron. 34:26-27). Such also are the approved of God, let them be condemned: "Hear the word of the Lord, ye that tremble at his word; Your brethren that hated you, that cast you out for my name's sake, said, Let the Lord be glorified; but he shall appear to your joy, and they shall be ashamed" (Isa. 66:5).

NOVEMBER 15

Tremble At His Word

... But this is the one to whom I will look; he who is humble and contrite in spirit and trembles at my word.

ISAIAH 66:2B

Further ... God himself cared for [those who reverenced] and watched over [them], that no distress, temptation, or affliction may overcome them and destroy them—"To this man will I look," said God, "even to him that is poor and of a contrite spirit, and that trembleth at my word." It is the same in substance with that in Isaiah 57: "For thus saith the high and lofty One that inhabiteth eternity, whose name is Holy; I dwell in the high and holy place, with him also that is of a contrite and humble spirit, to revive the spirit of the humble, and to revive the heart of the contrite ones." Yea, the way to escape dangers foretold, is to hearken to, understand, and fear the Word of God—"He that feared the word of the Lord among the servants of Pharaoh, made his servants and his cattle flee into the houses," and they were secured. But "he that regarded not the word of the Lord, left his servants and his cattle in the field," and they were destroyed by the hail (Exod. 9:20-25).

If at any time the sins of a nation or church are discovered and bewailed, it is by them that know and tremble at the Word of God. When Ezra heard of the wickedness of his brethren and had a desire to humble himself before God for the same, who were they that would assist him in that matter but they that trembled at the Word of God?—"Then," said he, "were assembled unto me every one that trembled at the words of the God of Israel, because of the transgression of those that had been carried away" (Ezra 9:4).

NOVEMBER 16

The Prophets Tremble At His Word

I hear [His Word], and my body trembles; my lips quiver at the sound; rottenness enters into my bones; my legs tremble beneath me ...

HABAKKUK 3:16A

As I have already hinted, from the author of them, they are the words of God. Therefore, you have Moses and the prophets, when they came to deliver their errand, their message to the people, still saying, "Hear the word of the Lord," [or] "Thus saith the Lord," and the like. So, when Ezekiel was sent to the house of Israel, in their state of religion, thus was he bid to say unto them, "Thus saith the Lord God"; "Thus saith the Lord God" (Ezek. 2:4, 3:11). This is the honor and majesty, then, that God hath put upon his written Word and thus he has done even of purpose. That we might make them the rule and directory of our fear and that we might stand in awe of and tremble at them. When Habakkuk heard the Word of the Lord, his belly trembled, and rottenness entered into his bones. "I trembled in myself," he said, "that I might rest in the day of trouble" (Hab. 3:16). The word of a king is as the roaring of a lion; where the word of a king is, there is power. What is it, then, when God, the great God, shall roar out of Zion and utter his voice from Jerusalem, whose voice shakes not only the earth, but also heaven? How doth holy David set it forth; "The voice of the Lord is powerful; the voice of the Lord is full of majesty" (Ps. 29:4).

NOVEMBER 17

God's Word: A Fire And A Hammer

"Is not my word like fire," declares the LORD*, "and like a hammer that breaks the rock in pieces?"*

JEREMIAH 23:29

[God's Word] ... is a Word that is fearful and may well be called the fear of the Lord, because of the subject matter of it. To wit, the state of sinners in another world; for that is it unto which the whole Bible bends itself, either more immediately or more mediately. All its doctrines, counsels, encouragements, threatenings, and judgments, have a look—one way or other—upon us, with respect to the next world, which will be our last state, because it will be to us a state eternal. This word, this law, these judgments, are they that we shall be disposed of by— "The word that I have spoken," says Christ, "it shall judge you (and so consequently dispose of you) in the last day" (John 12:48). Now, if we consider that our next state must be eternal, either eternal glory or eternal fire and that this eternal glory or this eternal fire must be our portion, [it will be] ... according as the words of God, revealed in the holy Scriptures, shall determine. Who will not but conclude that therefore the words of God are they at which we should tremble and they by which we should have our fear of God guided and directed, for by them we are taught how to please him in everything?

NOVEMBER 18

Rewarded Or Destroyed

For verily I say unto you, 'Till heaven and earth pass, one jot or one tittle shall in no wise pass from the law, till all be fulfilled.'

MATTHEW 5:18 KJV

[God's Word] ... is to be called a fearful Word because of the truth and faithfulness of it. The Scriptures cannot be broken. Here they are called the Scriptures of truth, the true sayings of God, and the fear of the Lord. For that every jot and tittle thereof is forever settled in heaven and stand more steadfast than doth the world. "Heaven and earth," said Christ, "shall pass away, but my words shall not pass away" (Matt. 24:35). Those, therefore, that are favoured by the Word of God, those are favoured indeed, and that with the favour that no man can turn away. But those that by the word of the Scriptures are condemned, those can no man justify and sit quiet in the sight of God. Therefore, what is bound by the text, is bound, and what is released by the text, is released. Also, the bound and released are unalterable (Dan. 10:21; Rev. 19:9; Matt. 24:35; Ps. 119:89; John 10:35). This, therefore, calleth upon God's people to stand more in fear of the Word of God than of all the terrors of the world. There wants even in the hearts of God's people a greater reverence of the Word of God than to this day appears among us. And this let me say, that want of reverence of the Word is the ground of all disorders that are in the heart, life, conversation, and in Christian communion. Besides, the want of reverence of the Word lays men open to the fearful displeasure of God: "Whoso despiseth the word shall be destroyed; but he that feareth the commandment shall be rewarded" (Prov. 13:13).

NOVEMBER 19

Guard Your Heart And Mouth

Keep your heart with all vigilance, for from it flow the springs of life.

PROVERBS 4:23

[Consider] ... all transgression begins at wandering from the Word of God. But ... [contrast what] David said, "Concerning the works of men, by the word of thy lips I have kept me from the paths of the destroyer" (Ps. 17:4). Therefore, Solomon said, "My son, attend to my words; incline thine ear unto my sayings; let them not depart from thine eyes; keep them in the midst of thine heart; for they are life unto those that find them, and health to all their flesh" (Prov. 4:20-22). Now, if indeed you would reverence the Word of the Lord and make it your rule and director in all things; believe that the Word is the fear of the Lord, the Word that stands fast forever. Without and against which God will do nothing, either in saving or damning of the souls of sinners. But to conclude this:

Know that those that have no due regard to the Word of the Lord and that make it not their dread and their fear; but the rule of their life is the lust of their flesh, the desire of their eyes, and the pride of life, [these] are sorely rebuked by this doctrine and are counted the fools of the world. For "lo, they have rejected the word of the Lord, and what wisdom is in them?" (Jer. 8:9). That there are such a people is evident, not only by their irregular lives but by the manifest testimony of the Word. "As for the word of the Lord," said they to Jeremiah, "that thou hast spoken to us in the name of the Lord, we will not hearken unto thee, but we will certainly do whatsoever thing goeth forth out of our own mouth" (Jer. 44:16-17).

NOVEMBER 20

Ashamed Of God's Word?

The one who rejects me and does not receive my words has a judge; the word that I have spoken will judge him on the last day.

JOHN 12:48

Are the words of God called by the name of the fear of the Lord? Are they so dreadful in their receipt and sentence? Then this rebukes them that esteem the words and things of men more than the words of God; as those do who are drawn from their respect of, and obedience to the Word of God. [They are drawn] by the pleasures or threats of men. Some there be who verily will acknowledge the authority of the Word yet will not stoop [bow] their souls thereto. Such, whatever they think of themselves, are judged by Christ to be ashamed of the Word; wherefore their state is damnable as the other. "Whosoever," said he, "shall be ashamed of me and of my words, in this adulterous and sinful generation, of him also shall the Son of man be ashamed, when he cometh in the glory of the Father, with the holy angels" (Mark 8:38).

And if these things ... [are] so, what will become of those that mock at, and professedly contemn, the words of God, making them as a thing ridiculous and not to be regarded? Shall they prosper that do such things? From the promises it is concluded that their judgment now of a long-time slumbers [sleeps] not. And when it comes, it will devour them without remedy (2 Chron. 36:15). If God, I say, hath put that reverence upon his Word as to call it the fear of the Lord, [then] what will become of them that do what they can to overthrow its authority, by denying it to be his Word, and by raising cavils [petty objections] against its authority? Such stumble, indeed, at the Word, being appointed thereunto, but it shall judge them in the last day (1 Pet. 2:8; John 12:48).

NOVEMBER 21

Fear Of The LORD As A Means Of Grace

The fear of the LORD is the beginning of wisdom, and the knowledge of the Holy One is insight.

PROVERBS 9:10

Having thus spoken of the object and rule of our fear, I should come now to speak of fear as it is a grace of the Spirit of God in the hearts of his people. But before I do that, I shall show you that there are divers sorts [different kinds] of fear besides. For man being a reasonable creature and having even by nature a certain knowledge of God has also naturally something of some kind of fear of God at times which, although it be not that which is intended in the text. Yet ought to be spoken to, that that which is not right may be distinguished from that that is.

There is, I say, several sorts or kinds of fear in the hearts of the sons of men. I mean besides that fear of God that is intended in the text and that accompanied eternal life. I shall here make mention of three of them.

First: There is a fear of God that flows even from the light of nature.

Second: There is a fear of God that flows from some of his dispensations to men, which yet is neither universal nor saving.

Third: There is a fear of God in the heart of some men that is good and godly but doth not for ever abide so. To speak a little to all these, before I come to speak of fear, as it is a grace of God in the hearts of his children.

NOVEMBER 22

Fear From The Light Of Nature

For although they knew God, they did not honor him as God or give thanks to him, but they became futile in their thinking, and their foolish hearts were darkened.

ROMANS 1:21

To the first, to wit, that there is a fear of God that flows even from the light of nature. A people may be said to do things in a fear of God, when they act one towards another in things reasonable and honest betwixt man and man, not doing that to others they would not have done to themselves. This is that fear of God which Abraham thought the Philistines had destroyed in themselves when he said of his wife to Abimelech, "She is my sister." For when Abimelech asked Abraham why he said of his wife, she is my sister.e replied, saying, "I thought surely the fear of God is not in this place and they will slay me for my wife's sake" (Gen. 20:11). I thought verily that in this place men had stifled and choked that light of nature that is in them. At least so far forth as not to suffer it to put them in fear, when their lusts were powerful in them to accomplish their ends on the object that was present before them. But this I will pass by, and come to the second thing, namely—

NOVEMBER 23

A Fearful But Unchanged Heart

Then the L*ORD said to him [Cain], "Not so! If anyone kills Cain, vengeance shall be taken on him sevenfold." And the* L*ORD put a mark on Cain, lest any who found him should attack him.*

GENESIS 4:15

To show that there is a fear of God that flows from some of his dispensations to men, which yet is neither universal nor saving. This fear, when opposed to that which is saving may be called an ungodly fear of God. I shall describe it by ... [what] follows—

There is a fear of God that causes a continual grudging, discontent, and heart-risings against God under the hand of God. And that is, when the dread of God in his coming upon men, to deal with them for their sins, is apprehended by them. And yet by this dispensation they have no change of heart to submit to God thereunder. The sinners under this dispensation cannot shake God out of their mind, nor yet graciously tremble before him. But through the unsanctified frame that they now are in, they are afraid with ungodly fear and so in their minds let fly against him. This fear oftentimes took hold of the children of Israel when they were in the wilderness in their journey to the promised land. Still, they feared that God in this place would destroy them. But not with that fear that made them willing to submit, for their sins, to the judgment which they fear, but with that fear that made them let fly against God. This fear showed itself in them, even at the beginning of their voyage and was rebuked by Moses at the Red Sea. But it was not there, nor yet at any other place, so subdued ... that it would rise again in them at times to the dishonor of God, and the anew [once more] making of them guilty of sin before him (Exod. 14:11-13; Num. 14:1-9).

NOVEMBER 24

Godly Fear Does Not Always Abide

And these are the ones sown on rocky ground: the ones who, when they hear the word, immediately receive it with joy. And they have no root in themselves, but endure for a while; then, when tribulation or persecution arises on account of the word, immediately they fall away.

MARK 4:16-17

The third thing that I am to speak to is, that there is a fear of God in the heart of some men that is good and godly but [it] does not forever abide so. Or you may take it thus—There is a fear of God that is godly but for a time. I shall show you what this fear is.

This fear is an effect of sound awakenings by the word of wrath which begets in the soul a sense of its right to eternal damnation. For this fear is not in every sinner; he that is blinded by the devil and that is not able to see that his state is damnable. He has not this fear in his heart but he that is under the powerful workings of the word of wrath as God's elect are at first conversion. He has this godly fear in his heart. That is, he fears that that damnation will come upon him which by the justice of God is due unto him, because he hath broken his holy law. This is the fear that made the three thousand cry out, "Men and brethren, what shall we do?" And [it] that made the [Philippian] jailer cry out and that with great trembling of soul, "Sirs, what must I do to be saved?" (Acts 16:30). The method of God is to kill and make alive, to smite and then heal. When the commandment came to Paul, sin revived, and he died, and that law which was ordained to life, he found to be unto death. That is, it passed a sentence of death upon him for his sins and slew his conscience with that sentence [Rom. 7:9].

NOVEMBER 25

Adam, Where Art Thou?

But the L*ORD* *God called to the man and said to him, "Where are you?"*

GENESIS 3:9

There is a fear of God that drives a man away from God—I speak not now of the atheist, nor of the pleasurable sinner, nor yet of these, and that fear that I spoke of just now. I speak now of such who through a sense of sin and of God's justice, fly from him of a slavish ungodly fear. This ungodly fear was that which possessed Adam's heart in the day that he did eat of the tree concerning which the Lord has said unto him, "In the day that thou eatest thereof, thou shalt surely die." For then was he possessed with such a fear of God as made him seek to hide himself from his presence. "I heard," said he, "thy voice in the garden, and I was afraid, because I was naked; and I hid myself" (Gen. 3:10). Mind it, he had a fear of God, but it was not godly. It was not that, that made him afterwards submit himself unto him. For that would have kept him from departing from him or else have brought him to him again, with bowed, broken, and contrite spirit. But this fear, as the rest of his sin, managed his departing from his God and pursued him to provoke him still so to do. By it he kept himself from God, by it his whole man was carried away from him. I call it ungodly fear because it begat in him ungodly apprehensions of his maker, because it confined Adam's conscience to the sense of justice only and consequently to despair.

The same fear also possessed the children of Israel when they heard the law delivered to them on Mount Sinai. It made them, saith the apostle to the Hebrews, that "they could not endure that which was commanded" (Heb. 12:20).

NOVEMBER 26

An Austere God

... I was afraid of you because you are a severe man. You take what you did not deposit, and reap what you did not sow.

LUKE 19:21

There is a fear of God, which, although it hath not in it that power as to make men flee from God's presence, yet it is ungodly. Because, even while they are in the outward way of God's ordinances, their hearts are by it quite discouraged from attempting to exercise themselves in the power of religion. Of this sort are they which dare not cast off the hearing, reading, and discourse of the word as others. No, nor the assembly of God's children for the exercise of other religious duties, for their conscience is convinced this is the way and worship of God. But their heart ... by this ungodly fear, is kept from a powerful gracious falling in with God. This fear takes away their heart from all holy and godly prayer in private and from all holy and godly zeal for his name in public. And there be many professors whose hearts are possessed with this ungodly fear of God and they are intended by the slothful one. He was a servant, a servant among the servants of God and had gifts and abilities given him, therewith to serve Christ, as well as his fellows. Yea and was commanded too, as well as the rest, to occupy till his master came. But what does he? Why, he takes his talent, the gift that he was to lay out for his master's profit and puts it in a napkin, digs a hole in the earth, and hides his lord's money and lies in a lazy manner at to-elbow all his days, not out of, but in his lord's vineyard. For he came among the servants also at last. By which it is manifest that he had not cast off his profession but was slothful and negligent while he was in it.

NOVEMBER 27

Be Not Afraid, Only Believe

But overhearing what they said, Jesus said to the ruler of the synagogue, "Do not fear, only believe."

MARK 5:36

This ungodly fear of God ... will not suffer the soul that is governed ... [by it] to trust only to Christ for justification of life. But will bend the powers of the soul to trust partly to the works of the law. Many of the Jews were, in the time of Christ and his apostles, possessed with this ungodly fear of God. For they were not as the former ... as the slothful servant, to receive a talent and hide it in the earth in a napkin. But they were an industrious people, they followed after the law of righteousness, they had a zeal of God and of the religion of their fathers. But how then did they come to miscarry? Why, their fear of God was ungodly. It would not suffer them wholly to trust to the righteousness of faith which is the imputed righteousness of Christ. They followed after the law of righteousness but attained not to the law of righteousness.

Wherefore? because they sought it not by faith but as it were by the works of the law. But what was it that made them join their works of the law with Christ, but their unbelief whose foundation was ignorance and fear? They were afraid to venture all in one bottom, they thought two strings to one bow would be best. And thus, betwixt two stools they came to the ground. And hence, to fear and to doubt, are put together as being the cause one of another. Yea, they are put ofttimes the one for the other. Thus, ungodly fear for unbelief: "Be not afraid, only believe," and therefore he that is overruled and carried away with this fear is coupled with the unbeliever that is thrust out from the holy city among the dogs.

NOVEMBER 28

Syncretism Forbidden

Ephraim is joined to idols, leave him alone.

HOSEA 4:17

This ungodly fear of God is [also] that which will put men upon adding to the revealed will of God their own inventions and their own performances ... as a means to pacify the anger of God. For the truth is, where this ungodly fear reigns, there is no end of law and duty. When those that you read of in the book of Kings were destroyed by the lions because they had set up idolatry in the land of Israel, they sent for a priest from Babylon that might teach them the manner of the God of the land. But behold when they knew it, being taught it by the priest, yet their fear would not suffer them to be content with that worship only. And again, "So these nations feared the Lord, and served their graven images" (2 Kings 17:33). It was this fear also that put the Pharisees upon inventing so many traditions: as the washing of cups, and beds, tables, and basins, with abundance of such other like gear. None knows the many dangers that an ungodly fear of God will drive a man into (Mark 7).

How has it racked and tortured the Papists for hundreds of years together! For what else is the cause but this ungodly fear at least in the most simple and harmless of them, of their penances, as creeping to the cross, going barefoot on pilgrimage, whipping themselves, wearing of sackcloth, saying so many Pater-nosters,[1] so many Ave-marias,[2] making so many confessions to the priest, giving so much money for pardons, and abundance of other the like, but this [is] ungodly fear of God?

---

1 Reciting The Lord's Prayer in Latin.

2 Reciting prayers to Jesus' mother, Mary, adapted from Luke 1:28.

NOVEMBER 29

God Be Merciful To Me The Sinner

But the tax collector, standing far off, would not even lift up his eyes to heaven, but beat his breast, saying, "God be merciful to me, a sinner!"

LUKE 18:13

I now come to show you what this fear does in the soul.

1. This fear makes a man judge himself for sin and to fall before God with a broken mind under this judgment; the which is pleasing to God, because the sinner by so doing justifies God in his saying and clears him in his judgment (Ps. 51).

2. As this fear makes a man judge himself and cast himself down at God's foot so ... [he] condoles and bewails his misery "I have surely heard Ephraim bemoaning himself," saying, "Thou hast chastised me and I was chastised, as a bullock unaccustomed to the yoke" (Jer. 31:19).

3. This fear makes a man lie at God's foot and puts his mouth in the dust, so there may be hope. This also is pleasing to God, now is the sinner as nothing and in his own eyes less than nothing: "He sitteth alone and keepeth silence," and "he putteth his mouth in the dust, if so be there may be hope" (Lam. 3:29).

4. This fear puts a man upon crying to God for mercy and that in most humble manner; now he sensibly cries, "God be merciful to me, a sinner" (Luke 18:13).

5. This fear makes a man that he cannot accept of that for support and succor which others that are destitute thereof will take up and be contented with. This man must be washed by God himself and cleansed from his sin by God himself (Ps. 51).

6. Therefore this fear goes not away until the Spirit of God doth change his ministration as to this, in leaving off to work now by the law, as afore, and coming to the soul with the sweet word of promise of life and salvation by Jesus Christ.

NOVEMBER 30

The Fear Of The Lord

The fear of the LORD is the beginning of wisdom and the knowledge of the Holy One is insight.

PROVERBS 9:10

[There is a] fear [that] is godly and the reason why it is godly is because the groundwork of it is good. I told you ... what this fear is; ... it is the fear of damnation. Now the ground for this fear is good as is manifest by these particulars.

1. The soul fears damnation and that is rightly because it is in its sins.

2. The soul fears damnation rightly because it hath not faith in Christ but is at present under the law.

3. The soul fears damnation rightly now, because by sin, the law and for want of faith, the wrath of God abides on it. But now, although thus far this fear of God is good and godly, yet after Christ, by the Spirit in the word of the gospel, is revealed to us. We are made to accept of him as so revealed and offered to us by a true and living faith. This fear, to wit, of damnation, is no longer good but ungodly. Nor does the Spirit of God ever work it in us again. Now we do not receive the spirit of bondage again to fear, [that is] to fear damnation. But we have received the spirit of adoption, whereby we cry, Father, Father. But I would not be mistaken when I say that this fear is no longer godly. I do not mean with reference to the essence and habit of it. For I believe it is the same in the seed which shall afterwards grow up to a higher degree and into a more sweet and gospel current and manner of working. But I mean reference to this act of fearing damnation, I say it shall never by the Spirit be managed to that work. It shall never bring forth that fruit more.

DECEMBER 1

Of Sin

The soul who sins shall die ...

EZEKIEL 18:20

Sin is the great block and bar to our happiness, the procurer of all miseries to man, both here and hereafter. Take away sin, and nothing can hurt us; for death, temporal, spiritual, and eternal, is the wages of it.

Sin, and man for sin, is the object of the wrath of God. How dreadful, therefore, must his case be who continues in sin! For who can bear or grapple with the wrath of God?

No sin against God can be little because it is against the great God of heaven and earth; but if the sinner can find out a little god, it may be easy to find out little sins.

Sin turns all God's grace into wantonness; it is the dare of his justice, the rape of his mercy, the jeer of his patience, the slight of his power, and the contempt of his love.

Take heed of giving yourself liberty of committing one sin, for that will lead thee to another; till, by an ill custom, it becomes natural.

To begin a sin, is to lay a foundation for a continuance; this continuance is the mother of custom, and impudence at last the issue.

The death of Christ gives us the best discovery of ourselves, in what condition we were, in that nothing could help us but that and the most clear discovery of the dreadful nature of our sins. For if sin be so dreadful a thing as to wring the heart of the Son of God, how shall a poor wretched sinner be able to bear it?

DECEMBER 2

Of Affliction

Not only that, but we rejoice in our sufferings, knowing that suffering produces endurance, and endurance produces character, and character produces hope, and hope does not put us to shame, because God's love has been poured into our hearts through the Holy Spirit who has been given to us.

ROMANS 5:3-5

Nothing can render affliction so insupportable as the load of sin; would you, therefore, be fitted for afflictions, be sure to get the burden of your sins laid aside and then what afflictions soever you may meet with will be very easy to you?

If thou canst hear and bear the rod of affliction which God shall lay upon thee, remember this lesson—thou art beaten that thou mayest be better.

The Lord uses his flail of tribulation to separate the chaff from the wheat.

The school of the cross is the school of light; it discovers the world's vanity, baseness, and wickedness and lets us see more of God's mind. Out of dark affliction comes a spiritual light.

In times of affliction, we commonly meet with the sweetest experiences of the love of God.

Did we heartily renounce the pleasures of this world, we should be very little troubled by our afflictions. That which renders an afflicted state so insupportable to many is because they are too much addicted to the pleasures of this life and so cannot endure that which makes a separation between them.

DECEMBER 3

Of Repentance And Coming To Christ

... how I did not shrink from declaring to you anything that was profitable, and teaching you in public and from house to house, testifying both to Jews and to Greeks of repentance toward God and of faith in our Lord Jesus Christ.

ACTS 20:20-21

The end of affliction is the discovery of sin and of that to bring us to a Saviour. Let us therefore, with the prodigal, return unto him, and we shall find ease and rest.

A repenting penitent, though formerly as bad as the worst of men, may, by grace, become as good as the best.

To be truly sensible of sin is to sorrow for displeasing of God; to be afflicted that he is displeased by us more than that he is displeased with us.

Your intentions to repentance and the neglect of that soul-saving duty, will rise up in judgment against you.

Repentance carries with it a divine rhetoric and persuades Christ to forgive multitudes of sins committed against him.

Say not with thyself, tomorrow I will repent; for it is thy duty to do it daily.

The gospel of grace and salvation is above all doctrines the most dangerous, if it be received in word only by graceless men—if it be not attended with a sensible need of a Saviour and bring them to him. For such men as have only the notion of it, are of all men most miserable—for by reason of their knowing more than heathens, this only shall be their final portion, that they shall have greater stripes.

DECEMBER 4

Of Prayer

But when you pray, go into your room and shut the door and pray to your Father who is in secret. And your Father who sees in secret will reward you. And when you pray, do not heap up empty phrases as the Gentiles do, for they think that they will be heard for their many words.

MATTHEW 6:6-7

Before you enter into prayer, ask your soul these questions—
To what end, O my soul, are you retired into this place?
Art you not come to discourse the Lord in prayer?
Is he present; will he hear you?
Is he merciful; will he help you?
Is your business slight; is it not concerning the welfare of your soul?
What words will thou use to move him to compassion?

To make your preparation complete, consider that you are but dust and ashes and he the great God and Father of our Lord Jesus Christ, that clothes himself with light as with a garment; that you are a vile sinner, he a holy God; that you are but a poor crawling worm, he the omnipotent creator.

In all your prayers forget not to thank the Lord for his mercies.

When you pray rather let your heart be without words, than thy words without a heart.

Prayer will make a man cease from sin, or sin will entice a man to cease from prayer.

Pray often, for prayer is a shield to the soul, a sacrifice to God and a scourge for Satan.

DECEMBER 5

Of The Lord's Day, Sermons, And Weekdays

The steadfast love of the L*ORD* *never ceases; his mercies never come to an end; they are new every morning, great is your faithfulness.*

LAMENTATIONS 3:22-23

Have a special care to sanctify the Lord's Day; for as you keep it, so it will be with you all the week long.

Make the Lord's Day the market for your soul; let the whole day be spent in prayer, repetitions, or meditations; lay aside the affairs of the other part of the week; let the sermon you have heard be converted, into prayer. Shall God allow you six days, and will you not afford him one?

In the church be careful to serve God, for you are in his eyes and not in man's.

You may hear sermons often and do well in practicing what you heard; but you must not expect to be told you in a pulpit all that thou ought to do. But be studious in searching the Scriptures and reading good books. What thou hear may be forgotten but what you read may better be retained.

Forsake not the public worship of God, lest God forsake you, not only in public, but in private.

What folly can be greater than to labour for the ... [food] that perishes and neglect the food of eternal life?

DECEMBER 6

Of Suffering

When he opened the fifth seal, I saw under the altar the souls of those who had been slain for the word of God and for the witness they had borne.

REVELATION 6:9

It is not every suffering that makes a martyr but suffering for the Word of God after a right manner. That is, not only for righteousness but for righteousness' sake. Not only for truth, but out of love to truth; not only for God's Word but according to it. To wit, in that holy, humble, meek manner, as the Word of God requires.

It is a rare thing to suffer aright and to have my spirit in suffering bent only against God's enemy, sin: sin in doctrine, sin in worship, sin in life, and sin in conversation.

The devil nor men of the world can kill thy righteousness or love to it. But by your own hand; or separate that and you asunder without your own act. Nor will he that does indeed suffer for the sake of it or out of love he bears ... [to it], be tempted to exchange it for the goodwill of all the world.

I have often thought that the best of Christians are found in the worst of times. And I have thought again that one reason why we are no better is because God purges us no more. Noah and Lot—who [were] so holy as they [were] in the time of their afflictions? And yet who so idle as they in the time of their prosperity?

DECEMBER 7

Of The Love Of The World

Do not love the world or the things in the world. If anyone loves the world, the love of the Father is not in him.

1 JOHN 2:15

Nothing more hinders a soul from coming to Christ, than a vain love of the world. And until a soul is freed from it, it can never have a true love for God.

What are the honors and riches of this world, when compared to the glories of a crown of life?

Love not the world; for it [the love of the world] is a moth in a Christian's life.

To despise the world is the way to enjoy heaven. And blessed are they who delight to converse with God by prayer.

DECEMBER 8

Of Death And Judgment

And it is appointed for many to die once, and after that comes judgment.

HEBREWS 9:27

As the devil labours ... to keep out other things that are good, so to keep out of the heart as much as ... [he can], the thoughts of passing from this life into another world. For he knows if he can but keep them from the serious thoughts of death, he shall the more easily keep them in their sins.

Nothing will make us more earnest in working out the work of our salvation than a frequent meditation of mortality. Nothing has greater influence for the taking off our hearts from vanities, and for the begetting in us desires after holiness.

O sinner, what a condition wilt you fall into when you depart this world! If you depart unconverted, you had better have been smothered the first hour you were born. You had better have been plucked one limb from another. You had better have been made a dog, a toad, a serpent; if you die unconverted and ... if you repent not.

A man would be counted a fool to slight a judge before whom he is to have a trial of his whole estate. The trial we have before God is of other-guise [outward appearance] importance. It concerns our eternal happiness or misery and yet dare we affront him?

The only way for us to escape that terrible judgment is to often pass a sentence of condemnation upon ourselves here.

DECEMBER 9

Of The Joys Of Heaven

He will wipe away every tear from their eyes, and death shall be no more, neither shall there be mourning, nor crying, nor pain anymore, for the former things have passed away.

REVELATION 21:4

There is no good in this life but what is mingled with some evil; honors perplex, riches disquiet, and pleasures ruin health. But in heaven we shall find blessings in their purity without any ingredient to embitter [but] with everything to sweeten them.

O! who is able to conceive the inexpressible, inconceivable joys that are there? None but they who have tasted them. Lord, help us to put such a value upon them here, that in order to prepare ourselves for them, we may be willing to forego the loss of all those deluding pleasures here.

How will the heavens echo of joy, when the bride, the Lamb's wife shall come to dwell with her husband forever!

Christ is the desire of nations, the joy of angels, the delight of the Father. What solace then must that soul be filled with that hath the possession of him to all eternity?

O! what acclamations of joy will there be when all the children of God shall meet together without fear of being disturbed by the antichristian and Cainish brood!

Is there not a time coming when the godly may ask the wicked what profit they have in their pleasure what comfort in their greatness and what knit in all their labour?

DECEMBER 10

Of The Torments Of Hell

And cast the worthless servant into the outer darkness. In that place there will be weeping and gnashing of teeth.

MATTHEW 25:30

Heaven and salvation are not surely more promised to the godly than hell and damnation is threatened to and executed on the wicked.

When once a man is damned, he may bid adieu to all pleasures.

O! who knows the power of God's wrath? none but [the] damned ones.

Sinners' company are the devil and his angels tormented in everlasting fire with a curse.

Hell would be a kind of paradise if it were no worse than the worst of this world.

As different as grief is from joy, as torment from rest, as terror from peace; so different is the state of sinners from that of saints in the world to come.

DECEMBER 11

Miscellaneous Bunyan Quotes

To receive instruction in wise dealing, in righteousness, justice, and equity.

PROVERBS 1:3

You have not lived today until you have done something for someone who can never repay you.

An idle man's brain is the devil's workshop.

In prayer it is better to have a heart without words than words without a heart.

If my life is fruitless, it doesn't matter who praises me, and if my life is fruitful, it doesn't matter who criticizes me.

He that is down needs fear no fall. He that is low, no pride; he that is humble, ever shall have God to be his guide.

To run and work the law commands but gives us neither feet nor hands. But better news the gospel brings, it bids us fly and gives us wings.

You can do more than pray, after you have prayed, but you cannot do more than pray until you have prayed. Pray often, for prayer is a shield to the soul, a sacrifice to God, and a scourge to Satan.

Pray and read, read and pray, for a little from God is better than a great deal from men.

DECEMBER 12

Miscellaneous Bunyan Quotes

Let the wise hear and increase in learning, and the one who understands obtain guidance.

PROVERBS 1:5

I am content with what I have, little be it, or much.

The fear of God is the beginning of wisdom and they that lack the beginning have neither middle nor end.

He who runs from God in the morning will scarcely find him the rest of the day.

What God says is best, though all the men in the world are against it.

Prayer is a sincere, sensible, affectionate pouring out of the soul to God, through Christ, in the strength and assistance of the Spirit for such things as God has promised.

Dark clouds bring water, when the bright bring none.

In times of affliction we commonly meet with the sweetest experiences of the love of God.

And, indeed, this is one of the greatest mysteries in the world; namely, that a righteousness that resides in heaven should justify me a sinner on earth.

The spirit of prayer is more precious than treasures of gold and silver.

Temptation provokes me to look upward to God.

DECEMBER 13

Miscellaneous Bunyan Quotes

Be not wise in your own eyes; fear the LORD, and turn away from evil.

PROVERBS 3:7

Prayer will make a man cease from sin or sin will entice a man to cease from prayer.

You have chosen the roughest road, but it leads straight to the hilltops.

His love is what makes us live, love, sing, and praise forever.

I was never out of my Bible.

In all your prayers forget not to thank the Lord for his mercies.

I will stay in jail to the end of my days before I make a butchery of my conscience.

I will stay in prison till the moss grows on my eye lids rather that disobey God.

He has given me rest by his sorrow and life by his death.

The more he cast away the more he had.

There is enough sin in the best prayer to send the whole world to hell.

DECEMBER 14

Miscellaneous Bunyan Quotes

Be not wise in your own eyes; fear the LORD, and turn away from evil.

PROVERBS 3:7

If you have sinned, do not lie down without repentance; for the want of repentance after one has sinned makes the heart yet harder and harder.

The reason why the Christians in this day are at such a loss as to some things is that they are contended with what comes from man's mouth without searching and kneeling before God to know of him the truth of things.

Nothing can hurt you except sin: nothing can grieve me except sin: nothing can defeat you except sin.

I preach deliverance to others, I tell them there is freedom, I tell them there is freedom while I hear my own chains clang. Therefore, I bind these lies and slanderous accusations to my person as an ornament. It belongs to my Christian profession to be vilified, slandered, reproached, and reviled and since all this is nothing but that, as God and my conscience testify, I rejoice in being reproached for Christ's sake.

Be of good cheer, Jesus Christ makes you whole.

To go back is nothing by death: but to go forward is fear of death and life everlasting beyond.

Hope is never ill when faith is well.

Prayer is a shield to the soul.

DECEMBER 15

John Bunyan's Last Sermon

Preached August 19, 1688, Taken From John 1:12-13

But to all who did receive him, who believed in his name, he gave the right to become children of God, who were born, not of blood nor of the will of the flesh nor of the will of man, but of God.

JOHN 1:12-13

These words have a dependence on what goes before, and therefore I must direct you to them for the right understanding of it. You have it thus,—"He came to his own, but his own received him not; but as many as received him, to them gave he power to become the sons of God, even to them which believe on his name; which were born, not of blood, nor of the will of the flesh, but of God." In the words before, you have two things—

First, some of his own rejecting him when he offered himself to them.

Secondly, others of his own receiving him, and making him welcome. Those that reject him he also passes by; but those that receive him, he gives them power to become the sons of God. Now, lest anyone should look upon it as good luck or fortune, he says, "They were born, not of blood, nor of the will of the flesh, nor of the will of man, but of God." They that did not receive him, they were only born of flesh and blood; but those that receive him, they have God to their father, they receive the doctrine of Christ with a vehement desire.

DECEMBER 16

The Wicked Desire Salvation, Sermon Cont.

Bear fruits in keeping with repentance. And do not begin to say to yourselves, "We have Abraham as our father." For I tell you, God is able from these stones to raise up children for Abraham.

LUKE 3:8

First, I will show you what he means by "blood." They that believe are born to it, as an heir is to an inheritance. They are born of God, not of flesh, nor of the will of man, but of God. Not of blood—that is, not by generation. Not born to the kingdom of heaven by the flesh; not because I am the son of a godly man or woman. That is meant by blood, (Acts 17:26), "He has made of one blood all nations." But when he says here, "not of blood," he rejects all carnal privileges they did boast of. The Pharisees boasted they were Abraham's seed. No, no, he says, it is not of blood. Think not to say you have Abraham to your father, you must be born of God if you go to the kingdom of heaven.

Secondly, "Nor of the will of the flesh." What must we understand by that? It is taken for those vehement inclinations that are in man to all manner of looseness, fulfilling the desires of the flesh. That must not be understood here. Men are not made the children of God by fulfilling their lustful desires; it must be understood here in the best sense. There is not only in carnal men a will to be vile, but there is in them a will to be saved also—a will to go to heaven also. But this it will not do; it will not privilege a man in the things of the kingdom of God. Natural desires after the things of another world, they are not an argument to prove a man shall go to heaven whenever he dies. I am not a free-willer, I do abhor it. Yet there is not the wickedest man but he desires some time or other to be saved.

DECEMBER 17

It All Depends on God, Sermon Cont.

So then it depends not on human will or exertion, but on God, who has mercy.

ROMANS 9:16

"It is not in him that wills, nor in him that runs, but in God that shews mercy;" there is willing and running, and yet to no purpose (Rom. 9:16). Israel, which followed the law of righteousness, has not obtained it. I do not understand, it is as if the apostle had denied a virtuous course of life to be the way to heaven. But a man without grace, though he have natural gifts, yet he shall not obtain privilege to go to heaven. Though a man without grace may have a will to be saved, yet he cannot have that will God's way. Nature cannot know anything but the things of nature. The things of God knows no man but by the Spirit of God. Unless the Spirit of God be in you, it will leave you on this side of the gates of heaven—"Not of blood, nor of the will of the flesh, nor of the will of man, but of God." It may be some may have a will, a desire that Ishmael may to be saved. Know this, it will not save your child. If it were our will, I would have you all go to heaven. How many are there in the world that pray for their children and cry for them and are ready to die; and all this will not do? God's will is the rule of all; it is only through Jesus Christ, "which were born, not of flesh, nor of the will of man, but of God."

Men that believe in Jesus Christ to the effectual receiving of Jesus Christ, they are born to it. They are born of God, unto God and the things of God before they receive God to eternal salvation. "Except a man be born again, he cannot see the kingdom of God."

DECEMBER 18

Ye Must Be Born Again, Sermon Cont.

Therefore, it says, "Awake, O sleeper, and arise from the dead and Christ will shine on you."

EPHESIANS 5:14

First, I will give you a clear description of it under one similitude or two. A child, before it is born into the world, is in the dark dungeon of its mother's womb. So, a child of God, before he be born again, is in the dark dungeon of sin, sees nothing of the kingdom of God. Therefore, it is called a new birth; the same soul has love one way in its carnal condition, another way when it is born again.

Secondly, as it is compared to a birth, resembling a child in his mother's womb, so it is compared to a man being raised out of the grave. And to be born again is to be raised out of the grave of sin—"Awake, thou that sleepest, and arise from the dead, and Christ shall give thee life." To be raised from the grave of sin is to be begotten and born (Rev. 1:5). There is a famous instance of Christ—"He is the first-begotten from the dead, he is the first-born from the dead;" unto which our regeneration alludes. That is, if you be born again by seeking those things that are above, then there is a similitude betwixt Christ's resurrection and the new birth. Which were born, which were restored out of this dark world and translated out of the kingdom of this dark world into the kingdom of his dear Son and made us live a new life. This is to be born again and he that is delivered from the mother's womb, it is the help of the mother. So, he that is born of God, it is by the Spirit of God.

DECEMBER 19

Results Of The New Birth, Sermon Cont.

For everyone who lives on milk is unskilled in the word of righteousness, since he is a child.

HEBREWS 5:13

I must give you a few consequences of a new birth.

First, a child, you know is incident to cry as soon as it comes into the world. For if there be no noise, they say it is dead. You that are born of God and Christians, if you be not criers then there is no spiritual life in you. If you be born of God, you are crying ones; as soon as he has raised you out of the dark dungeon of sin, you cannot but cry to God, What must I do to be saved? As soon as ever God had touched the jailor, he cries out, "Men and brethren, what must I do to be saved?" Oh! How many prayerless professors are there in London that never pray? Coffeehouses will not let you pray, trades will not let you pray, looking glasses will not let you pray; but if you were born of God you would.

Secondly, it is not only natural for a child to cry but it must crave the breast. It cannot live without the breast. Therefore, Peter makes it the true trial of a newborn babe; the newborn babe desires the sincere milk of the Word, that he may grow thereby. If you be born of God, make it manifest by desiring the breast of God. Do you long for the milk of promises? A man lives one way when he is in the world, another way when he is brought unto Jesus Christ; (Isa. 66), "They shall suck, and be satisfied." If you be born again, there is no satisfaction till you get the milk of God's Word into your souls; (Isa. 66:11).

DECEMBER 20

More Results Of The New Birth, Sermon Cont.

And I adorned you with ornaments and put bracelets on your wrists and a chain on your neck. And I put a ring on your nose and earrings in your ears and a beautiful crown on your head.
EZEKIEL 16:11-12

Thirdly, a child that is newly born, if it does not have other comforts to keep it warm than it had in its mother's womb, it dies. It must have something got for its succor. So, Christ had swaddling clothes prepared for him. So those that are born again, they must have some promise of Christ to keep them alive. Those that are in a carnal state warm themselves with other things. But those that are born again, they cannot live without some promise of Christ to keep them alive, as he did to the poor infant in Ezekiel 17, "I covered thee with embroidered gold." And when women are with child what fine things will they prepare for their child! O but what fine things has Christ prepared to wrap all in that are born again! O what wrappings of gold has Christ prepared for all that are born again! Women will dress their children, that everyone may see them, how fine they are. So, he said in Ezekiel 16:11—"I decked thee also with ornaments, and I also put bracelets upon thine hands, and a chain on thy neck. And I put a jewel on thy forehead, and earrings in thine ears, and a beautiful crown upon thine head;" and he said in the thirteenth verse, "thou didst prosper to a kingdom."

Fourthly, a child when it is in its mother's lap, the mother takes great delight to have that which will be for its comfort; so, it is with God's children, they shall be kept on his knee; (Isa. 66:11), "They shall suck and be satisfied with the breasts of her consolation." Verse 13 declares, "As one whom his mother comforteth, so will I comfort you." There is a similitude in these things that nobody knows of but those that are born again.

DECEMBER 21

More Results Of The New Birth, Sermon Cont.

For those whom he foreknew he also predestined to be conformed to the image of his Son ...

ROMANS 8:29

Fifthly, there is usually some similitude betwixt the father and the child. It may be the child looks like its father. So those that are born again, they have a new similitude, they have the image of Jesus Christ (Gal. 4.). Every one that is born of God has something of the features of heaven upon him. Men love those children that are like them most usually. So does God his children; therefore, they are called the children of God. But others do not look like him, therefore they are called Sodomites. Christ describes children of the devil by their features; the children of the devil, his works they will do. All works of unrighteousness are the devil's works. If you are earthly, you have borne the image of the earthly; if heavenly, you have borne the image of the heavenly.

Sixthly, when a man has a child, he trains him up to his own liking, he learns the custom of his father's house. So are those that are born of God; they have learned the custom of the true church of God, there they learn to cry, My Father and my God. They are brought up in God's house, they learn the method and form of God's house for regulating their lives in this world.

DECEMBER 22

One More Result Of The New Birth, Sermon Cont.

For you did not receive the spirit of slavery to fall back into fear, but you have received the Spirit of adoption as sons, by whom we cry, "Abba! Father!"

ROMANS 8:15

Seventhly, children, it is natural for them to depend upon their father for what they want. If they want a pair of shoes, they go and tell him. If they want bread, they go and tell him. So should the children of God do. Do you want spiritual bread? Go tell God of it. Do you want strength of grace? Ask it of God. Do you want strength against Satan's temptations? Go and tell God of it. When the devil tempts you, run home and tell your heavenly Father. Go pour out your complaints to God. This is natural to children. If anyone has wronged them, they go and tell their father. So do those that are born of God, when they meet with temptations go and tell God of them.

DECEMBER 23

Please Open To Us

Afterward the other virgins came also, saying, "Lord, lord, open to us."

MATTHEW 25:11

What I have written before is to make a strict inquiry whether you be born of God or not. Examine by those things I laid down before of a child of nature and a child of grace. Are you brought out of the dark dungeon of this world into Christ? Have you learned to cry, My Father? (Jer. 3:19), "And I said, Thou shalt call me thy Father." All God's children are criers. Can you be quiet without you have a belly full of the milk of God's Word? Can you be satisfied without you have peace with God? Pray you consider it and be serious with yourselves.

If you have not these marks, you will fall short of the kingdom of God, you shall never have an interest there; there is no intruding. They will say, "Lord, Lord, open to us; and he will say, I know you not." No child of God, no heavenly inheritance. We sometimes give something to those that are not our children, but not our lands. O do not flatter yourselves with a portion among the sons unless you live like sons. When we see a king's son play with a beggar, this is unbecoming. So, if you are the king's children, live like the king's children. If you be risen with Christ, set your affections on things above, and not on things below. When you come together, talk of what your Father promised you. You should all love your Father's will and be content and pleased with the exercises you meet with in the world. If you are the children of God, live together lovingly. If the world quarrels with you, it is no matter; but it is sad if you quarrel together.

DECEMBER 24

Final Sermon's Final Summons

Therefore, preparing your mind for action, and being sober-minded, set your hope fully on the grace that will be brought to you at the revelation of Jesus Christ.

1 PETER 1:13

Do you see a soul that has the image of God in him? Love him, love him. Say, this man and I must go to heaven one day. Serve one another, do good for one another. And if any wrong you, pray to God to right you and love the brotherhood. Lastly, if you are the children of God, learn that lesson: "Gird up the loins of your mind as obedient children, not fashioning yourselves according to your former conversation. But be ye holy in all manner of conversation." Consider that the holy God is your father and let this oblige you to live like the children of God, that you may look your Father in the face with comfort another day.

DECEMBER 25

Pilgrim's Progress Aphorisms

Keep your heart with all vigilance for from it flow the springs of life.

PROVERBS 4:23

This hill, though high, I covet to ascend;
The difficulty will not me offend.
For I perceive the way to life lies here.
Come, pluck up, heart; let's neither faint nor fear.
Better, though difficult, the right way to go,
Than wrong, though easy, where the end is woe.

A man there was, though some did count him mad, the more he cast away the more he had.

I have given him my faith, and sworn my allegiance to him; how, then, can I go back from this, and not be hanged as a traitor?

The man that takes up religion for the world will throw away religion for the world.

I seek a place that can never be destroyed, one that is pure, and that fades not away and it is laid up in heaven, and safe there, to be given, at the time appointed, to them that seek it with all their heart. Read it so, if you will, in my book.

It is always hard to see the purpose in wilderness wanderings until after they are over.

For to speak the truth, there are but few that care thus to spend their time but choose rather to be speaking of things to no profit.

DECEMBER 26

Pilgrim's Progress Aphorisms, Cont.

But he said to them, "It is I; do not be afraid."

JOHN 6:20

"But were you not afraid, good sir, when you see him come with his club?" "It is my duty," said he, "to distrust mine own ability, that I may have reliance on him that is stronger than all.

Is there anything more worthy of our tongues and mouths than to speak of the things of God and heaven?

God's grace is the most incredible and insurmountable truth ever to be revealed to the human heart. That is why God has given us his Holy Spirit to superintend the process of more fully revealing the majesty of the work done on our behalf by our Saviour. He teaches us to first cling to, and then enables us to adore with the faith he so graciously supplies, the mercy of God. This mercy has its cause and effect in the work of Jesus on the cross.

There is in Jesus Christ more merit and righteousness than the whole world has need of.

Christian may have entered the Valley of Humiliation overconfident and puffed up with false pride. But he departs with humble reliance on the Word of God and prayerful gratitude to the Lord of the Highway who has come to his aid and saved him from the Destroyer. He goes forward with his sword drawn. He has learned his lesson and now relies consciously on God's Word for protection.

The law, instead of cleansing the heart from sin, doth revive it, put strength into, and increase it in the soul, even as it does discover and forbid it, for it does not give power to subdue.

DECEMBER 27

Pilgrim's Progress Aphorisms, Cont.

So that your faith might not rest in the wisdom of men but in the power of God.

1 CORINTHIANS 2:5

Mr. Worldly-Wiseman is not an ancient relic of the past. He is everywhere today, disguising his heresy and error by proclaiming the gospel of contentment and peace achieved by self-satisfaction and works. If he mentions Christ, it is not as the Saviour who took our place, but as a good example of an exemplary life. Do we need a good example to rescue us, or do we need a Saviour?

Wake up, see your own wretchedness, and fly to the Lord Jesus. He is the righteousness of God, for he himself is God. Only by believing in his righteousness will you be delivered from condemnation.

I stopped being watchful and diligent. I rushed after my own lusts. I sinned against the light of the Word and the goodness of God. I have grieved for the Spirit and he is gone. I tempted the devil, and he came to me. I have provoked God to anger, and he has left me. I have so hardened my heart that I cannot repent.

Prudence asked further, "Do you not still carry some of the baggage from the place you escaped?""Yes, but against my will. I still have within me some of the carnal thoughts that all my countrymen, as well as myself, were delighted with. Now all those things cause me to grieve. If I could master my own heart, I would choose never to think of those things again. But when I try only to think about those things that are best, those things that are the worst creep back into my mind and behaviour."

DECEMBER 28

Does "All" Mean "All?"

And I, when I am lifted up from the earth, will draw all people to myself.

JOHN 12:32

"All that the Father giveth me." This word is often used in Scripture. And is to be taken more largely or more strictly even as the truth or argument for the sake of which it is made use of will bear. Wherefore, that we may the better understand the mind of Christ in the use of it here. We must consider that it is limited and restrained only to those that shall be saved. To wit, to those that shall come to Christ; even to those whom he will "in no wise cast out." Thus, the words all to Israel, is sometimes to be taken, although sometimes it is taken for the whole family of Jacob. "And so all Israel shall be saved" (Rom. 11:26). By all Israel here, he intends not all of Israel, in the largest sense; "for they are not all Israel which are of Israel;" "neither because they are of the seed of Abraham, are they all children. But, In Isaac shall thy seed be called. That is, they which are the children of the flesh, these are not the children of God. But the children of the promise are counted for the seed" (Rom. 9:6-8).

This word ALL, therefore, must be limited and enlarged, as the truth and argument, for the sake of which it is used will bear. Else we shall abuse Scripture, and readers, and ourselves, and all. "And I, if I be lifted up from the earth," said Christ, "will draw ALL men unto me" (John 12:32). Can any man imagine, that by ALL, in this place, he should mean all and every individual man in the world, and not rather that all that is consonant to the scope of the place?

DECEMBER 29

Two Different Groups Of "All"

For God has consigned all to disobedience, that he may have mercy on all.

ROMANS 11:32

And if, by being "lifted up from the earth," he means, as he should seem, his being taken up into heaven. And by it "drawing ALL men after him," he meant a drawing them unto that place of glory. Then must he mean by ALL men, those and only those that shall in truth be eternally saved from the wrath to come. "For God hath concluded them all in unbelief, that he might have mercy upon all" (Rom. 11:32). Here again you have all and all, two alls. But yet a greater disparity between the all made mention of in the first place and that all made mention of the second. Those intended in this text are the Jews, even all of them, by the first all that you find in the words. The second all doth also intend the same people; yet only so many of them as God will have mercy upon. "He hath concluded them all in unbelief, that he might have mercy upon all." The all also in the text, is likewise to be limited and restrained to the saved, and to them only. And again;—

The word "giveth," or "hath given," must be restrained, after the same manner, to the same limited number. "All that the Father giveth me." Not all that are given, if you take the gift of the Father to the Son in the largest sense. For in that sense there are many given to him that shall never come unto him. Yea, many are given unto him that he will "cast out." I shall therefore describe first in what sense the gift in the text must be taken.

DECEMBER 30

The Father's Gift To The Son

Ask of me, and I will make the nations your heritage, and the ends of the earth your possession.

PSALM 2:8

Because then, all the men, yea, all the things in the world, must be saved. "All things," he said, "are delivered unto me of my Father" (Matt. 11:27). This, I think, no rational man in the world will conclude. Therefore, the gift intended in the text must be restricted to some, to a gift that is given by way of specialty by the Father to the Son.

It must not be taken for ALL, that in any sense are given by the Father to him. Because the Father hath given some, yea, many to him, to be dashed in pieces by him. "Ask of me," said the Father to him, "and I shall give thee the heathen for thine inheritance, and the uttermost parts of the earth for thy possession." But what must be done with them? Must he save them all? No! "Thou shalt break them with a rod of iron; thou shalt dash them in pieces like a potter's vessel" (Ps. 2:9). This method he used not with them that he saved by his grace, but with those that himself and saints shall rule over in justice and severity (Rev. 2:26-27). Yet, as you see, "they are given to him." Therefore, the gift intended in the text must be restricted to some, to a gift that is given by way of specialty by the Father to the Son.

In Psalm 18 he saith plainly, that some are given to him that he might destroy them. "Thou hast given me the necks of mine enemies; that I might destroy them that hate me" (v. 40). These, therefore, cannot be of the number of those that are said to be given in the text; for those, even ALL of them, shall come to him, "and he will in no wise cast them out."

DECEMBER 31

Judas: A Gift To Jesus!

While I was with them, I kept them in your name, which you have given me. I have guarded them, and not one of them has been lost except the son of destruction, that the Scripture might be fulfilled.

JOHN 17:12

Some are given to Christ, that he by them might bring about some of his high and deep designs in the world. Thus, Judas was given to Christ. To wit, that by him, even as was determined before, he might bring about Christ's death and so the salvation of his elect by his blood. Yea, and Judas must manage this business as that he must lose himself for ever in bringing it to pass. Therefore, the Lord Jesus, even in his losing of Judas, applies himself to the judgment of his Father. If he had not in that thing done that which was right, even in suffering of Judas so to bring about his master's death, by so doing, bring about his own eternal damnation also.

"Those," said he, "that thou gavest me, I have kept, and none of them is lost, but the son of perdition; that the Scripture might be fulfilled" (John 17:12). Let us, then, grant that Judas was given to Christ, but not as others are given to him, not as those made mention of in the text; for then he should have failed to have been so received by Christ and kept to eternal life. Indeed, he was given to Christ; but he was given to him to lose him, in the way that I have mentioned before. He was given to Christ, that he by him might bring about his own death, as was before determined; and that in the overthrow of him that did it. Yea, he must bring about his dying for us in the loss of the instrument that betrayed him, that he might even fulfill the Scripture in his destruction, as well as in the salvation of the rest. "And none of them is lost, but the son of perdition; that the Scripture might be fulfilled."

Christian Focus Publications

Our mission statement –

STAYING FAITHFUL

In dependence upon God we seek to impact the world through literature faithful to His infallible Word, the Bible. Our aim is to ensure that the Lord Jesus Christ is presented as the only hope to obtain forgiveness of sin, live a useful life and look forward to heaven with Him.

Our Books are published in four imprints:

CHRISTIAN FOCUS

popular works including biographies, commentaries, basic doctrine and Christian living.

CHRISTIAN HERITAGE

books representing some of the best material from the rich heritage of the church.

MENTOR

books written at a level suitable for Bible College and seminary students, pastors, and other serious readers. The imprint includes commentaries, doctrinal studies, examination of current issues and church history.

CF4•K

children's books for quality Bible teaching and for all age groups: Sunday school curriculum, puzzle and activity books; personal and family devotional titles, biographies and inspirational stories – because you are never too young to know Jesus!

Christian Focus Publications Ltd,
Geanies House, Fearn, Ross-shire,
IV20 1TW, Scotland, United Kingdom.
www.christianfocus.com